PROGRESS IN EDUCATION, VOLUME 21

PROGRESS IN EDUCATION

Series Editor: Robert V. Nata

This series presents substantial results from around the globe in selected areas of educational research. The field of education is consistently on the top of priority lists of every country in the world, yet few educators are aware of the progress elsewhere. Many techniques, programs and methods are directly applicable across borders.

This series attempts to shed light on successes wherever they may occur in the hope that many wheels need not be reinvented again and again.

Progress in Education, Volume 1
ISBN: 1-56072-836-1

Progress in Education, Volume 2
2001. ISBN: 1-56072-934-1

Progress in Education, Volume 3
2001. ISBN: 1-59033-016-1

Progress in Education, Volume 4
2001. ISBN: 1-59033-089-7

Progress in Education, Volume 5
2002. ISBN: 1-59033-251-2

Progress in Education, Volume 6
2002. ISBN: 1-59033-321-7

Progress in Education, Volume 7
2002. ISBN: 1-59033-429-9

Progress in Education, Volume 8
2002. ISBN: 1-59033-439-6

Progress in Education, Volume 9
2003. ISBN: 1-59033-539-2

Progress in Education, Volume 10
2003. ISBN: 1-59033-579-1

Progress in Education, Volume 11
2003. ISBN: 1-59033-690-9

Progress in Education, Volume 12
2003. ISBN: 1-59033-781-6

Progress in Education, Volume 13
2004. ISBN: 1-59454-090-X

Progress in Education, Volume 14
2007. ISBN: 978-1-60021-554-5

Progress in Education, Volume 15
2007. ISBN: 1-60021-673-0 (Hardcover)
2008. ISBN: 978-1-60741-926-6 (E-book)

Progress in Education, Volume 16
2008. ISBN: 978-1-60456-098-5

Progress in Education, Volume 17
2009. ISBN: 978-1-60692-505-8

Progress in Education, Volume 18
2010. ISBN: 978-1-60876-117-3 (Hardcover)
2010. ISBN: 978-1-61122-572-3 (E-book)

Progress in Education, Volume 19
2010. ISBN: 978-1-60876-169-2

Progress in Education, Volume 20
2010. ISBN: 978-1-61668-742-7 (Hardcover)
2010. ISBN: 978-1-61668-803-5 (E-book)

Progress in Education, Volume 21
2011. ISBN: 1-56072-934-1(Hardcover)
2010. ISBN: 978-1-61728-444-1 (E-book)

PROGRESS IN EDUCATION, VOLUME 21

ROBERT V. NATA

EDITOR

Nova Science Publishers, Inc.
New York

For permission to use material from this book please contact us:
Telephone 631-231-7269; Fax 631-231-8175
Web Site: http://www.novapublishers.com

NOTICE TO THE READER

The Publisher has taken reasonable care in the preparation of this book, but makes no expressed or implied warranty of any kind and assumes no responsibility for any errors or omissions. No liability is assumed for incidental or consequential damages in connection with or arising out of information contained in this book. The Publisher shall not be liable for any special, consequential, or exemplary damages resulting, in whole or in part, from the readers' use of, or reliance upon, this material. Any parts of this book based on government reports are so indicated and copyright is claimed for those parts to the extent applicable to compilations of such works.

Independent verification should be sought for any data, advice or recommendations contained in this book. In addition, no responsibility is assumed by the publisher for any injury and/or damage to persons or property arising from any methods, products, instructions, ideas or otherwise contained in this publication.

This publication is designed to provide accurate and authoritative information with regard to the subject matter covered herein. It is sold with the clear understanding that the Publisher is not engaged in rendering legal or any other professional services. If legal or any other expert assistance is required, the services of a competent person should be sought. FROM A DECLARATION OF PARTICIPANTS JOINTLY ADOPTED BY A COMMITTEE OF THE AMERICAN BAR ASSOCIATION AND A COMMITTEE OF PUBLISHERS.

Additional color graphics may be available in the e-book version of this book.

LIBRARY OF CONGRESS CATALOGING-IN-PUBLICATION DATA

ISBN: 978-1-61728-115-0

ISSN: 1535-4806

Published by Nova Science Publishers, Inc. † New York

CONTENTS

PREFACE

This series presents substantial results from around the globe in selected areas of educational research. The field of education is consistently on the top of priority lists of every country in the world, yet few educators are aware of the progress elsewhere. Many techniques, programs and methods are directly applicable across borders.

This series attempts to shed light on successes wherever they may occur in the hope that many wheels need not be reinvented again and again.

Recently there has been a dramatic influx of new immigrants in urban schools in the United States. Therefore, Chapter 1 focuses on using children's literature that discusses their psychosocial needs, as a strategy to support young immigrant children in their urban schools. First, the authors introduce the need and the significance of this topic by highlighting the increase in immigrants in urban education as a statement of a problem and addressing their psychosocial needs as one possible solution to the problem. Second, the authors discuss the theoretical framework as the underpinnings for their selection. Third, the authors discuss the empirical and historical research, as the framework for the selection of children's literature for early elementary years to foster interpersonal understanding of the immigrant child facing psychosocial adjustments. Fourth, the authors analyze the children's literature they have selected using the stated theoretical and empirical underpinnings. Fifth, the authors recommend to urban teachers that three educational principles be applied to the selection of the books, discussion of those books, and follow up activities related to the books. Last, they conclude by summarizing their main message to urban educators.

In China, the development of higher education is even more attractive than the development of social economy. Chinese colleges bear the responsibility of training higher talents for the great developing country which thus demands a high-qualified and well-structured teaching staff. Therefore, each college in China has paid great attention on the construction of teaching staff. However, with the ever-increasing completeness of market economic system and the enhancement of the sense of self-realization for the college teachers in China, the turnover rate of college teachers is greater and greater. It is consequently a critical issue for the colleges to treat such a fact correctly and take countermeasures to deal with it.

For most of the existing literatures in China, there is a popular view that teachers turnover rate negatively influences college performance which has not received enough empirical tests. Chapter 2 tries to empirically test the relationship between teachers turnover rate and college performance in China. Taking the scores on students education and the scores on scientific research adapted from the data in "Appraisal of Chinese Colleges: 2002-2005" as the variables measuring college performance, and taking the data of teachers turnover rate for Chinese colleges in the same period collected from "the Statistical Table of Chinese College Teachers" as the independent variable, the paper empirically finds that there is an inversed U-shaped curve relationship between the two variables. Specifically speaking, for Chinese colleges, when the teachers turnover rate is lower than 3.3%, teachers turnover has positive effect on college performance, while when the teachers turnover rate is higher than 3.3%, there is a negative relationship between the two variables.

The empirical result shows that a reasonable teachers turnover is helpful to the construction of Chinese colleges. That is because such a fact can bring new concepts, new methods and new behavior modes to the new colleges which can be very helpful to the old modes. However, when the rate is higher than a certain level, some core teachers begin to leave and the remaining teachers feel depressed. Therefore, too higher turnover rate will negatively affect college performance. For college managers in China, instead of simply lowering teachers turnover rate as possible, it is necessary for them to control teachers turnover rate in a certain degree in order to improve college performance.

As discussed in Chapter 3, conversations regarding the "achievement gap" fail to consider the historical, economic, sociopolitical and moral backdrop that created the "education debt" experienced by African-Americans. These conversations around the "achievement gap" do not take into consideration the systemic inequities that have accumulated over centuries, resulting in African Americans' cumulative denial of quality learning opportunities (Ladson-Billings, 2006). As a result, many African American students are not afforded access to adequate resources to achieve at the levels comparable to their white counterparts. Despite the legacy of the systematic inequity, many African American parents, historically and presently, continue to successfully pursue quality formal learning opportunities for their children. Using qualitative data from high achieving African American mathematics students matriculating through undergraduate mathematics programs, the authors argue that African-Americans have both historically and currently utilized social and cultural capital to produce high academic achievers, in spite of the "educational debt". The central question guiding this research is how have African American parents of urban public school students empowered themselves in ways that address the educational debt? Results suggest that African-American parents instilled values, advocated for their children and mobilized various resources to positively impact their children's achievement.

Using data from the National Education Longitudinal Study of 1988 (NELS: 88/2000), this study investigated whether grade retention is associated with postsecondary education attendance and bachelor degree completion. Three questions are addressed in Chapter 4: 1) Is grade retention associated with postsecondary education attendance and BA degree completion? 2) Is timing of retention associated with postsecondary education attendance and BA degree completion differently? and 3) Do students who were retained but persisted to graduate from high school differ in postsecondary education attendance and BA degree completion from continuously promoted students?

Findings indicated that the experience of grade retention was significantly associated with lower rates of postsecondary education attendance and BA degree completion when sociodemographic factors, academic achievement, and school factors in eighth grade were taken into account. Both early and late retention were significantly associated with lower rates of postsecondary education attendance and BA degree completion. However, late retention (between fourth and eighth grades) was more strongly linked to lower rates of postsecondary education and BA degree completion than early retention (between first and third grades). Among participants who have a high school diploma, retained participants have a lower rate of BA degree completion than those who were never retained. However, there is no significant difference in postsecondary education attendance between retained and never retained participants.

Urban poverty; high mobility and displacement in and out of neighborhoods; inadequate funding to adequately cover the educational, social, and health needs of children and their families; and high teacher turnover are just some of the vital challenges of urban schools and communities. Too often, schools and teachers are inadequately prepared for the social, political, and economic conditions impacting the lives of their urban students, families, and communities. To be a meaningful part of the commitment to the struggle toward social, economic, cultural, and racial justice, schools must respond by transforming their focus and strategies to work more intimately with their urban communities, community-based organizations, and if applicable, nearby colleges and universities.

In so doing, urban education can move toward a more democratic form of education with input from all involved. Schools can build trust and collaboration with local community members, community organizations, and higher education. The transformation of not only urban education but also of communities toward a more clear form of social justice and equity underlies this approach.

Chapter 5 begins by discussing theories of community strengths and community oriented pedagogy that underlie this approach. The chapter describes the values that develop in collaboration and that frame the work of such urban education strategies. It illustrates school-community-university connections by giving brief descriptions of several such programs, and describes more fully three exemplary models. And finally, the chapter synthesizes the key outcomes of utilizing this school-community-university collaborative approach to urban education.

The chapter mainly serves as a review of literature and of successful programs, but will also include the study of three exemplary programs which will be featured as models of successful school-community-university collaborations.

Best management practices (BMPs) for urban landscapes, including school grounds and college campuses, are often based on production agriculture methods rather than current research in the field of urban horticulture. In particular, the overuse of organic amendments in landscape situations results in soil subsidence, poor plant health, and nutrient overload, which in turn can impact aquatic systems downstream. Instead of using a crop production model for managing urban soils, we should mimic natural processes seen in forest ecosystems. Chapter 6 will outline the problems inherent in short-term (crop production model) management practices in urban landscapes that contribute to the shortened life span of landscape trees and shrubs. A new paradigm for sustainable landscape management will be presented based on the relatively young science of urban horticulture. The application of these site-appropriate methods to school and college landscapes provides ideal educational opportunities for school children, college students, and neighborhood volunteers. Not only will these BMPs improve the health and sustainability of soil and plant systems, they will also increase landscape resistance to invasive species and opportunistic pests. The result – a community-managed landscape requiring less fertilizer, fewer pesticides, and less labor – represents a truly sustainable model.

Chapter 7 presents the use of Reinforcement Learning (RL) in two real-life problems. The use of RL seems to be adequate for many real problems in which there is a long-term goal to achieve clearly defined by means of rewards, and the way of achieving that goal is by means of some interactive actuations to change the state of the environment that characterizes the problem. However, the practical use of RL also involves some associated problems. This chapter presents the experience of the authors to deal with those difficulties in order to successfully solve the tackled problems, as it is shown in the obtained results.

There are twomain branches of reinforcement learning: methods that search directly in the space of value functions that asses the utility of the behaviors (*Temporal Difference Methods*); and methods that search directly in the space of behaviors (*Policy Search Methods*). When applying Temporal Difference (TD) methods in domains with very large or continuous state spaces, the experience obtained by the learning agent in the interaction with the environment must be generalized. The generalization can be carried out in two different ways. On the one hand by discretizing the environment to use a tabular representation of the value functions (e.g. Vector Quantization Q-Learning algorithm). On the other hand, by using an approximation of the value functions based on a supervised learning method (e.g. CMAC Q-Learning algorithm). Other algorithms use both approaches to benefit from both mechanisms, allowing a higher performance. This is the case of the Two Step Reinforcement Learning algorithm. In the case of Policy Search Methods, the Evolutionary Reinforcement Learning algorithm has shown promising in RL tasks. All these algorithms present different ways to tackle the problem of large or continuous state spaces. In Chapter 8, the authors organize and discuss different generalization techniques to solve this problem. Finally, the authors demonstrate the usefulness of the different algorithms described to improve the learning process in the Keepaway domain.

The detection and filtering of communication signals possessing time-frequency (tf) diversity is considered in this chapter. When viewed as an optimization problem in tf space, multiple intelligent agents are used to learn characteristic features of the transmitted signals. The agents are shown to detect and reconstruct specific signals possessing tf diversity in a co-ordinated manner.

The intelligent agents sensing this particular communications environment control a group of narrowband radio receivers. Multiple agent reinforcement learning is used to effectively co-ordinate agent behaviour as they respond to information retrieved from the tf environment. This approach has a further advantage of potentially increasing the rate of information processing following training, due to the parallel nature of the multiple agent implementation.

A review of some of the complex issues inherent in multiple agent reinforcement learning is presented in Chapter 9. The concept of agent mediation in a multi-agent reinforcement learning environment is introduced.

Intelligent agents define the management and specialist tasks. Each is sensitive to different features of the signal of interest (SOI) likely to be present in the tf fragments detected. These include energy threshold agents, demodulator agents, spectral content agents and signal envelope agents which are introduced and discussed. A two-stage learning algorithm incorporating firstly, multi-agent clustering in the tf space. This is followed by a second phase consisting of an optimization of team membership by agents leading on to the reconstruction of one or more SOI.

Two multi-agent systems are introduced as examples that attempt to detect and filter signals possessing known features of interest contained within the wider received spectral band. Various learning policies are investigated and the performance of the systems are considered.

Finally, advantages and some of the co-ordination issues involved in the fusion of spatially diverse agent information are also discussed.

In: Progress in Education, Volume 21
Editor: Robert V. Nata, pp. 1-24

ISBN: 978-1-61728-115-0
© 2011 Nova Science Publishers, Inc.

Chapter 1

CHILDREN'S LITERATURE AND UNDERSTANDING IMMIGRANT CHILDREN

Navaz Peshotan Bhavnagri[1] and Lindsey Willette[2]
[1]College of Education, Wayne State University, Detroit, Michigan
[2]Archdiocese of Detroit, Most Holy Trinity School, Detroit, Michigan

Abstract

Recently there has been a dramatic influx of new immigrants in urban schools in the United States. Therefore, this chapter focuses on using children's literature that discusses their psychosocial needs, as a strategy to support young immigrant children in their urban schools. First, we introduce the need and the significance of this topic by highlighting the increase in immigrants in urban education as a statement of a problem and addressing their psychosocial needs as one possible solution to the problem. Second, we discuss the theoretical framework as the underpinnings for our selection. Third, we discuss the empirical and historical research, as the framework for the selection of children's literature for early elementary years to foster interpersonal understanding of the immigrant child facing psychosocial adjustments. Fourth, we analyze the children's literature we have selected using the stated theoretical and empirical underpinnings. Fifth, we recommend to urban teachers that three educational principles be applied to the selection of the books, discussion of those books, and follow up activities related to the books. Last, we conclude by summarizing our main message to urban educators.

Introduction: Increase in Immigrants

The movement of migration around the world has significantly increased in the recent years. The immigrant population of the United States has increased by 13 million people during the decade of 1990's (Capps, Passel, Perez-Lopez & Fix, 2010), and then an additional 6.9 million between 2000 and 2008 (Migration Policy Institute, 2010). In 2008, the immigrant population in the United States was almost 35 million, which was 12% of the population, as reported by Organization for Economic Cooperation and Development (OCED, 2008).

The 2000 US census data indicates that this massive migration resulted in one out of every five children under the age of eighteen, or 14 million children, in the United States were either immigrants themselves or are children of immigrant parents (Bornstein, Deater-

Deckard & Lansford, 2007). By the year 2005-2006, 22% of all immigrant children were kindergarteners and preschoolers and almost a quarter of young children of five and under (24%) had an immigrant parent (Fortuny, Capps, Sims & Chaudhary, 2010). By 2007, which is the latest demographic data currently available on children, there were 22% or 16,548,000 children in immigrant families in USA (Kids Count Data Center, 2010).

Given this dramatic increase of immigrant children it undoubtedly has impacted schools. This is particularly true of urban schools because immigrant children and families are more likely to live in urban areas. Lollock (2000) reports that according to 2000 Census almost half of the foreign born lived in a central city in a metropolitan area (45.1%), while slightly more than one quarter of the native population (27.5%) lived in a central city.

Given these demographics, Rong and Priessle (1998) openly admit that it is no easy task for urban schools to fully address the needs of rapidly increasing numbers of immigrant children, especially if they speak little or no English, which is often the case thus facing linguistic and academic challenges. For example, according to the Office of English Language Acquisition, Language Enhancement and Academic Achievement for Limited English Proficient Students (OELA, 2010) there was 0% growth in the numbers of students with Limited English Proficiency (LEF) in the year 1995 –96. However, a decade later, in the year 2005-06 alone, there was an increase of 57.17% in LEF students.

Therefore, as an urban educator, it is of paramount importance to support these immigrant children who are facing so many challenges in their urban schools. Besides limited proficiency in English and academic adjustments to a different educational system they also have to make psychosocial and interpersonal adjustments. For example, upon arrival they have no friends (Pryor, 1998; Rubin & Bhavnagri, 2001). They are therefore lonely in their strange surroundings such as their new home, school and neighborhood (Kirova, 2001), given that they have left behind many of their personal and precious possessions which make them feel so much at home. Thus using children's literature that discusses their psychosocial and interpersonal adjustments is a strategy to support both young immigrant children and their nonimmigrant peers to adjust to each other in their urban schools.

As a result, first, we have introduced above the significant increase in immigrant children as a challenge to urban teachers. Furthermore, we have suggested that using children's literature, which address immigrant children's interpersonal and psychosocial needs as one possible solution to this challenge. Second, we discuss the theoretical framework as the underpinnings for our selection of children's literature for early elementary children. Third, we discuss the empirical and historical research the framework as the underpinnings for the same selection. Fourth, we analyze our selection of children's literature, using the stated theoretical and empirical underpinnings. Fifth, we recommend to urban teachers that three educational principles be applied to the selection of the books, discussion of those books, and follow up activities related to the books. Last, we conclude by summarizing our main message to urban educators.

Our Theoretical Framework

Our first theoretical framework for selecting children's books is based on *empirically developed models on immigrant acculturation* (e.g., Garza & Gallegos, 1985; Rueschenberg & Buriel, 1989). These models suggest that immigrants do not simply shed old values for new ones as accepted previously (e.g., Gordon, 1964; Handlin, 1951); rather, they selectively maintain some of their old values and practices, modify some, and alter others.

We agree with Rueschenberg and Buriel's (1989) findings that acculturation is not an all or none process. The Mexican families in their study did not simply totally assimilate, but instead they selectively acculturated only on the external family variables such as their interactions outside the home but maintained their own culture on intra-familial variables, such as their relationships and interactions within family members. These results suggest, and we too agree, that acculturation is a multi-dimensional and a differentiated process.

Many of the books we chose also address this selective acculturation process outside their home. Examples include finding a new home (e.g., *My Diary from Here to There, Good-bye, 382 Shin Dang Dong, A Piece of Home)* and maintaining their own culture, such as ethnic food, cultural artifacts and values from the old country when interacting within family members (e.g., *Who Belongs Here? An American Story, My Chinatown, Hannah is My Name, Lights for Gita, A Very Important Day).*

Garza and Gallegos (1985), acculturation model supports our view that the environment has differential impact on each immigrant, and each immigrant has a personal choice to the degree of acculturation. (e.g., *The Name Jar, Hannah is My Name,* and *America My New Home* show a range of impact the new environment makes on immigrant children and their families. These stories also depict the choices each immigrant child makes as to the degree of his or her acculturation.) Based on the above works, we too view that acculturation is selective, nuanced, differentiated, multifaceted and complex.

Bhatnagar (1983) in his discussion of educating immigrants identifies three paradigms for examining the adjustment of immigrants. In the assimilation paradigm, the immigrant adopts the ways of the host nation, including its language, traditions and mannerisms. Over time, the immigrants have become like the members of the host society. In the adjustment paradigm, the immigrant adopts some of the ways of the host society and also retains their original cultural values and traditions. In the integration, paradigm, both the immigrant and the host members make adjustments.

We subscribe to the integration paradigm mentioned by Bhatnagar. For example, the first author of this chapter in her immigrant research with others (Patel, Power & Bhavnagri, 1996) has viewed acculturation as a bi-directional process in which the new immigrants modify the mainstream culture, and at the same time individuals in the mainstream culture also change to effectively adjust the immigrants' ways. We recommend that this integration paradigm be used when the stories are read, for we attempt not only to reach out to the immigrant child to accept the ways of the host country but we also reach out to children from the host culture to accept the immigrant child (e.g., *My Name is Yoon, The Name Jar, Angel Child, Dragon Child).* This paradigm thus promotes bi-directional interpersonal understanding between children.

Thus this paradigm leads to our second theoretical framework, namely *Selman's theory of Interpersonal Understandings* (Selman, 1980). This theory addresses the coordination of one's own social perspective with the social perspective taking of others. As a young child develops, he has different levels of understanding of friendships (Selman & Schultz, 1990).

Children at level 0 (3 to 6 years old) have an egocentric understanding of friendship. Friendship is understood as physical actions, such as someone who offers toys to them. Thus, a friend is a person with whom they are currently having momentary physical interactions. They do not understand friendship in psychological terms, such as a friend is a confidant with whom you have an emotional intimacy. They are thus unable to differentiate between psychological and physical attributes. For example, a close friend is one who is in literal close physical proximity when playing and not someone for whom they feel psychological closeness. Furthermore, they admire the physical attributes of their friend and not their psychological attributes.

Children at level 1 (5 to 9 years old) have a unilateral understanding of friendship, namely as a one-way assistance. Unlike level 0, now they do understand that individual's have psychological needs and attributes (e.g., thoughts, feelings, motives). They further understand that their psychological perspective is separate and different when compared to others. However, the child considers a friend is someone who does what he or she wants him to do, and not consider at all what the friend's wants and psychological needs. In terms of closeness, it is no more only a person's physical proximity such as he is my friend because he lives near by. Now a person is my friend because he meets my needs.

The stories we selected took into account the developmental levels of interpersonal understanding and perspective taking of young children (e.g., stories such as *Marianthe's Story, My Diary from Here to There* and *From Far Away* encourages perspective taking). This is especially true when stories are read and the teacher draws children's attention to illustrations depicting protagonist's emotions and then invites children to explain how they would feel if they were put in that same situation. We on one hand acknowledge the developmental limitations of young children in friendship making and taking on the perspective of the immigrant protagonist. However, on the other hand, we suggest using the provocative verbal dialogue by the teacher to scaffold the young child to move from level 0 to level 1.

Thus this scaffolding leads to our third theoretical framework, namely *Vygotsky's Socio Historical Theory* (Vygotsky, 1978). Vygotsky's theory recommends that an appropriate educational verbal discourse between a teacher who is an expert and a child who is a novice can facilitate the child to move from a lower level of zone of proximal development (lower ZPD) to a higher level of zone of proximal development (upper ZPD)(Berk & Winsler, 1995). This interpersonal level of verbal and social interactions, also called shared cognition or co-construction of knowledge (Wertsch & Rogoff, 1984), contributes to internalization at the intrapersonal level (Wink & Putney, 2002). During story telling, this scaffolding and moving the child to upper ZPD should be applied when the children participate in verbal teacher-child interactions. Such inter personal interactions could facilitate children internalizing an understanding, empathy and perspective taking of an immigrant child.

According to Vygotsky, physical tools like the children's books can expand children's memory and focused attention (Bodrova & Leong, 1996). Our book selection is such that during storytelling, the teacher can deliberately activate her student's memory by helping students remember similar situations. She can also expand their empathy and perspective taking by focusing their attention on emotional scenarios the protagonist confronts during acculturation. Additionally, the teacher should focus children's attention on the protagonists' uses of physical tools. For example, discuss how the protagonists have emotional attachments to familiar personal artifacts from their old country that activate their memory and self regulate their loss, fear and loneliness when being uprooted from their old country (e.g., blanket made by grandmother, Hannah's bracelet to her friend Janie so that she will remember Hannah, a grandmother's gift of a wooden block in a pouch to Unhei that is placed next to grandmother's photos, Jangmi's hand painted scrolls, painted fans, silk cushions and straw mats.

Our Empirical and Historical Research Framework

Our first empirical research is based *on studies on children's literature and children's social interpersonal understandings* conducted by Bhavnagri and her colleagues. Bhavnagri and Samuels' (1996a, 1996b) study used children's books that promoted pro-social thinking of multiple social skills including empathy, perspective taking and forming friendships. All these skills were discussed in Selman's Theory of Interpersonal Understanding and were considered in our selection of books. We also have built on Molenda and Bhavnagri's (2008) work, where books were read to low-income, urban and inner city bilingual immigrant children, to promote pro-social interpersonal behaviors.

Our second empirical research is based *on immigrant studies conducted by Bhavnagri and her colleagues*. The books selected here are based on Rubin and Bhavnagri's (2001) focus group research findings about immigrant students, such as them missing their family members. These authors found a common theme that all the immigrant participants "deeply missed many of their close family members who were still in their home country" (p. 310). They have then recommended, that, "educators need to show empathy and understanding for immigrant student's circumstances". The authors of this chapter have therefore have suggested educational dialogue to promote empathy.

Bhavnagri and her colleague's historical research (Bhavnagri & Krolikowski, 2000; Bhavnagri, Krolikowski & Vaswani, 2006) on immigrant children, as well as international empirical research on low income, at risk, vulnerable urban children (Bhavnagri & Vaswani, 1999) have documented that when the teachers actively and deliberately use community-linked strategies then they are very effective in supporting immigrant and at risk urban children's well being. For example, during the Reform Era (1870 -1920), kindergarten teachers utilized community businesses, services and resources to optimize immigrant kindergartener's development; and visiting teachers in public schools did home and community visits to immigrant children and families, resulting in prevention and ameliorating immigrant children's failure.

Another example, when schools have collaborated with an available community agency (e.g., international institute), which in turn is working very closely with other community agencies, (e.g., social service agencies, radio stations, foreign-language press, immigration office, youth organizations, legal agencies, employment agencies, universities) and other community personnel (e.g., family life educators, vocational counselors, social workers, English translators, community organizers), then such schools are highly successful in supporting and mobilizing their teachers to facilitate immigrant children's academic, social and personal adjustments (Bhavnagri, Krolikowski & Vaswani, 2006). Based on these findings, we strongly support that teachers use public libraries as a valuable community resource and public librarian as an expert in selecting suitable children's books that promote interpersonal understanding between immigrant and non-immigrant children. Our selection too was based on books available in public libraries.

Other researchers have supported the findings of Bhavnagri's and her colleagues' work. For example, Pryor et al's (1998) research on immigrant children's psychological and social adjustment in urban schools also supports Rubin and Bhavnagri's findings. Pryor et al also reported that, "the children acutely feel the loss of their friends and family back home" (p.6). Kirova's (2001) phenomenological research also reported on immigrant children's following emotions. First, immigrant children feel alone and lonely because they feel the loss of familiar home, friends and every day comforting and treasured objects. Second, they felt different from others; specifically, they lacked the ability to fit with their peer groups and communicate effectively. The authors of this chapter have therefore attempted to discuss the protagonist immigrant children's psychological needs, particularly the range of emotions they undergo during their process of acculturation.

Pryor, Ginn-Clark, Kostrzewa, Asher, Palmer, and Gaba (1998) research findings are that the sense of loss is much more significant for parents than their children. The authors agree with Pryor et al (1998), that immigrant parents have to cope with challenges such as, lack of private transportation, finding quality higher education in order to be retrained but on a limited budget, and lack of competencies in English, all of which marginalizes them and reduces the prospects of immediate employability (Bhavnagri, 2001). As a result, they take low paying and labor intensive jobs, resulting in economic stress. Pryor et al., further reports that many immigrants scrimp and save to send remittances to their close relatives back home. They are lonely and isolated. Some have come first, hoping to bring their family later. Pryor, (2001) stated that when immigrant parents were interviewed, less than twenty percent reported that they were completely happy with their lives. This was particularly true of those who had grueling jobs for which they were over qualified missed their life in their homeland.

Theilheimer's (2001) study has reported that the use of children's books resulted in immigrant students sharing their emotions. As a result, the immigrant students improved their communication with others; and others in turn gained a deeper understanding and perspective of the immigrant students. Based on these findings, we too suggest that children's books be used to identify emotions of the immigrant protagonists and support non-immigrant students to gain an understanding and perspective of immigrant students.

Many of the challenges reported in all these immigrant studies were depicted in the stories we chose. On the other hand, there is also ample evidence that despite these adversities and challenges the immigrant families are resilient, on the whole optimistic, and are diligently striving towards positive adjustments in the new country, especially if they receive support from extended family and community members (e.g., Bhavnagri, 2001; Bhavnagri & Krolikowski, 2000; Bhavnagri, Krolikowski & Vaswani, 2006, Rubin & Bhavnagri 2001; Johns 2001; Watson 2001). The children's books that we discuss also portray immigrant parents facing multiple challenges but also being very resilient in effectively coping with the challenges confronted in a new country.

Given all these empirical findings, we chose books that address the following challenges. (1) How does the immigrant protagonist children copes with initial emotions, such as loss of familiar home, and the loneliness of missing their friends, family, neighborhood, village and a whole cultural life style (e.g., *Spoken Memories, Sumi's First Day of School Ever, Who Belongs Here? An American Story*)? (2) How does the protagonist immigrant children cope when they are teased because of their limited English (e.g., *Painted Words, Angel Child, Dragon Child*) and because they have unusual names, which are tied to their self identity (e.g., *My Name is Yoon, The Name Jar, Good-bye, 382 Shin Dang Dong, Angel Child, Dragon Child*)? (3) How does the protagonist immigrant child and their parents cope when they feel lonely and get separated from family members, such as when fathers arrive first in

USA (e.g., *Spoken Memories, My Diary from Here to There*)? (4) How do the parents of the protagonists cope with economic stress and hardships, like taking low paying and labor-intensive jobs (e.g., *Hannah is My Name*)? (5) How do children and their parents of the protagonists demonstrate that they are resilient, optimistic and can integrate to the new country, resulting in all happy endings (e.g., *Hannah is My Name, A Piece of Home, From Far Away*)?

Children's Literature

Baghban (2007) states that picture books can help elementary immigrant school children with the acculturation process they undergo when entering into the Unites States. Hence in this section, we provide a discussion of books suitable for early elementary children, where the main characters are immigrant children. Besides summarizing the central content of these books, we use our theoretical and empirical framework to further analyze how its content can promote interpersonal understanding between immigrant and nonimmigrant children. The specific concepts referring to our theoretical and empirical framework are italicized to facilitate the reader to easily identify the linkages to the framework.

We do not claim that this is a comprehensive list of all possible books. Our books were chosen based on availability via public library, given that urban teachers would also have access to public libraries. These books are discussed under the following immigrant related categories: (1) unwanted uprooting; (2) adjusting to a new country; (3) accepting identity, and (4) naturalization. The sequential order of presenting these four categories follows the time line of the entire process of acculturation. For example, first, they are uprooted from their own country. Next, they have to adjust to this country. Then they gradually accept their new identity. Finally, they formalize this acculturation process by going through the naturalization ceremony of becoming citizens.

Unwanted Uprooting

Immigrant children often do not have a choice when it comes to them leaving their home country and immigrating to a new country. This change can be initially unsettling and difficult but the immigrant children have the resiliency to adjust to the new circumstances. Books like *My Diary from Here to There* by Perez, *Good-bye, 382 Shin Dang Dong* by Park and Park, *A Piece of Home* by Levitin, and *Who Belongs Here? An American Story* by Knight deal with this unwanted uprooting. In the beginning of these books, the main characters are in their home country and are faced with the impending move and all of the challenges and stresses associated with it.

For example, in *My Diary from Here to There,* Amada overhears her parents' discussion about leaving Mexico. She uses her diary as a *physical tool to regulate her feelings,* which gives her resiliency, when her father leaves his home in Mexico to look for work in the United States. Amada worries about the relocation of her family, leaving friends, making new friends and *acculturation* to living in the United States. The story includes *emotional issues such as fear, worry, stress, separation of family, relocation, leaving other family members and friends, not being able to take all treasured items and the adjustment when once settled in the new country.*

My Diary from Here to There has a protagonist from an upper elementary grade and not an early elementary grade. Despite it, we chose this book because it has great potential in helping children understand the emotions one goes through when uprooted from their home. Teachers can solicit children's personal experiences as to how they regulate their emotions such as fear, worry and loneliness in order to relate to Amada's emotions when immigrating.

In *Good-bye, 382 Shin Dang Dong*, Jangmi moves to America and experiences feelings similar to that of Amada. She finds it difficult to say goodbye to relatives and friends, plus she misses the food, customs, and beautiful things from her home in Korea. On the plane ride, Jangmi is worried because she does not speak any English. Her father teaches her an English word, rose. Her name Jangmi in Korean language means rose. When asked if she would like to adopt Rose as her American name, Jangmi refuses saying she likes her Korean name. This response clearly illustrates her resistance and her resilience to the pressures of mainstream culture. As stated in the immigrant theoretical framework, that it is not uncommon *for immigrants to maintain some of their old values when adapting to a new country and undergoing the acculturation process.*

Jangmi pines for home as soon as she arrives; comparing the foreign things in America to the lovely and comforting things she was familiar with in Korea. This directly relates to Kirova's (2001) research that states immigrant *children feel lonely and uprooted* because of the everyday objects they had to leave behind. Once settled into their new home, Jangmi makes friends with the girl next door. She has newly developed feeling of hope about her new home and her new life in the United States. Eventually, Jangmi seems to be willing to adopt some American ways. The major focus of this book is on the impending and then actual move to America. The book concludes without addressing a lot of the adjustment that Jangmi will still have to undergo to integrate into the American culture.

In *A Piece of Home,* Gregor's family is getting ready to leave Russia to join other family members in the United States. Gregor is faced with a very daunting task when his father tells him that he can take only one special belonging. He struggles with the decision, recalling fond memories of the treasures he has. He finally chooses to bring a blanket that his great-grandmother made, despite his family trying to dissuade him from carrying such a bulky item. His blanket is a *physical tool for Gregor, which not only provides him physical comfort but more importantly, provides him also emotional comfort* and resiliency when he makes the move.

Gregor worries about his family's move and wishes he could go back to Russia during the plane ride to America. Kirova's (2001) study reported that immigrant children not only miss everyday objects of comfort, but deeply miss their family and friends as well. Upon the family's arrival, their relatives from United States are overjoyed and happily greet them. After a shaky encounter with his cousin, Gregor soon makes friends.

Who Belongs Here? An American Story is an inspiring tale of a frightened and sad young Cambodian refugee boy named Nary, who shows resiliency by fleeing to Thailand with his grandmother and uncle. His bravery is portrayed through his long travel and subsequent stay in a refugee camp. Then he endures another long trip, arriving in the United States with his makeshift family, to be granted a new freedom.

His trial and tribulations are still not over. Now, in the United States, Nary encounters a *language barrier* and has many frustrating days addressing the daunting task of learning

English. He also encounters bullies at school who call him inappropriate ethnic names and he is worried about his *inability to fit in with his peers*. Nary and his teacher then plan a lesson so that his classmates can get an idea on what it is like to be a refugee and he eventually makes friends with the other children at his school. Nary also learns how to write in Khmer so that he can keep in touch with family members who are still in Cambodia.

Despite this story being about a refugee child, we chose to include it for the following reasons. Firstly, immigrant children also encounter some psychosocial adjustments similar to refugee children, like Nari (e.g., *stress in learning a new language and being accepted by peers)*. Secondly, Nary is portrayed as an active competent child, who strives hard for his own social, emotional, language and academic development. He thus demonstrates resiliency and coping strategies also found in immigrant children. Bhavnagri (2001) as a guest editor to the special theme issue on: "The Global Village: Migration and Education" in *Childhood Education* reports that resiliency was a common theme among immigrants, especially if they received support from others. In Nary's case, he is resilient because he has his teacher and the presence of his make shift family to support him. Thirdly, this story suggests that teachers in collaboration with the new child can actively and effectively use strategies to integrate a refugee or an immigrant child into a classroom.

Adjusting to a New Country

Immigrant children have to cope with changes associated with drastic moves. Books that address coping with change and demonstrating resiliency of the children are *Marianthe's Story* by Aliki, *Hannah is My Name* by Yang, *Sumi's First Day of School Ever* by Pak, *My Chinatown* by Mak, *America, My New Home* by Gunning, and *Lights for Gita* by Gilmore.

Marianthe's Story has two stories included in one book. The first story is titled, *Painted Words*. This story deals with Marianthe's first day of school and the many challenges she faces related to *acculturation*. For example, she has to *learn how to adapt and adjust in an English-speaking classroom* when she speaks no English herself. Another example, she *lacks friends,* and is subjected to teasing such as name calling, sniggers, nudging and whispering about her, particularly done by one classmate. She thus experiences hurt and *loneliness*.

The second story is titled *Spoken Memories* in which Marianthe is well adjusted to her classroom and her classmates. Her English has adequately developed and she is able to participate in life story time. Marianthe uses a framed photograph holding it close to her heart, to remember what her life was in her home country, namely Greece. Vygotsky would explain this type of use of a photograph, as young children needing pictorial symbols and physical artifacts to prompt their memory and deliberately activate their thinking (Bodrova & Leong, 1996).

This book does address many common concerns and tribulations that immigrants face. The story setting in *Spoken Memories* is about a rural immigrant Greek girl coming from a developing agrarian society. For example, Marianthe walks two hours to get to the nearest school, hauls fresh water to her village from a spring and is discriminated because she is a girl who wants to go to school. This would be an excellent book to discuss if the teacher has an immigrant rural child from a developing country who has led a life similar to Marianthe.

Hannah is My Name focuses on a family's struggle to become legal residents of the United States. While they are waiting for their green cards to come from the government, the family faces *economic stress*. This economic stress is portrayed, for example, when Hannah's parents express their worries that they may not be able to provide the necessities for their daughter, such as food and milk. Another example, Hannah likes books like *Curious George* and reads it from the shelf of Woolworth. She hides her disappointment from her father when she has to return it on the shelf. Thus the implied message is that they cannot afford it. Still another example, of economic hardship is that the father walks home, implying that the family cannot afford the cost of daily transportation, after completing his laborious low paying job of washing dishes in a diner. Moreover, he is walking, wearing second hand shoes that are falling apart.

Her dad's job situation is similar to what Pryor's (2001) research findings reported, namely that immigrant parents have grueling jobs and some immigrants are stressed because they are struggling economically. Hannah's parents are additionally stressed, because they are fearful and have anxieties that they will be discovered in America without their green cards and will be forced to leave.

Hannah cares and consoles her distressed weeping mother because she lost her job. This situation is parallel to Rubin and Bhavnagri's (2001) findings about Chaldean immigrant family related stressors, impacting their adolescent offspring. Chaldean adolescents expressed their care and concern for their parents who had limited employable skills and limited English, just like Hannah's mother, by economically supporting them. Hannah, who is a young child, too expressed care and concern for her mother by stroking her hair, telling her not to worry, and finally suggesting that she does not need any new toys or new shoes. Furthermore, Hannah too like the Chaldean immigrants had to live in small, crowded urban apartments due to limited income.

The story ends after an anxious wait of over two years. The family is overjoyed when their green cards finally arrive and they *integrate* into their new culture. The end of the book also hints about the gradual shift in identity from Chinese to Chinese American. A sensitive discussion of all the immigrant issues addressed in this book can help students gain *empathy, understanding and perspective taking about immigrants and their acculturation process.*

In *Sumi's First Day of School Ever,* Sumi finds her school to be a lonely, scary and mean place. During recess, Sumi starts a friendship with another girl who sits beside her in the dirt and draws objects similar to what she is drawing. Sumi's portrayal of friendship suggests that she is at *Selman's level 0,* because her entire friendship is based on her physical proximity. It is a brief parallel activity with their verbal interactions focused for that moment only, which physically draws them together. The teacher should discuss this strategy of participating in doing similar activities side by side to promote friendship making between immigrant and non-immigrant children.

Bhavnagri and Samuels' (1996a, 1996b) study has established that through storybook discussions, teachers can promote pro-social thinking such as understanding of how to make friends, taking another child's perspective and understanding others emotions. Therefore the teacher should through storybook discussions promote an understanding of an immigrant child's perspective (e.g., *child wants to make friends*) and an understanding of their emotions (e.g., *fear, worry, and loneliness*).

This book does not explicitly say that Sumi is an immigrant but she has limited proficiency in English, like that of a newly arrived immigrant child. Additionally, the book addresses the psychosocial needs and challenges of immigrant children. However, it is plausible, that Sumi is an American citizen, raised in an ethnic and non-English speaking household. Thus she could be a child of immigrant parents or even a two or three generation descendant of an immigrant.

My Chinatown is about one year of a Chinese boy's life presented in a poem format starting in winter, and continuing until next winter rolls around again. The boy reminisces and longs for "home", by comparing his current home in New York Chinatown with his original home back in China. The poem mentions his grandmother in China, his reluctance to schooling and learning English, his family's quick departure to the United States, the things that had to be left behind, as well as the boy gradually adjusting to the United States. This book thus does a commendable job giving *perspective on the boy's personal emotions* but it does not shed light on any interpersonal relationships with peers that the boy has during his acculturation process.

Gunning's *America, My New Home* has twenty-three poems depicting a young Jamaican village girl's adjustment to specific events in a busy city. These poems express the *fear and loneliness* the character initially feels. She gradually learns the Queen's English and experiences commonplace events such as the subway, circus and amusement parks in the United States. We believe the teacher will need to help students connect and integrate the individual elements in each poem in order for them to comprehend the continuity between poems into a complete story.

In *Lights for Gita*, a young girl is celebrating Diwali, festival of lights for the first time away from her home country of India. Gita thinks that the November gloom her new host country gives off is nothing like the glow that New Delhi exhorts for the celebration. Gita's family undergoes multiple set backs while getting readying for Diwali, such as freezing rain preventing the family from setting off fireworks and inhibiting Gita's friends from attending her party. Finally, the storm knocks out power in the house. Therefore, the only lights available for Diwali are the diyas that are lit. The horrible weather on Diwali makes Gita *long for her old home, familiar things and especially her grandmother* who is still in New Delhi.

Gita gradually accepts the fate of the day and experiences joy when her lit up diyas beat out the unexpected darkness that fell upon her. This story thus symbolizes the meaning of festival of light as giving hope and conquering psychological darkness. That is one of the true meanings of Diwali for all and now especially for Gita. The story also suggests that when *immigrants hold on to their religion, familiar customs and spiritual rituals, it then provides them with resiliency, comfort and the ability to overcome despair when adjusting to the challenges of the new country.*

Accepting Identity

Many immigrant children must make adjustments to the American perceived oddity of their ethnic names as well as the language barriers they face to avoid being marginalized by the major culture. In *The Name Jar* by Choi and *My Name is Yoon* by Recorvitis, girls are uncomfortable with their ethnic derived names and undergo self-identity and self-acceptance transformations. *I Hate English* by Levine concentrates on a girl's resistance to learn the English language. Surat's book *Angel Child, Dragon Child* deals with the oddity of an ethnic name as well as a language barrier and *From Far Away* by Munsch describes a young girl's identity adjustment when arriving in a new country.

Every child at birth has a right to a name, according to United Nation's Convention on the Rights of the Child, article 7 (Convention Right Information Network, 2010), thus codifying the importance of having a name. It is a right to one's identity and thus it is not an easy decision to change one's name. Hence, it should be no surprise when individuals choose to resist and refuse to change their names.

In *The Name Jar,* Unhei experiences teasing on the school bus on her way to her first day of school. She fingers the block of wood with her name on it given to her lovingly by her grandmother, while she was crying. She uses it as a Vygotskian physical tool to activate her grandmother's memory of loving words, and as a physical object to clutch and settle her nervousness and excitement of the first day. When she is introduced to her classmates, she chooses not to say her name because she worries that no one will be able to pronounce it. She sets out to choose an Americanized name because she does not want to be different from other American kids and because she *fears that she is unable to fit in with her peers.*

Her resilient mother reassures her that "That you *are* different, Unhei. That's a good thing" thus celebrating her individuality and empowering her daughter's self esteem. Her mother subscribes to the *integration paradigm,* which states that immigrants take on some customs of the host country while also holding onto some of their preliminary cultural beliefs, values and traditions (Bhatnagar, 1983).

Unhei's classmates are cooperating with her wish to find an American name by suggesting names, which they put into a big jar. She integrates well into the classroom community and seems to make friends easily. After she and her classmates work on finding an American name, she finally settles on her Korean name, Unhei. Her decision suggests her being resilient to accepting her Korean identity despite being a minority. She feels accepted by her peers from the majority culture even though she has a Korean name, and feels psychologically secure and empowered enough to retain her original name.

My Name is Yoon is a story about a young Korean girl who adamantly and repeatedly opposes writing her name, which in Korean means Shining Wisdom, in the English alphabet. She prefers to write her name using the Korean script. Her refusal to write her name in English is her way of resisting an identity change. Furthermore, she is lonely, has no friends and expresses her desire to go back to her home country, which is a frequent desire during an immigrant's acculturation process. She psychologically copes with her reality, through daydreaming and transforming herself into other items. Whenever, asked to write her name in English, she instead writes the name of the object she is currently imagining that she is. However, her flights of imagination actually result in expanding her English vocabulary.

Over time with parental support, teacher's understanding and acceptance, and by her making friends, she gradually begins to like America. An immigrant's adjustment is always facilitated by a social support network of family, friends and community members (Bhavnagri, 2001; Bhavnagri & Krolikowski, 2000; Bhavnagri, Krolikowski & Vaswani, 2006), which Yoon also experiences.

She also accepts her new identity and understands that she is different from other children and that is "good". As a result, she no longer feels a need to express her revolt by refusing to write her name in English. Finally, she happily writes her name using the English alphabet. Now she feels psychologically secure, for the story ends by her claiming that even when written in English, "It still means Shining Wisdom". This newfound change is a testament to Yoon's adaptability and resilience to changing circumstances over time, demonstrating final self-acceptance.

In *I Hate English,* Mei Mei has a very difficult time accepting the fact that she can't think and talk in Chinese anymore. She refuses to speak in school even though she understands most of what the teacher says. After school, she goes to a Chinatown Learning Center and does everything in Chinese. One day a teacher arrives at the Center to help Mei Mei with English. Mei Mei is suddenly faced with overwhelming emotions when the teacher comes across a word in English that Mei Mei does not know in Chinese. She fears that she will lose something about herself because of this lack of understanding.

The adjustment process is very difficult for her, but with a determined teacher Mei Mei eventually comes to an acceptance with the language. The integration paradigm, which *emphasizes bi-directionality,* is highlighted when Mei Mei and her teacher *both have to make modifications in the way they think and act. They reach out to each other's cultures to facilitate Mei Mei's adjustment.* This bi-directionality in adjustment is limited to the adult child interaction. Unfortunately, this story does not address bi-directionality in adjustment during child-child interaction which results in interpersonal understandings.

In *Angel Child, Dragon Child,* Ut, whose given name is Nguyen Hoa, and her family came to America but they were forced to leave their mother back home in Vietnam because of limited money. When Ut and her sisters start their new school American children immediately tease them because they look different from all of the other children in the schoolyard. The teasing continues because of Ut's clothing, her name, and because she responds to her teacher in Vietnamese. When she feels isolated and alone, Ut pulls out a small picture of her mother. This Vygotskian *physical tool* helps Ut remember the loving words her mother spoke to her before she left Vietnam, and therefore finally helps her accept her Vietnamese nickname and heritage.

The days pass as the family continues to try to adjust, while deeply missing their mother. An altercation occurs one day between Ut and Raymond, a cruel boy who teases Ut. Ut and Raymond are then forced to sit together until they come to an understanding of each other, which ultimately leads to an unlikely friendship between the two. The peer support that Raymond shows Ut empowers her to accept her identity, which then further propels Raymond to be adamant about the school hosting a Vietnamese fair and raising enough money for Ut's mother to be reunited with the rest of her family. This book draws attention *to making friends and missing family members,* two very common immigrant issues. It additionally demonstrates that a non-immigrant child can be *empathetic to the emotional needs* of an immigrant child.

In *From Far Away,* Saoussan writes a letter to her reading buddy describing how her family had to flee their country of origin, due to war and ended up in Canada. She tells of her struggles with the *language barrier* and not understanding simple social norms, like asking to use the bathroom. She also describes her fearful first experience with Halloween and how it brought many terrified memories of the war in her home country. Saoussan explains that a year has passed since her arrival into Canada and she has learned English, made friends and likes school.

She tells her reading buddy that Canada is a nice place, which allows readers to see that she has made a good adjustment. When she tries to change her name to Susan her mother resists that idea, thus indicating that she is not willing to let her daughter loose her ethnic identity. Bhatnagar (1983) would say that Saoussan was subscribing to the assimilation paradigm while her mother was subscribing to the integration paradigm. This book is written in a very simple text, which makes it easy for young children to understand. Even though this book is about a refugee child we decided to include this book because a lot of the adjustment issues presented in *From Far Away* are parallel to the adjustment issues that an immigrant child faces.

Naturalization

Immigrants who come to the United States with intentions to make this country their permanent residence must go through the naturalization process. Many immigrants view this as a joyous time for celebration. Even though the immigrants are officially becoming citizens of the United States, it does not mean that they will give up their ethnic identities, traditions, and beliefs. *The American Wei* by Pomerance and *A Very Important Day* by Herold both deal with the naturalization process.

In *The American Wei,* Wei Fong is a young boy who is very excited because his family is getting ready to go to the courthouse to be sworn in as American citizens. It is a doubly lucky day for him because he also loses his first tooth in front of the courthouse. Since he cannot find it on his own, all the other people becoming American citizens join him in searching for his missing tooth. The guard at the entrance is pressuring the crowd to get inside the courthouse because the ceremony is about to begin, when an old woman proudly finds the tooth. All the tooth searchers make their way into the building and the naturalization process begins. After the ceremony the family heads back home and celebrates with friends and family, and that night the tooth fairy makes a visit to Wei Fong.

A Very Important Day follows twelve families as they make their way down to a New York courthouse, on a very snowy day, so that they can be sworn in as American citizens. Many of the people hoping to be sworn never had to worry or deal with snow in their home countries, while others are very used to it. All families do some comparing and contrasting of the United States to their countries of origin.

Both these books are very *developmentally appropriate* for young children. For example, losing a first tooth is especially exciting for all young children, an authentic experience to which they can easily relate. However, these books do not examine the interpersonal understandings of an immigrant child or antecedent factors that lead to naturalization. Despite this lack of focus on the antecedents that lead to naturalization and becoming an American citizen, we chose to include these books for two reasons. First, they are so celebratory and festive in nature and which young child does not enjoy celebration and festivity? Second, it completes the entire acculturation process with a specific scripted ceremony, which is worth discussing especially when the immigrant child participates in this celebratory process. It is like a fairytale ending, with a clear finale, which too has a happy conclusion.

Educational Recommendations for Urban Teachers

We recommend that the urban teachers should apply the three principles mentioned below to the following three procedures: (a) the selection of books, (b) asking provocative discussion questions and comments when telling of these stories, and (c) finally designing related participatory activities. Hence we have books, discussions and activities as sub-headers linking the principles to the above stated procedures.

Principle One: Developmentally Appropriate Practices

Books. Copple and Bredekamp (2009) define developmentally appropriate practices (DAP) as "meeting children where they are" (which Vygotsky calls lower ZPD) and "enabling them to reach goals that are both challenging and achievable" (xii) (which Vygotsky calls moving them to their upper ZPD). Our practice of selecting *books* and *discussing* them by asking challenging questions is based on Vygotsky's theory. Hence, we are applying DAP.

Discussions. Here are examples of DAP questions to ask, thus "enabling them to reach goals that are both challenging and achievable" and that can move students to their upper ZPD. In the book titled, *Hannah is My Name,* teachers can ask questions relating to the fearful flee Hannah and her father have from the police, such as "What has happened to make Hannah and her father have to leave so quickly? How do you think that made Hannah feel? How would that make you feel? How does Hannah feel now about the hotel guard (who warned them about the police coming and helped them escape though a back entrance)?" Questions similar to that challenge scaffold students to deeply reflect beyond the surface level of the text, and finally imagine and visualize experiences beyond their daily mundane life. Thus it is stretching their mental capacities and moving them to their upper ZPD, which is DAP.

Additionally, we recommend that that we meet children "where they are" on Selman's developmental theory, namely at the level 0, but then via discussion of the books, we move them to level 1. For example, in *My Diary from Here to There,* a teacher can ask questions such as "When Amada leaves Mexico to immigrate to the United States, can she still remain best friend with Michi who remains behind in Mexico?" Since young children view friendship as physical proximity and do not have a full understanding about the psychological connection friends have, they are most likely to respond, "No, they cannot remain best friends." Teachers can then scaffold children to level 1 by asking about their friends in another classroom or school. Young children can be scaffolded to realize that friends may not always be in close physical proximity at all times and yet remain friends. Teachers can then connect the children's responses to an explanation as to how Amada and Michi can also remain friends, even though they will both be living in different countries. Applying Selman's developmental theory integrated with Vygotsky's scaffolding to move children to their upper ZPD is truly a DAP.

We also recommend one of the core consideration in DAP, which is to know each child as an individual and be responsive to individual variation (Copple & Bredekamp, 2009). Through out this chapter, we have been advocating to be responsive through appropriate discussion of books to the individual variations in the psychosocial needs of new immigrants.

Activities. We recommend activities such as role-playing related to literacy, which is undergirded by developmental theories and thus can be regarded as DAP. This recommendation based on the first author's earlier works where the children role played to learn the different elements of a story (Creech & Bhavnagri, 2002). This role-playing was grounded in the principles of child development and Vygotskian concepts of scaffolding to upper ZPD. Furthermore, Epstein (2009) states that developmentally, children do explore shared emotions and empathic responses indirectly through role-play. They attribute their own emotions and the emotions of others' to characters when they pretend. According to

Epstein, stories can help children reflect on these feelings and spark discussions that promote perspective taking.

There are studies that state that dramatic play contributes to the creation of positive relations among peers, which is necessary in interpersonal understanding. It thus establishes that dramatic play is a highly developmentally appropriate activity. For example, in case studies by Kaufman (1994), additional resources, such as hand mirrors, jewelry, pull toys, manipulatives and additional baby dolls, were added into the housekeeping area of an imaginative play center in a kindergarten classroom which helped a five year old girl develop friendships and create positive relationships among her peers by learning how to act out, and enjoy, different roles with the assistance of her teacher.

According to Wood (2007), dramatic play corners are essential instruments for expression of feelings. Therefore based on Wood's expertise and Kaufman's study, we recommend that the teacher add additional resources as props related to the stories read (e.g., clothing, artifacts, and house wares similar to what the protagonists used in their old country, literacy and art materials to pretend diary keeping, packing boxes and suitcases for moving, and the many objects which had favorite memories of the protagonist attached to it), to support and facilitate the children to integrate elements of the story in their spontaneous child initiated dramatic play. Additionally, the teacher may have to take on a role from the story, to initiate, facilitate and sustain the dramatic play episodes. Smilansky's (1976) famous research calls that inside intervention.

Teachers can also initiate structured role-playing the following types of scenarios from the stories. For example, role play the first interaction between Gregor and his cousin in *A Piece of Home,* or the playground interaction and subsequent friend making with a classmate in *My Name is Yoon,* or when Jangmi gets an impromptu visit from her new neighbor next door and makes her first American friend in *Goodbye, 382 Shin Dang Dong.*

McLennan (2008) recommends when dramatic activities (e.g., child-initiated spontaneous dramatic play or teacher-initiated structured role playing) are executed repeatedly they can promote feelings of empathy and understanding for other people's points of view and situations. Hence we recommend that the above dramatic play and role playing should not be a single event while still expecting expect empathy and understanding from the students. Teachers would need to find time to repeatedly role play the same scenarios from the story and thus move the child gradually from 0 level to level 1.

Principle Two: Evidence Based Practice

Books. Buysse and Wesley (2006) in their treatise on evidence-based practice in the early childhood field have stated that educational interventions should be based on scientific research on the effectiveness of practices. Therefore, based on the scientific research by Bhavnagri and Samuel's (1996a), where they successfully used children's books as an intervention strategy to promote pro-social thought and perspective thinking, we too are recommending the very same intervention for understanding the immigrant children. Furthermore, we selected only those children's books where the content was aligned to the empirical research findings on immigrants' adjustment and acculturation process. Additionally, our practice of selecting children's literature is based on theoretical models and paradigms, which were developed on empirical research as well.

Buysse and Wesley also recommend that the characteristics of individual children and their families, their values, circumstances and context be integrated into all decisions related to educational practices. We therefore selected books, which actively reflected the characteristics of immigrant children and their families, their values, and the circumstances and context unique to their immigrant experience.

Discussions. We recommend discussion questions be based on relevant research. For example, Shure and Spivack's research focuses on interpersonal competence, which is the exact focus of this chapter (Shure & Spivack, 1980; Shure, 1989). They reported that causal, consequential and alternative thinking were effective, resulting in social problem solving and interpersonal understanding, but alternative thinking was the most effective. We recommend the teachers ask questions on causal thinking (e.g., In *The Name Jar* what happens on the bus ride to school that makes Jangmi decide not to tell the students in her class her name?), consequential thinking (e.g., If Jangmi had decided to change her name how do you think that would affect her relationship with her mother and with her classmates?), and alternative thinking (e.g., Jangmi's classmates tried to help her adjust by making a name jar for her. What are some other ways that the children in Jangmi's class could help her adjust?).

Another example, based on the research of first author and her colleague, we recommend that teacher-child social interactions be promoted: (1) during opening of the story, (2) teacher's modeling story reading, (3) children reciting or retelling the story and (4) closing the story with children's elaborations (Mason, McCormick & Bhavnagri, 1986). They report that it fostered more child initiated questions and helped children to clarify their lack of understanding.

Activities. da Silvia and Villas-Boas' (2006) study of two multicultural elementary school classes concluded that art education fostered a positive viewpoint among students regarding respect for cultural and ethnic groups different from their own. They propose that using art, as a tool to achieve the global development of students, can be an important facet for promoting intercultural education. Based, on their proposal we recommend art activities should be based on specific scenarios to promote respect and integration of all students in the urban education setting based on research. For example, art can be used as a medium to express the feelings and emotions of the protagonist in *Marianthe's Story,* which ultimately led to the other children in the protagonist's class accepting her as a friend and a member of their classroom community.

Turner and Brown (2008) used small group discussions based on student led dialogue regarding one of three scenarios. Scenarios presented to the students were about (a) a new student joining the class in the middle of the school year; (b) going away on a family vacation in another country where the language is foreign and being separated/lost without the other members in the family; and (c) hearing bad news about their family member who was the sole provider of income for the family losing their job. The study concluded that empathy, and meaningful changes in attitude towards refugee and immigrant children were increased among student participants when they were asked, "How does it feel?" Then the teacher led the students to participate in a whole class interactive discussion, based on their small group discussions. Thus this research focused on immigrant and refugees can be converted into similar small group discussions during show and tell or similar whole class storyboard discussion activity.

Principle Three: Culturally Appropriate Practices

Books. Derman-Sparks and Edwards (2010), who are experts in anti-bias education for young children, argue that the majority of books only show the lives of the dominant culture and a much greater focus needs to be given to books that highlight diversity. We therefore recommend that teachers use our book selection because it highlights the diversity of cultures within the immigrant population, which are typically marginalized.

Derman-Sparks and Edwards (2010) also argue that that very young children lack accurate information about the lives and culture of people other than themselves. They recommend and so do we, that several cultures be appropriately represented in books. For example, our selections do accurately reflect the immigrant child's culture from her home country (e.g., cultural household objects, food and clothing; cultural attitudes towards parents, teachers, and friends; cultural significance of their name; and cultural values towards learning to read and write). The books also accurately portray the sub cultures of the immigrants in the USA (e. g., life in ethnic immigrant neighborhoods) and the USA's mainstream culture (e. g., educational culture of American schools).

Our selection of books was also undergirded by the first author's personal experiences and her writings on cultural diversity. Since she is an immigrant, she used her life experiences to determine the authenticity and appropriate representation of the protagonists' experiences. She has written about variations in parent-child styles of interactions and child rearing practices in diverse cultures (Bhavnagri, 1986). She in collaboration with her colleagues, has advocated that adults be culturally sensitive and responsive to very young children, as young as infants and toddlers, so that there is a cultural continuity and support for family's child rearing practices (Bhavnagri, & Gonzalez-Mena 1997; Gonzalez-Mena, & Bhavnagri, 2000), Gonzalez-Mena, & Bhavnagri, 2001).

We have the same recommendations here, namely for kindergarten and early elementary teachers to select books which are culturally sensitive and responsive. Given that there are nuanced variations in the socialization goals across cultures (Gonzalez-Mena, 2008), we recommend that teachers select books that respect the child's home culture while also specifically showing parents' goals for socialization in a positive light. For example, our selections positively depict numerous situations where parents have specific socialization goals based on their cultural values (e.g., helping child learn a new language, coping with teasing by explanations, expecting child to become responsible by participating in labor intensive adult chores, providing reasons to retain her original name from her own culture, taking children to ethnic markets, encouraging children to be an integral part of family singing, reunions, and cultural celebrations, such as Diwali). Such selections contribute to cultural understanding and cultural competence among children.

Discussions. The strategies for discussion are culturally, appropriate based on two approaches. The first approach is to ask discussion questions about the story that parallels the lives of all the urban students, showing them the similarities between the characters and themselves, regardless of the cultures. For example, children have at some time experienced positive emotions (e.g., happiness, sense of achievement, pride, affection), and negative emotion (e.g., fear, worry, loneliness, stress, rejection, teasing). Hence ask questions, such as "Have you ever felt that way? When did you feel that way? What did you then do? Who did you tell?" We recommend that we then discuss that the story characters, although from different cultures, have similar emotions.

Derman-Sparks and Edwards (2010) warns us that sometimes these differences among children can lead to learning incorrect ideas or stereotypes about cultural identity. The second approach, therefore, is to discuss the elements of the protagonists' life that are unfamiliar or different from the lives of the children in the classroom. Some examples include "Does your mommy shop at a place called Chinatown? Where does she shop? Name some grocery stores where she shops. What groceries does Hannah's mommy buy? What groceries does your mommy buy? Tell me one thing that Hannah's mommy buys that your mommy does not buy. What food does Hannah's family have for dinner? What foods do they eat when they celebrate the arrival of their green cards? What do you eat when you celebrate Thanksgiving?"

Activities. One approach is to do individual cultural activities related to a book. Many scholars suggest adding cultural materials in the classroom as a strategy to promote cultural activities. For example, Derman-Sparks and Edwards (2010) suggest adding materials in the classroom that broaden their cultural knowledge. Kaufman's findings and Wood's expertise resulted in similar advice to provide materials to make it a DAP, thus addressing the first principle.

Still other scholars suggest to have clear well-developed goal oriented cultural activities, and not simply adding cultural materials. For example, Copple and Bredekamp (2009) recommend that the teachers provide activities that allow for cultural exploration because when teachers respect diversity it promotes all children's positive cultural identity. Shareff and Gonzalez-Mena (2008) suggest doing an activity similar to role–playing, which they call mingling, followed by self-reflection journal writing, to promote cultural awareness and sensitivity. Pryor (2001) also recommends that teachers should incorporate celebrations and lessons about the immigrants' culture that will help the newcomers feel valued and at home.

Therefore, here are some examples of possible individual cultural art activities related to the stories we chose. Children can make replicas of: (1) cultural artifacts that the protagonist had left behind (Chinese lanterns, Mexican piñatas); (2) cultural artifacts they brought with them as physical tools to remember (Korean pouch, Korean wooden block, Chinese fan, Chinese hand painted scroll, Chinese mat, Greek and Korean family members framed photographs), (3) cultural tools they use to cope with adjustment that is culturally acceptable in USA (like making a name jar to find an American name) or artifacts which are culturally associated with USA (constructing classroom identification cards that are similar to the green cards), (4) cultural art from immigrant's country of origin (Rangoli, a floor design decoration done during Diwali in India).

A second possibility could be developing a full thematic unit on the culture of an immigrant child. Such a thematic unit can give immigrant students a chance to be peer teachers among their classmates while providing students an opportunity to learn the richness that different cultures have to offer. For example, a thematic unit about the Chinese culture can feature books we mentioned already such as *Hannah is My Name, My Chinatown, I Hate English* and *An American Wei.* Ashley's *Cleversticks* is a book that can be added to this list.

In *Cleversticks,* Ling Sung is a new student who does not enjoy his time at school nor does he enjoy interacting with the other students. When his cookie breaks into small pieces, Ling Sung uses two paintbrushes as chopsticks to pick up pieces, which amazes his teachers and classmates. His unique talent is a natural thing for him since that's the way he eats at home. Ling Sung gets to be the star of the day as he tries to teach the others in his class how to eat using chopsticks. Afterwards, Ling Sung develops a better relationship with his fellow classmates.

We recommend the following activities to develop a thematic unit related to the above listed books: (1) that *Chopsticks* be followed up by an activity introducing chopsticks to students of non-Oriental descent, (2) cooking Chinese cuisine (e.g., making pot stickers, egg rolls, and stir-fry containing Chinese vegetables like Bok Choy), (3) promoting dramatic play using Chinese kitchen utensils and ingredients to the housekeeping area (e.g., Wok, Chinese uncooked noodles), (4) art activities making Chinese replica (e.g., Chinese lantern, fans, scrolls, paper dragons), (5) moving and listening to Chinese music, (6) field trips to Chinese cultural places (e.g. museums displaying Chinese artifacts, Chinese grocery stores, Chinese laundry, Chinese restaurants) and culminating finally in (7) celebration of Chinese new year with a parade and festivity.

Conclusion

To summarize and conclude, when all three principles are applied to books, discussion and activities then young children can develop a deeper interpersonal understanding between immigrant and non immigrant children. The selected books do not portray the immigrant children as helpless victims unable to cope with acculturation, but as resilient and competent children who do make healthily psychosocial adjustments.

Therefore, our main message and plea to the teachers are as follows: "Please, be sensitive and cognizant of an immigrant child's psycho-social adjustment during acculturation. Kindly, use the positive messages from these books and the strategies that we have suggested, to help all urban children, immigrant as well as non-immigrant, to develop an understanding, empathy and a perspective of an immigrant child who is undergoing the integration process. Thank You."

References

Aliki, (1998). *Marianthe's story. Painted words.* New York: Greenwillow Books.

Aliki, (1998). *Marianthe's story. Spoken memories.* New York: Greenwillow Books.

Ashely, B. (1992). *Cleversticks.* New York: Crown.

Baghban, M. (2007). Immigration in childhood: using picture books to cope. *The Social Studies,* **98**, 2, 71-76.

Berk, L. E. & Winsler, A. (1995). *Scaffolding children's learning: Vygotsky and early childhood education.* Washington, DC: National Association for the Education of Young Children.

Bhatnagar, J. (Ed.). (1983). *Educating Immigrants.* London: Croom Helm.

Bhavnagri, N. (1986). *Mother-infant interactions in various cultural settings.* In L. G. Katz (Ed.), Current topics in early childhood: Vol 6, (1-32). Norwood, NJ: Ablex.

Bhavnagri, N. P. (2001). The Global Village: Migration and education. *Childhood Education.* **77**, 5, 256-259.

Bhavnagri, N. P. & Samuels, B. G. (1996a). Children's literature and activities promoting social cognition of peer relationships in preschoolers. *Early Childhood Research Quarterly,* **11**(3), 307-331.

Bhavnagri, N. P. & Samuels, B. G. (1996b). Making and keeping friends: A thematic unit to promote understanding of peer relationships in young children. *Childhood Education,* **72** (4), 2.

Bhavnagri, N. P. & Gonzalez-Mena, J. (1997). The Cultural Context of Infant Caregiving. *Childhood Education,* **74**(1), 2-8.

Bhavnagri, N. P. & Vaswani, T. G. (1999). Expanding roles of teachers for the 21st Century: An Indian Context. *Childhood Education,* **75**, 297-303.

Bhavnagri, N. P. & Krolikowski, S. (2000). Home-community visits during an era of reform: 1870-1920. *Early Childhood Research and Practice.* **2**, 1, 1-39. Retrieved on Jan 6, 2010. http://ecrp.uiuc.edu/v2n1/bhavnagri.html.

Bhavnagri, N. P., Krolikowski, S. & Vaswani, T. G. (2006). Interagency Collaboration For Culturally Diverse Immigrant Children and Families: A Case Study with Historical and Contemporaneous *Perspective Childhood Education.,* **83**. 6-11.

Bodrova, E. & Leong, D. J. (1996). *Tools of the mind.* Englewood Cliffs, N. J: Merrill

Bornstein, M. C., Deater-Deckard K. & Lansford, E. (2007). Introduction: Immigrant families in contemporary societies. In: E., Lansford, K., Deater-Deckard, M. C., Bornstein, *Immigrant families in contemporary societies.* New York: The Guilford Press.

Buysse, V. & Wesley, P. W. (2006). *Evidence-based practice in the early childhood field.* Washington D.C.: Zero to Three.

Capps, R., Passel, J. S. & Perez-Lopez, D. Fix, M. (2010). *The new neighbors: A Users' guide to data on immigrants in U.S. communities.* The Urban Institute Washington, DC. Retrieved on Jan 6, 2010. http://www.urban.org/url.cfm?ID=310844.

Choi, Y. (2001). *The name jar.* New York: Dell Dragonfly Books.

Creech, N. & Bhavnagri, N. P. (2002) Teaching elements of story through drama to first graders. *Childhood Education.,* **79**, 4, 219-224.

Convention Right Information Network (2010). Convention on the Rights of the Child. Retrieved on Jan 17, 2010. (http://www.crin.org/docs/resources/treaties/uncrc.asp).

Copple, C. & Bredekamp, S. (2009) *Developmentally appropriate practice in early childhood programs: Serving children from birth through age 8.* Washington, D. C.: NAEYC.

da Silva, J. L. & Villas-Boas, M. A. (2006). Research note: promoting intercultural education through art education. *Intercultural Education.,* **17**, 1, 95-103.

Derman-Sparks, L. & Edwards, J. O. (2010). *Anti-Bias education for young children and ourselves.* Washington, D. C.: NAEYC.

Epstein, A. S. (2009). *Me, You, and Us: Social-Emotional Learning in Preschool.* Ypsilanti, MI: HighScope Press.

Fortuny, K., Capps, R., Sims M. & Chaudhary, A. (2010) *Children of Immigrants: National and State Characteristics.* Brief 9, August. *Retrieved Jan,* **6**, 2010. http://www.urban.org/uploadedpdf/411939_childrenofimmigrants.pdf.

Garza, R. T. & Gallegos, P. I. (1985). Environmental influences and personal choice: A humanistic perspective on acculturation. *Hispanic Journal of Behavioral Sciences*, **7**, 365-379.

Gilmore, R. (1994). *Lights for Gita.* London: Mantra Publishing, Ltd.

Gonzalez-Mena, J. (2008). *Diversity in early care and education: Honoring differences, 5th* *edition.* Washington, D. C.: NAEYC.

Gonzalez-Mena, J. & Bhavnagri, N. P. (2000). Diversity and infant/toddler caregiving. *Young Children, 55(5),* 31-34.

Gonzalez-Mena, J. & Bhavnagri, N. P. (2001) Helping ECE professionals understand cultural differences in sleeping practices. *Child Care Information Exchange.* March/April, 138, 91-93. 76.

Gordon, M. (1964). *Assimilation in American life.* New York: Oxford University Press.

Gunning, M. (2004). *America, my new home.* Honesdale, PA: Wordsong.

Handlin, O. (1951). *The uprooted.* Boston: Little, Brown. Hepburn, K. S. (2004). *Building culturally and linguistic competent services to support young children, their families, and school readiness.* Baltimore: Ann Casey E. Foundation.

Herold, M. R. (1995). *A very important day.* New York: Morrow Junior Books.

Johns, S. Using the Comer Model to educate immigrant children. *Childhood Education.,* **77,** 5, 268-274.

Kaufman, B. A. (1994). Day by day: playing and learning. *International Journal of Play Therapy.* **3,** 1, 11-21.

Kids Count Data Center (2010). Retrieved Jan 17, 2010 from http://datacenter.kidscount.org/data/acrossstates/Rankings.aspx?loct=2&by=v&order=a& ind=115&dtm=445&tf=18

Kirova, A. (2001). Loneliness among Immigrant Children: Implication for Classroom practice *Childhood Education.,* **77,** 5, 260-267.

Knight, M. B. (1993). *Who belongs here? An American story.* Gardiner, ME: Tilbury House.

Levine, E. (1989). *I hate English.* New York: Scholastic.

Levitin, S. (1995). *A piece of home.* New York: Dial Books.

Lollock, L. (2000). *The Foreign Born Population in the United States: March.*

Current Population Reports, P20-534, U.S. Census Bureau, Washington, D. C. Mak, K. (2002). *My Chinatown.* New York: HarperCollins.

Mason, J., McCormick, C. & Bhavnagri, N. (1986). How are you going to help me learn: Lesson negotiation between a teacher and preschool children. In D. Yaden, Jr. & S.Templeton (Eds.), *Metalinguistic awareness and beginning literacy* (159-172). Portsmouth: Heinemann.

McLennan, D. M. P. (2008). The benefits of using sociodrama in the elementary classroom: promoting caring relationships among educators and students. *Early Childhood Education Journal.,* **35,** 451-456.

Migration Policy Institute. (2010). 2008 *American community survey and census data on the foreign born by state.* Retrieved Jan 17, 2010 from http://www.migrationinformation.org/DataHub/acscensus.cfm.

Molenda, C. F. & Bhavnagri N. P. (2009). Cooperation Through Movement Education and Children's Literature. *Early Childhood Education Journal,* **37,** 153-159.

Munsch, R. (1995). *From far away.* Toronto: Annick Press. Organization for Economic Cooperation and Development (OECD, 2008). *A profile of immigrant population in the 21st century: Data from OCED countries.* Retrieved Oct 30, 2009, from http://browse.oecdbookshop.org/oecd/pdfs/browseit/8108011E.PDF

Office of English Language Acquisition, Language Enhancement and Academic Achievement for Limited English Proficient Students (OELA, 2010) Retrieved Jan 6, 2010, from http://www.ncela.gwu.edu/files/uploads/4/GrowingLEP_0506.pdf.

Pak, S. (2003). *Sumi's first day of school ever.* New York: Viking.

Park, F. & Park, G. (2002). *Good-bye, 382 Shin Dang Dong.* Washington, D. C.: National Geographic Society.

Patel, N., Power, T. G. & Bhavnagri, N. P. (1992) Socialization values and practices of Indian immigrant parents: Correlates of modernity and acculturation. *Child Development,* **67**, 302-313.

Perez, A. I. (2002). *My diary from here to there.* San Francisco: Children's Book Press.

Pomeranc, M. H. (1998). *The American Wei.* Park Ridge, IL: Albert Whitman.

Pryor, C., (2001) New Immigrants and Refugees in American Schools: Multiple Voices. *Childhood Education.,* **77**, 5, 275-283.

Pryor, C. B., Ginn-Clark A., Kostrzewa, K., Asher. D., Palmer, R. & Gaba, M. (1998). *Integrating immigrant and refugee children into urban schools.* Detroit MI: Wayne State University. Skillman Center for Children, Occasional Papers.

Recorvitis, H. (2003). *My name is Yoon.* New York: Farrar, Straus and Giroux.

Rong, X. L. & Priessle. J. (1998*). Educating immigrant students: What we need to know to meet the challenges.* Thousand Oaks, CA: Corwin Press.

Rubin, L. & Bhavnagri, N. P. (2001). Voices of recent Chaldean adolescent immigrant's experiences. *Childhood Education.,* **77**, 5, 308-312.

Rueschenberg, E. & Buriel, R. (1989) Mexican American family and functioning and acculturation: A family systems perspective. *Hispanic Journal of Behavioral Science.,* **11**, 3, 232-244.

Selman, R. (1980). *The growth of interpersonal understanding. New* York: Academic.

Selman, R. L. & Schultz, L. H. (1990). *Making a friend in youth: Developmental Theory and Pair Therapy.* New York: Aldine De Grueter.

Shareef, I. & Gonzalez-Mena, J. (2008). *Practice in building bridges: Companion resource to diversity in early care and education, 5th edition.* Washington, D. C. NAEYC.

Smilansky, S. (1968). *The effects of sociodramatic on disadvantaged preschool children.* New York: Wiley.

Shure, M. B. (1989). Interpersonal competence training. In W. Damon (Ed.), *Child development today and tomorrow* (pp. 393-408). San Francisco: Jossey-Bass.

Shure, M. B. & Spivack, G. (1980). Interpersonal problem solving as a mediator of behavioral adustment in preschool and kindergarten children. *Journal of Developmental Psychology,* I, 29-44.

Surat, M. M. (1983). *Angel child, dragon child.* New York: Scholastic.

Theilheimer, R. (2001). Bi-directional learning through relationship building. *Childhood Education.,* **77**, 5, 284-288.

Turner, R. N. & Brown, R. (2008). Improving children's attitudes towards refugees: an evaluation of a school-based multicultural curriculum and an anti-racist intervention. *Journal of Applied Social Psychology.,* **38**, 5, 1295-1328.

Vygotsky, L. (1978). *Mind in society: The development of higher psychological processes.* Cambridge: Harvard University Press.

Watson, D. C. Characteristics of Hmong immigrant students: The response of a university/ elementary school collaboration. *Childhood Education.,* **77**, 5, 303-307.

Wertsch, J. B. & Rogoff, B. (1984). Editors' notes. In B. Rogoff & J. B. Wertsch (Eds.), *Children's learning in the "zone of proximal development."* San Francisco: Jossey-Bass.

Wink, J. & Putney, L. (2002). *Vision of Vygotsky.* Boston: Allyn and Bacon.

Wood, C. (2007). *Yardsticks: Children in the classroom ages 4-14.* Turner Falls, MA: Northeast Foundation for Children.

Yang, B. (2004). *Hannah is my name.* Cambridge, MA: Candlewick Press.

In: Progress in Education, Volume 21
Editor: Robert V. Nata, pp. 25-54

ISBN: 978-1-61728-115-0
© 2011 Nova Science Publishers, Inc.

Chapter 2

EMPIRICAL STUDY ON THE RELATIONSHIP BETWEEN TEACHERS TURNOVER RATE AND COLLEGE PERFORMANCE: EVIDENCE FROM CHINA

*Zhang Changzheng[1], Li Huai-zu[2] and Cao Yu-ping[2],**

[1]School of Management and Economics, Xi'an University of Technology,
Xi'an 710054, China
[2]School of Management, Xi'an Jiaotong University, Xi'an 710049, China

Abstract

In China, the development of higher education is even more attractive than the development of social economy. Chinese colleges bear the responsibility of training higher talents for the great developing country which thus demands a high-qualified and well-structured teaching staff. Therefore, each college in China has paid great attention on the construction of teaching staff. However, with the ever-increasing completeness of market economic system and the enhancement of the sense of self-realization for the college teachers in China, the turnover rate of college teachers is greater and greater. It is consequently a critical issue for the colleges to treat such a fact correctly and take countermeasures to deal with it.

For most of the existing literatures in China, there is a popular view that teachers turnover rate negatively influences college performance which has not received enough empirical tests. This paper tries to empirically test the relationship between teachers turnover rate and college performance in China. Taking the scores on students education and the scores on scientific research adapted from the data in "Appraisal of Chinese Colleges: 2002-2005" as the variables measuring college performance, and taking the data of teachers turnover rate for Chinese colleges in the same period collected from "the Statistical Table of Chinese College Teachers" as the independent variable, the paper empirically finds that there is an inversed U-shaped curve relationship between the two variables. Specifically speaking, for Chinese colleges, when the teachers turnover rate is lower than 3.3%, teachers turnover has positive

---

* E-mail address: zcz7901@163.com

effect on college performance, while when the teachers turnover rate is higher than 3.3%, there is a negative relationship between the two variables.

The empirical result shows that a reasonable teachers turnover is helpful to the construction of Chinese colleges. That is because such a fact can bring new concepts, new methods and new behavior modes to the new colleges which can be very helpful to the old modes. However, when the rate is higher than a certain level, some core teachers begin to leave and the remaining teachers feel depressed. Therefore, too higher turnover rate will negatively affect college performance. For college managers in China, instead of simply lowering teachers turnover rate as possible, it is necessary for them to control teachers turnover rate in a certain degree in order to improve college performance.

Keywords: College teachers, Turnover, College performance.

1. Introduction

As a widespread phenomenon in modern organizations, turnover is exerting much stronger effect on organizations. For colleges, one of the special organizations in modern society, the conclusion still holds. Compared with the traditional occupations, the requirements on college teachers are obviously much higher. For new college teachers, after the entrance into the college, they must receive much training in order to take hold of the professional knowledge, skills, ability and other characteristics (KSAOs) for performing their positions. Such a KSAOs barrier makes it very difficult for the colleges to acquire the high-qualified teachers in the labor market, especially the teachers in the critical positions are more difficult to get. If a college has a relatively much higher turnover rate, then the daily teaching and research work flow will be inevitably interrupted by the turnover of teachers. Consequently, a series of problems will occur, for example, the very experienced teachers are very scarce, and on the contrary, the new entrants can not integrate into the extant teachers team without a longer training and corporation. Therefore, the colleges with a too higher turnover rate will find it is too difficult to get the advantage under the ever-increased competition. As a consequence, the extant students and the potential students will have a much lower satisfaction degree and the social evaluation will decrease too. All in all, the teachers' turnover logically will bring great threats on the operation efficiency and objective achievements.

However, it should be indicated that not all the teachers' turnover will exert bad effect on the operation efficiency or the performance of the colleges. In one side, teachers' turnover can promote the information & knowledge exchange among different colleges. Under a certain condition, the existence of teachers' turnover makes it possible for the colleges to substitute the lower-qualified college teachers with the higher-qualified ones. Due to the new entrants, new knowledge, new concepts and new teaching know-how, which are very critical to the success of the colleges, will be brought into the new colleges, and thus the work efficiency of the colleges teachers will increase. In the other hand, the teachers' turnover may weaken the extant and traditional operation modes and all kinds of rules which at a large degree deter the innovation of colleges. As we all know, innovation is the core concept in the age of so-called knowledge economy, especially for the special organization, the colleges. That is to say, for the colleges, teachers' turnover may be not always a bad thing.

In this paper, the authors propose that within a certain range, there is an inversed U-shaped curve relationship between teachers' turnover rate and colleges performance. The paper is arranged as follows. Part two provides a summary on the studies on the relationship between employees turnover and organizational performance; Part three puts forward a model integrating the two variables, i.e. teachers' turnover rate and college performance, and further provides a theoretical hypothesis; Part four takes the scores on students education and the scores on scientific research adapted from the data in "Appraisal of Chinese Colleges: 2002-2005" as the variables measuring college performance, and take the data of teachers turnover rate for Chinese colleges in the same period collected from "the Statistical Table of Chinese College Teachers" as the independent variable, and further empirically finds that there is an inversed U-shaped curve relationship between the two variables; The final part is the conclusion.

2. Literature Review

The issue of turnover is the key topic in the research field of business management, organizational behavior and psychology, and the relevant literature is very rich. However, except for very limited examples, most of the research takes it natural that turnover is a negative behavior which needs strict constraint, and thus the research focus is the influencing factors of turnover behavior which naturally ignores the real effect of turnover behavior on the organizations. What is more, there is scarcely any the research directly investigating the relationship between teachers' turnover rate and colleges performance. The most relevant literature is shown as follows.

2.1. Research Summarization on the Relationship between Turnover Rate and Organizational Performance

(1) There is no significant relationship between the two. Takao Kato & Cheryl Long (2005) constructs a regression model on CEO turnover by adopting the financial and accounting data of the Chinese listed firm from 1998 to 2002, and empirically finds that the turnover rate of CEO has nothing to do with firm performance at all under the condition of without any large controlling shareholders. Baster& IZA Bonn (2006) makes study on the effect of CEO turnover on the football team performance by adopting the data of the Holland football team from 1986 to 2004. The empirical results show that the leave of CEO does not improve the performance of the football team. Many other studies based on the data of the listed firms indicate that though there is an positive effect of CEO turnover on firm performance statistically, the absolute size is too small. De Paola, Maria and Scoppa, In the paper of Vincenzo (2008), sport data are used to study the effects of manager replacement on firm performance. Using match results of the major Italian soccer league ("Serie A"), they analyze the effects of coach (manager) changes in terms of team performance. From the preliminary estimates, including year and team fixed effects, it emerges that changing the coach produces a positive effect on a number of measures of team performance. However, this effect turns out to be statistically insignificant once we

take into account the fact that the firing of a coach is not an exogenous event, but it is triggered by a "dip" in team performance. Using as an instrument for coach change the number of remaining matches in the season (which is a proxy for the residual length of the coach contract) Two-Stages Least Squares estimations do not show any significant effect of coach change on team performance.

(2) There is a positive relationship between the two. Job matching theory (Jovanovic, 1979) predicts that workers less suitable for the firm leave earlier; hence, there is room for labor turnover to improve performance by clearing the workforce of poor worker-job matches. McEvoy and Cascio's (1987) meta-analysis of twenty-four reported correlations between performance and turnover concluded that 'good performers are ... less likely to leave ... than are poor performers', which supports the main prediction of job matching theory (p. 758). Williams and Livingstone's (1994) further meta-study of turnover supported McEvoy and Cascio (1987) and proved an even stronger negative relationship between worker individual performance and voluntary turnover when pay is contingent on performance. Mark J. Roberts & James R. Tybout (1997) regard that the short-term effect of turnover is not clear. The reason is that the new comers need a adaption process, and thus their productivity can not significantly exceed the employees who leave the position. From a long-term perspective, the quality of the new comers is almost higher than that of the employees who leave the position, and thus the re-allocation of human resource will finally improve the organizational performance. Many empirical study indicate that the turnover of senior employees will have negative effect on firm performance, while the younger employees' turnover has unclear effect on firm performance, and such a fact is most obvious in manufacturing industry. Bingley &Westergaard-Nielsen (2004) find that turnover rate improves firm performance, while the employment rate has the negative effect. W. S. Siebert & N. Zoubanov (2006) adopts the fixed effects framework and excludes the influence of CEO quality from the production regression model, and empirically find that no matter the employment rate or the turnover rate both have positive effect on productivity.

(3) There is a negative relationship between the two. The human resource management literature has traditionally viewed labor turnover in a negative light. Human capital theories of labor turnover point to loss of firm-specific human and social capital (Dess and Shaw 2001). Organizational theories point to disruptive changes in organization (Carroll and Harrison, 1998). This negative view is supported by the results of several empirical studies. For example, Huselid (1995) finds high labor turnover negatively linked to labor productivity in his sample of 968 U.S. firms. Also Baron, Hannan and Burton (2001) find turnover to be "disruptive" in their study of hi-tech start-ups in California in the early 1990s. John M. Levine & Richard L. Moreland (1992) take the project team members as the object, and empirically conclude that if the information on the task skills of new team members is not provided sufficiently to the other team members, then turnover will lead to the breakage of the mutual memory system of the team and thus lead to the decrease of team performance. Pekka Ilmakunnas, Mika Maliranta & Jari Vainiomäki (2003) investigate the relationship between employees's turnover and the increase of the total factor productivity by adopting the data of Finland manufacturing firms. The

results show that employees' turnover rate has negative effect on the increase of total factor productivity. The reason is that the leave of employees leads to the change of "person-position" match which will affect the increase of the total factor productivity. In the work of By McElroy(2001) et al, data were collected from 31 regional subunits of a national financial services company to examine differential effects of 3 types of turnover (voluntary, involuntary, and reduction-in-force) on measures of organizational subunit performance, and each form of turnover exhibited adverse effects on subunit performance. Loretta A. Terry & William Allan Kritsonis (2008) indicates that school staffing problems are primarily due to excessive demand resulting from a "revolving door"—where large numbers of qualified teachers depart their jobs for reasons other than retirement and their positions are filled with unprepared and unqualified teachers. What is more, many other studies have concentrated on quits specifically, and have found a negative impact of quits on firm performance, including Mefford (1986) for plants of a multinational manufacturing firm, Alexander, Bloom and Nuchols (1994) for U.S. hospitals, Batt (2002) for U.S. Call centers, McElroy, Morrow and Rude (2001) for branches of a U.S. financial company, and Kersley and Martin (1997) for the sample of firms in the 1990 UK Workplace Employee Relations Survey (WERS). The explanations generally revolve around the loss of firm-specific human capital to quits.

(4) There is a contingent relationship between the two. Considering the effect of employees' turnover on the efficiency of the organization, Dalton & Tudor (1979) classifies turnover behavior into functional turnover and dysfunctional turnover according to the organization's evaluation on the employees. The key of such a method is up to how the organization evaluates the employees who leave the position, since the different evaluation will lead to different sorting results. Miller (1987) indicates that the evaluation on the employees who leave the position, namely the operational definition of the negative or positive effect on the organization, should be considered from the following 3 aspects: ①The quality of the employees who leave the position; ②The difficulty of substituting the employees who leave the position; ③The importance degree of the vacant positions due to the leave of the employees. Robert M. Hussey (2005) constructs a theoretical model focusing on the relationship among job creation, job extinction and labor productivity which indicates that the relationship between employees' turnover and labor productivity is up to the future job prospect, and he empirically tests the conclusion. W. Stanley Siebert & Arnaud Chevalier (2006) applies the panel data of 347 British textile fabric retailers from 1995 to 1999 in order to investigate the effect of employees' turnover on the productivity, and empirically demonstrates that there is an inversed U-shaped curve relationship with a critical transition point of 20%. According to the result, when the employees' turnover rate is lower than 10%, there is a positive relationship between the two, while when the employees turnover rate is higher than 20%, there is a negative relationship between the two. W. Stanley Siebert et al. (2006) study the impact of labor turnover on labor productivity using a panel dataset of 347 shops belonging to a large UK clothing retailer over1995-1999. For the within-shop link, holding constant the shop's permanent characteristics, they observe an inverted U-shape effect of labor turnover on productivity. The productivity-maximizing rates of

FTE-adjusted quits and hires are each about 20% per year, improving productivity by 2.5% compared to the zero turnover level. They explain the difference between this optimal level of labor turnover and its observed average (quits and hires each around 10%) through the costs of hiring estimated at about £600 per hire. By contrast, between shops, there is a positive link between average rates of turnover and average productivity, suggesting that an unobservable management quality factor generates both high turnover and productivity.

2.2. Commentary on the Literature

The scholars who hold the view of "No relationship" regard that there is no necessary significant relationship between employees' turnover and organizational performance. They indicate that the fact of employees' turnover is the necessary result and practical need called "get rid of the stale and take in the fresh" during the running process of an organization, which will not necessarily lead to better or worse performance. Organizational performance is determined to a larger degree by the change of the other factors instead of the change of turnover rate. The other possible reason is that, turnover has both negative and positive effect on organizational performance, but in most conditions, the strength of them are rather equal which always leads to that there is no significant relationship between the two.

The scholars who hold the view of "Positive relationship" regard that the fact of turnover is helpful to the organizational metabolism and process reform which can bring new ideas, new thinking way and new behavior modes into the organization, which can improve the efficient allocation and utilization of resources and thus increase the organizational performance. Of course, the scholars also recognize the negative effect of turnover on organizational morale and the normal organizational process. However, such effects are attributed as the secondary effects, and the positive effects are the leading role. As a matter of fact, such empirical result may have some relation with the industry they choose. Compared with the vocation of college teachers, such a view may not be true.

The scholars who hold the view of "Negative relationship" regard that the traditional mutual memory system of the team is damaged by the leave of team members which can not be repaired in a short term. Such scholars though accept the positive effect of turnover, they pay more attention to the negative effect on organizational performance. The final balance between the negative and positive effects is the pure evil effect on organizational performance.

Though the contingent view is of more practical meaning, many scholars express very cautious attitude. Taking the utility theory as the departure point, Boudreau & Berger (1985) regard that only the organization has compared the productivity and substitution cost of the employees who leave the positions with the productivity and employment cost of new employees correctly, can the effect of employees' turnover on organizational performance be judged precisely. However, because part of the turnover cost of the employees who leave the positions is indirect cost, the precise judge is very difficult.

According to the discussion above, the relationship between turnover rate and organizational performance is very complexed. If we adopt different industries and different research assumptions in different periods, there will be different conclusions. For the industry of higher education, whether the employees' turnover can lead to the change of colleges performance or not needs us to analyze in depth considering the nature of the colleges and teachers. In addition, at present there is no such a well-accepted conclusion can be referred to. From a certain perspective, the research on the relationship between teachers' turnover rate and colleges performance in China has both the practical and theoretical meanings. For Chinese colleges, it is still a question, namely, what is the effect on colleges performance of the turnover of college teachers?

3. Model and Research Hypothesis

Turnover can be voluntary turnover and passive turnover (i.e. being fired). For chinese college teachers, till today, there are very examples of being fired. Therefore, the model assumes that the turnover of college teachers is voluntary turnover, and its decisional power is up to teachers themselves. Of course, the death of teachers is not included also.

3.1. Model Construction

The basic idea of the model is to take job tenure as the mediation variable and discuss the relationship between teachers' turnover rate and colleges performance. The specified process is shown as follows. First, by the assumptions on the payment system of Chinese colleges teachers, the relationship between job tenure and individual performance of an college teacher is investigated. The deduced result is there is an inversed U-shaped relationship between the two variables. Second, taking the assumption that the performance of individual teacher is consistent with the performance of the whole college, or at least there is a strong positive relationship between the two, the inversed U-shaped relationship between teachers' turnover rate and college performance is concluded. Finally, according to the reverse relationship between job tenure and teachers' turnover rate in a college, the inversed U-shaped curve relationship between college teachers' turnover rate and college performance is deduced. During the model analysis process, one of the most critical assumptions is that the relationship between individual teacher's performance and the whole college's performance.

The model assumes that the payment of a college teacher is determined by three factors, respectively wage on general skills of a teacher (W_a), the fit between the teacher's specialized human capital and the college (Y), and the share of the teacher's pay to the college residual (λ). Lazear (1979) indicates that in order to retain the employees critical to the organization, the organization usually intends to delay the payment, which shows that the organization will offer a pay lower than the employee's marginal productivity when the employee is in his or her early phase of the working life, while offer a pay much higher than the employee's marginal productivity when the employee is in his or her later phase of the working life. In order to reflect such a fact, the paper assumes that with the increase of the teacher's tenure (T) in the same college, the share of the teacher's payment to the college residual will increase too. The human capital theory expects that the on-the-job training will improve the specialized skills of the employees, so the so-called teacher-college fitness will change with the increase of job tenure of the teacher. If the delayed payment system is not designed reasonably, or the individual teacher's performance is not observed precisely, then with the increase of job tenure, the job burnout and turnover intention of the teacher will be stronger.

If it is true, job tenure has a unclear effect on colleges performance which is hard to judge directly. According to the discussion above, the wage of a teacher can be defined as follows.

$$W = W_a + \lambda(T)Y(T) \tag{1}$$

According the Information-seeking Theory, in order to assure the emergence of turnover behavior, the model assumes that the external wage is a random variable. That is to say, for a college teacher, the wage on general skills (W_a) is affected by a special random variable (θ) which satisfies the normal distribution described as $N(0,1)$. If the following condition is satisfied, then the teacher will choose to leave.

$$W_a > W \Longleftrightarrow \lambda Y \tag{2}$$

According to equation (2), when a teacher faces a better fluctuation of the market wage, if the fluctuation exceeds the profit share brought by the specialized skills of the teacher, then the teacher will choose to quit. No matter the human capital model or the delayed payment model both show that the possibility of an employee's turnover will decrease with the increase of job tenure, since the profit share of the employee is the increment function of fitness of the specialized human capital. Such a conclusion is confirms with the reality well.

3.2. Model Analysis an Hypothesis

Because the decision on the issue of turnover is not only affected by both the external and internal environment factors, but determined by the individual characteristic factors. Specialized speaking, the most critical personal factor is personal ability. Facing the very special college policy and external environment, teachers with different ability have different reaction and job pressure, and thus their turnover decision process and results are different too. Therefore, there is an absolute need to introduce individual ability into the model.

The above very simple model can be expanded into the more generalized conditions, in which there are two kinds of teachers, i.e., high-qualified teachers and low-qualified teachers. Compared with the lower-qualified teachers, the higher-qualified teachers have higher fitness between teachers and college and higher generalized capital, i.e., $Y_1 > Y_2$, $W_{a1} > W_{a2}$. If the type of the teachers can be observed, the higher-qualified teachers will face better and more external job alternatives. According to the common sense, it can be assumed that higher-qualified teachers will have higher profit share than the lower-qualified teachers ($\lambda_1 > \lambda_2$), since the former always perform better than the later. Further, the model assumes that the two kinds of teachers face different market demands, and then the random variables of the payment for the generalized skills are different, respectively can be shown as $\theta_1 \sim N(\theta^*_1, \delta_1)$ and $\theta_2 \sim N(\theta^*_2, \delta_2)$, of which $E(\theta_1) > E(\theta_1)$ holds. Consequently, according their own types, college teachers will make the decisions on whether quit or not based on the following equation.

The condition for the higher-qualified teachers to quit: $\lambda_1 Y_1 < \theta_1$.

The condition for the lower-qualified teachers to quit: $\lambda_2 Y_2 < \theta_2$.

If the college can not provide the higher-qualified teachers with better profit share, then the higher-qualified teachers will intend to quit. Under this condition, the higher-qualified teachers will persist in seeking the market opportunities until they find a college that can completely match their productivity. Following such a logic, the higher-qualified college teachers are more apt to turnover. It is needed to be mentioned that if the profit share of the teachers has nothing to do with their performance in a college, then job tenure will be the signal of their productivity. Such a fact usually means that the teachers with longer teachers in such a college without any performance-based payment may be rather lower.

This simple model shows that the relationship between college performance and college teachers' turnover rate depends on the payment system of the colleges. If the college can precisely measure the performance of the teachers, and accordingly afford the payments, then we can expect that a longer job tenure will improve the specialized human capital of college teachers and decrease the lazy behavior which can improve the college performance finally. On the contrary, if the payment system can not make sure that the most capable teachers get the relative higher payment, then the self-selection mechanism will lead to that such colleges will own only the lower-qualified teachers.

Figure 1 describes the relationship between job tenure and teachers' productivity. The model assumes that there are two kinds of teachers, respectively higher-qualified teachers (A=1) and lower-qualified teachers (A=0). Of which, the productivity of higher-qualified teachers is always relatively higher, and comparatively speaking, the possible change range is much greater than that of the lower-qualified teachers.

For higher-qualified teachers in China, at the beginning of their job tenure, they have not recognized the specific status of the payment system of the college, and therefore, the effect of the payment system has not occurred. The higher-qualified teachers will actively project themselves and invest much in the specialized human capital of the college, just as all the other new entrants in the college. Due to the subjective effort and objective capability, the productivity of the higher-qualified teachers will increase rapidly. However, with the increase of the job tenure, because the higher-qualified teachers have recognized that the college, just as the other colleges in China, does not follow the rule of "more pay for more work", instead, the college just gives priority to seniority and has the propensity of equalization. At this time, higher-qualified teachers intend to be involved in job burnout, and their specialized human capital investment decreases much. However, because in one hand, each college has its own rigid performance appraisal requirements, and in the other hand, in order to get the better employment opportunity, they have to retain their performance higher than the average level of the productivity of the lower-qualified teachers.

On the contrary, for the lower-qualified teachers, the habit of "giving priority to seniority" and the propensity of "getting an equal share regardless of the work done " in many Chinese colleges are favorable. Therefore, the lower-qualified teachers have the motivation to enhance the investment in the specialized human capital and they work with more effort. Consequently, With the increase of job tenure, the productivity of lower-qualified teachers will increase gradually. However, due to their poor capability, their growth rate is rather slow which is shown as the very small slope for the lower-qualified teachers in figure 1.

The model can further reasonably assume that there are the same number of the two kinds of teachers. In the first phase of the college running, the average performance of the college is the average value of the productivity of the two kinds of teachers. Because the change of the higher-qualified teachers' productivity is greater, the change of the final college performance leans to the productivity of the higher-qualified teachers. However, in the second phase, the turnover behavior has occurred. In China, many colleges can not observe the productivity of the teachers precisely, and thus the higher-qualified teachers with higher performance can not be rewarded completely. With the delay of the job tenure, the higher-qualified teachers usually face better external job alternatives, and compared with the lower-qualified teachers, they will have a bigger possibility of choosing to leave. Consequently, with the continuous running of the college, the number of the lower-qualified teachers in such a college will exceed that of the higher-qualified teachers. Under this condition, the average performance of the college will lean to the change orientation of the performance of the lower-qualified teachers. However, because the change rate of the higher-qualified teachers' performance is obviously greater than that of the lower-qualified teachers, the final average performance of the college is up to the change status of the higher-qualified teachers' performance. Following such a logic, the model concludes that due to the self-selection mechanism, there is an inversed U-shaped curve relationship between job tenure and the college performance. Further, due to the reverse relationship between job tenure and turnover rate, it can be concluded that there is an inversed U-shaped curve relationship between turnover rate and college performance, too (See in figure 2).

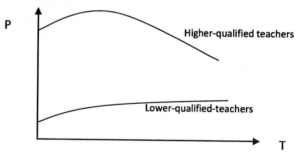

Figure 1. Relationship between teachers' job tenure and job performance.

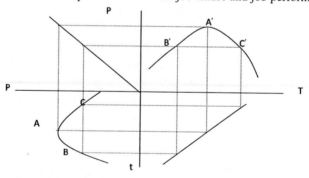

Figure 2. Relationship between turnover rate and college performance.

According to the model result, the paper can provide the research hypothesis:

H1: There is an inversed U-shaped curve relationship between teachers' turnover rate and college performance.

4. Empirical Test

4.1. Data Source

As we all know, the two missions of the colleges are teaching and scientific research. According to the "Evaluation on Chinese colleges (2002-2005)", a report edited by Wu Sulian, Lu Jia & Guo Shilin in Guangdong Management Science Academe, the paper chooses the change rate of the scores on students education (y_1) and the change rate of the scores on scientific research (y_2) as the dependent variables. Because their research report only mentions the data of the top 100 colleges, the colleges that can not be always the top 100 for every year during the four years are not included in our sample. Just for simplicity, the paper give each college in the sample a code (See Appendix 1 and Appendix 2). During the later analysis process, each college is called by its code.

4.2. Data Processing

Because the statistical data is not complete and perfect, there is an absolute need to deal with the missing data at first. The traditional missing data processing methods mainly include Bypassing Meta-group Method, Filling Missing Value by Hand Method, Total Constant Variable Method, Method of Average Attributes, Probability Estimation Method, and so on. However, such methods do not make full use of the information on the interlink among the data, and thus there exit the obvious shortcomings, such as lower precision, greater error.

a. Data Amending

Under the condition of existing many unclear characteristics, the correlation coefficients can reflect the correlating degree between some attributes of the research objectives. Based on this idea, we can analyze many characteristics, such as data structure type and data distribution law by applying the correlation coefficients, and further amend the missing value according to the information derived from the analysis. The method is ①to take out the column or row which includes the missing data (x), ②to make correlation analysis respectively on the rows and columns of the residual array, ③to find the maximum correlation coefficient between the row or column in which the missing data resides and the other rows or columns (r), ④to construct a equation in which the correlation coefficient including x equals to r, and then resolve equation on x. Finally, we can find the most suitable amending value for the missing data.

In order to make the data elements are comparable, it is needed to carry out data standardization. To set X as a data block with n vectors (i.e. $X_1, X_2, \cdots, X_n$) and s dimensions, namely, each vector has s items. $X_j = (X_{1j}, X_{2j}, \cdots, X_{nj})^T \in R^s, j = 1, 2, \cdots, n$. Of which, X_{i0j0} is the missing data which needs to be amended. Just for simplicity, the row sector is expressed by $b_i(i = 1, \cdots, s)$, and column vector is shown as $a_j(j = 1, \cdots, n)$.

$$
a_1 \quad \ldots \quad a_{j0} \quad \ldots \quad a_n
$$

$$
X = \left\{
\begin{array}{ccccc}
x_{11} & \cdots & x_{1i} & \cdots & x_{1n} \\
\vdots & \vdots & \vdots & \vdots & \vdots \\
x_{i01} & \cdots & x_{i0j0} & \cdots & x_{i0n} \\
\vdots & \vdots & \vdots & \vdots & \vdots \\
x_{s1} & \cdots & x_{sj0} & \cdots & x_{sn}
\end{array}
\right\}
\begin{array}{c}
b_1 \\
\vdots \\
b_{i0} \\
\vdots \\
b_s
\end{array}
\tag{3}
$$

The first step: To get rid of the $i0$ row in X, then data block A can be reached.

$$
a_1^* \quad \ldots \quad a_2^* \quad \ldots \quad a_3^*
$$

$$
A = \left\{
\begin{array}{ccccc}
x_{11} & \cdots & x_{1j0} & \cdots & x_{1n} \\
\vdots & \vdots & \vdots & \vdots & \vdots \\
x_{(i0-1)1} & \cdots & x_{(i0-1)j0} & \cdots & x_{(i0-1)n} \\
x_{(i0+1)1} & \cdots & x_{(i0+1)j0} & \cdots & x_{(i0+1)n} \\
\vdots & \vdots & \vdots & \vdots & \vdots \\
x_{s1} & \cdots & x_{sj0} & \cdots & x_{sn}
\end{array}
\right\}
\begin{array}{c}
b_1 \\
\vdots \\
b_{(i0-1)} \\
b_{(i0+1)} \\
\vdots \\
b_s
\end{array}
\tag{4}
$$

To define the correlation coefficients between column $j0$ and the other columns:

$$
r_{j0t} = r(a_{j0}^*, a_1^*), l = 1,2,\cdots,n; l \neq j
$$

$$
r_{j0t} = \frac{\sum_{t=1}^{s}(x_{tj0} - \overline{x_{j0}})(x_{tl} - \overline{x_l})}{\sqrt{\sum_{t=1}^{s}(x_{tj0} - \overline{x_{j0}})^2} * \sqrt{\sum_{t-1}^{s}(x_{tl} - \overline{x_l})^2}} \qquad l = 1,2,\cdots,n; l \neq j
\tag{5}
$$

In equation (5), $\overline{x_{j0}} = \dfrac{1}{s}\sum_{t=1}^{s}x_{tj0}; \overline{x_l} = \dfrac{1}{s}\sum_{t=1}^{s}x_{tl},$ $l = 1,2,\cdots,n; l \neq j$.

To set : $r_{i0} = \max_{i \leq l \leq n} r_{i01}$.

The second step: to get rid of the $j0$ column in X, then data block B can be reached.

$$
a_1 \ldots \quad a_{(j0-1)} \quad a_{(j0+1)} \quad \ldots \quad a_n
$$

$$B = \begin{cases} x_{11} & \cdots & x_{1(jo-1)} & x_{1(j0+1)} & \cdots & x_{1n} \\ \vdots & \vdots & \vdots & \vdots & \vdots & \vdots \\ x_{i01} & \cdots & x_{i0(j-1)} & x_{i0(j0+1)} & \cdots & x_{i0n} \\ \vdots & \vdots & \vdots & \vdots & \vdots & \vdots \\ x_{s1} & \cdots & x_{s(j0-1)} & x_{s(j0+1)} & \cdots & x_{sn} \end{cases} \begin{matrix} b_1 \\ \vdots \\ b_{(i0-1)} \\ \vdots \\ b_s \end{matrix} \tag{6}$$

To define the correlation coefficients between $i0$ row and the other rows:

$$r_{i0k} = r(b_{i0}^*, b_k^*), k = 1,2,\cdots,s; k \neq i0$$

$$r_{i0k} = \frac{\sum\limits_{t=1}^{n}(x_{i0t} - \overline{x_{i0}})(x_{kt} - \overline{x_k})}{\sqrt{\sum\limits_{t=1}^{n}(x_{i0t} - \overline{x_{i0}})^2 * \sum\limits_{t=1}^{n}(x_{kt} - \overline{x_k})^2}} \tag{7}$$

$$\overline{x_{i0}} = \frac{1}{n}\sum\limits_{t=1}^{n} x_{i0t}; \overline{x_k} = \frac{1}{n}\sum\limits_{t=1}^{n} x_{kt}, k = 1,2,\cdots,s; k \neq i0$$

In equation (7),

To set: $r_{k0} = \max\limits_{1\leq k\leq s} r_{i0k}$.

The third step: to resolve the equation on the missing data X_{i0j0}.

When $r_{l0} > r_{k0}$ holds, we adopt the data block A, and the following equation can be reached:

$$r_{l0} = \frac{\sum\limits_{t=1}^{s}(x_{tj0} - x_{j0})(x_{tl0} - \overline{x_{l0}})}{\sqrt{\sum\limits_{t=1}^{s}(x_{tj0} - \overline{x_{j0}})^2 * \sum\limits_{t=1}^{s}(x_{tl0} - \overline{x_{l0}})^2}} \tag{8}$$

$$\overline{x_{j0}} = \frac{1}{s}\sum\limits_{t=1}^{s} x_{tj0}; \overline{x_{l0}} = \frac{1}{s}\sum\limits_{t=1}^{s} x_{tl0}$$

In equation (8),

When $r_{l0} \leq r_{k0}$ holds, we adopt data block B, then the following equation can be reached:

$$r_{k0} = \frac{\sum\limits_{t=1}^{n}(x_{i0t} - \overline{x_{i0}})(x_{k0t} - \overline{x_{k0}})}{\sqrt{\sum\limits_{t=1}^{n}(x_{i0t} - \overline{x_{i0}})^2 * \sum\limits_{t=1}^{n}(x_{k0t} - \overline{x_{k0}})^2}} \tag{9}$$

In equation (9), $\overline{x_{i0}} = \frac{1}{n}\sum_{t=1}^{n} x_{i0t}, \overline{x_{t0}} = \frac{1}{n}\sum_{t=1}^{n} x_{k0t}$.

The fourth step: to get the amending data X_{i0j0} by adopting equation (8) and equation (9).

The fifth step: to output X_{i0j0}.

The sixth step: to adopt the inverse process of the above data standardization in order to return to the original data.

According to the above steps, the missing data is amended as table 1.

b. Abnormal Data Elimination

If we observe the data in Appendix 1 and Appendix 2, it can be found that some data may be the abnormal data. Till today, scholars all over the world are exploring the methods of excluding the influence of the abnormal values, for example, some of them investigate the data processing method of excluding the abnormal values in variable measurement, regression analysis, data simulation and time series analysis. Most of them do this thing form two perspectives, namely, excluding the abnormal values and robustness test. The next part combines the two perspectives paying the attention to the generalized methods of excluding the abnormal values with the consideration of statistical robustness.

Table 1. Amending results of the missing data

Code	2003		2004	
	y_1	y_2	y_3	y_2
81	-2.34	-3.23	——	——
88	——	——	4.28	6.02
91	-12.3	-18.1	-5.87	-9.77
95	——	——	6.22	11.47
96	——	——	7.23	4.62
99	-3.56	-8.34	-9.34	-10.98

Discrimination gross error:

$$|v_\delta| > (k_p + k_m)s \tag{10}$$

The measurement precision of k_m in equation (10) is given by $k_m \geq \frac{1}{\sqrt{n}}$.

For the asymmetrical distribution, the confidence factors in two the two ends should be different, respectively set as k_u and k_l. Consequently, the discrimination gross error is as follows.

$$-k_l s > v_j - \bar{x} > k_u s \tag{11}$$

Therefore, its asymmetrical distribution range can be estimated according to equation (12).

$$\bar{x} - \alpha k \sigma \pm ks = \bar{x} - (\alpha \pm 1)ks = \bar{x}_{-k_l s}^{-+k_u s}$$
$$k_l = (1+\alpha)k \quad ; \quad k_u = (1-\alpha)k \tag{12}$$

In equation (12), k and α are respectively distribution coefficient and asymmetrical coefficient relatively to the distribution mid-point. Similarly, the measurement precision of k should be expanded at least by $\dfrac{1}{\sqrt{n}}$.

This part uses β distribution representing the statistical rule of all the data in this research. Such a method is helpful to express both the unimodal and monoclinal valley, and describe its all kinds of symmetrical and asymmetrical distributions by using a single probability distribution, which especially confirms with the boundedness feature of the erro, namely, $X \sim \beta_x(\delta, h), x \in [a, b]$. The distribution density is as follows.

$$\beta_x(\delta, h) = \frac{(\frac{x-a}{b-a})^{\delta-1}(\frac{1-(x-a)}{b-a})^{h-1}}{(b-a)B(\delta, h)} \tag{13}$$

It's normalized expression is:

$$\beta(\delta, u) = \frac{u^{\delta-1}(1-u)^{h-1}}{B(\delta, h)} \tag{14}$$

In equation (14), $u = \dfrac{x-a}{b-a}$, and $B(\delta, h) = \dfrac{\Gamma(\delta+h)}{\Gamma(8)\Gamma(h)}$ is β function, and $\Gamma(*)$ is Γ function; $\delta > 0$; h>0.

β distribution morphologies: (1) Symmetrical distribution, g=h. Normal distribution, β (4,4); Uniform distribution, $\beta(1,1)$; arcsine distribution, $\beta(0.5, 0.5)$; Kurtosis distribution, g=h>4; Trapezoidal distribution to triangle distribution, 1<g=h≤2.5; U distribution, g<1, h<1.

(2) Asymmetrical distribution, g≠h. Right angle distribution, $\beta(2,1)$ or $\beta(1,2)$; J distribution, (g-1) (h-1)<0.

Parameter estimation:

$$\hat{\delta} = \bar{u}\left\{\frac{\bar{u}(1-\bar{u})}{s_u^2} - 1\right\}$$

$$\hat{h} = (1-\bar{u})\left\{\frac{\bar{u}(1-\bar{u})}{s_u^2} - 1\right\}$$

(15)

Distribution range estimation :

$$[a,b] = \left[\bar{x} \pm (1 \pm \alpha)ks\right]$$

(16)

The distribution coefficient :

$$k = \frac{\delta + h}{2\sqrt{\dfrac{\delta h}{\delta + h + 1}}}$$

(17)

The asymmetrical coefficient :

$$\alpha = \frac{\delta - h}{\delta + h}$$

(18)

As long as we estimate the parameters (g,h) and then calculate (k,α), then we can judge the abnormal data according to equation (11) and equation (12).

According to the discussion above, the specific steps of eliminating the abnormal data are shown as follows.

(1) Preliminary analysis: to normalize the data and make description.

(2) To select the discrimination criterion: the selection of the discriminate criterion is based on the data volume, probability distribution, or (g, h), $(\hat{\gamma}_3, \hat{\gamma}_4)$ and the suspicious data. When n>30 holds, equation (15) to equation (18) should be adopted, and equation (12) should be followed.

(3) To calculate the discrimination statistic: to calculate (g, h) and (α, k) according to the selected discrimination criterion. During the process, it is needed that the results should not be influenced by the abnormal data.

(4) To confirm the discrimination critical value: Usually, we should confirm the critical value of the above statistic under the given significance level by referring to the table. Under the large sample, it is recommended that we should make sure the critical value according to β distribution.

(5) To judge and eliminate the abnormal data: to compare the critical value with the statistic, if it exceeds the range of critical value, then the responding abnormal data can be deleted.

4.3. Canonical Correlation Analysis

a. Analysis Process

According to the research design, college performance is measured by the scores on students education (y_1) and the scores on scientific research (y_2); while the natural wastage of college teachers is expressed as x_1, and the voluntary turnover rate of college teachers is shown as x_2. In the next part, the relationship between the two variables is investigated by the method of canonical correlation analysis.

To set the two random vectors, $x = (x_1, x_2, \cdots, x_p)'$ and $y = (y_1, y_2, \cdots, y_q)'$, and the covariance matrix of x, y is:

$$\operatorname{cov}\begin{bmatrix} x \\ y \end{bmatrix} = \Sigma = \begin{bmatrix} \sum_{11} & \sum_{12} \\ \sum_{21} & \sum_{22} \end{bmatrix} \tag{19}$$

In order to investigate the canonical correlation relationship between the two groups variables, x and y, let's consider the following linear·combination,

$$\begin{cases} u = a'x = a_1 x_1 + a_2 x_2 + \cdots + a_p x_p \\ v = b'y = b_1 y_1 + b_2 y_2 + \cdots + b_q y_q \end{cases} \tag{20}$$

Equation (20) means that we should strive for calculating a & b which can make the correlation coefficient between u and v, i.e. $r = \dfrac{\operatorname{cov}(u, v)}{\sqrt{\operatorname{var}(u)\operatorname{var}(v)}}$, get the maximum value under the condition of x, y and given.

Table 2. The elimination results of the abnormal data

Code	2002		2003		2004	
	x_1	x_2	x_1	x_2	x_1	x_2
51	—	—	0.41	9.44	—	—
67	0.07	0.07	—	—	—	—
72	0.03	1.26	—	—	—	—
77	0.39	1.77	0.14	0.56	—	—
89	0.00	0.90	0	0.28	0.32	0.50
90	0.12	0.12	0.50	1.13	—	—
91	0.26	0.35	0.38	0.85	0.06	0.73

To normalize the random variables u and v,

$$\begin{cases} \mathrm{var}(u = \mathrm{var}(a'x) = a'\sum_{11} a = 1) \\ \mathrm{var}(v) = \mathrm{var}(b'y) = b'\sum_{22} b = 1 \end{cases} \tag{21}$$

And it can be indicated that,

$$r = \mathrm{cov}(u,v) = a'\,\mathrm{cov}(x,y)b = a\sum_{12} b \tag{22}$$

Consequently, under the constraint of equation (21), let's strive for calculating $a \in R_p$, $b \in R_q$ which will make equation (22) get the maximum value.

To construct a lagrange function:

$$L = a'\sum_{12} b - \frac{\lambda}{2}\left[a'\sum_{11} a - 1\right] - \frac{\mu}{2}\left[b'\sum_{22} b - 1\right]$$

To get the first partial derivative of L, and set it equals zero, then the following equation set can be reached,

$$\begin{cases} \dfrac{\partial L}{\partial \alpha} = \sum_{12} b - \lambda \sum_{11} a = 0 \\ \dfrac{\partial L}{\partial b} = \sum_{21} a - \mu \sum_{22} b = 0 \end{cases} \tag{23}$$

By applying equation (22), we can get $\lambda = a'\sum_{12} b = b'\sum_{21} a = \mu$, which is equal with the correlation coefficient between u and v, i.e. r. Consequently, the problem is further changed into how to resolve the following equation set,

$$\begin{cases} \sum_{12} b - \lambda \sum_{11} a = 0 \\ \sum_{21} a - \lambda \sum_{22} b = 0 \end{cases} \tag{24}$$

Then a_{ij} and b_{jk} can be reached, and the canonical variables of u_k and v_k can be calculated.

For all the reached canonical variables, it is needed for us to provide the significance test. Only the canonical variable that meets the test requirements can be used for economic analysis.

Here is the test statistic,

$$Q_j = -\left[n - j - \frac{1}{2}(p+q+1)\right]\ln\left[\prod_{i=j}^{p}(1-\lambda_i)^2\right] \tag{25},$$

Which is λ^2 distributed with the degree of freedom $f = (p-j+1)(q-j+1)$.

Before the data processing with computers, we calculate out that the data inflexion of the sample by adopting step by step searching is 3.3% under the criterion (significance level) of 0.0001.

To input data with the preliminary treatment into the computers, and carry out the canonical correlation analysis by adopting the CANCORR process of SAS, the results are shown as table 3 and table 4.

Table 3. The canonical correlation coefficient and the standard error (A)

Pair number	R	Standard error	Eigen value
1	0.9746	0.0009	128.9238
2	0.9014	0.0012	76.2375

Table 4. The canonical correlation coefficient and the standard error (B)

Pair number	R	Standard error	Eigen value
1	0.9823	0.0010	398.7230
2	0.9702	0.0013	290.7426

Table 5. Correlation coefficients test result (A)

Pair number	Degree of Freedom	χ^2	χ^2 critical value ($\alpha = 0.05$)
1		292.3151	98.9230
2		118.4238	46.2224

Table 6. Correlation coefficients test result (B)

Pair number	Degree of Freedom	χ^2	χ^2 critical value ($\alpha = 0.05$)
1		263.7466	87.3489
2		163.8524	72.3478

The canonical correlation coefficient and its test results when turnover rate is greater than 3.3% are shown in table 3, while the canonical correlation coefficient and its test results when turnover rate is lower than 3.3% are shown in table 4.

According to table 3 and table 4, the two canonical correlation coefficients are both higher, which show that the two canonical variables are closely related. But if we want to know the significance degree of the correlations between the canonical variables, it is needed for us to carry out χ^2 test on the correlation coefficients. The specific method is to compare the χ^2 statistic with the critical value and according the comparative results, the significance degree of the correlation coefficients between the canonical variables is confirmed. The test result when turnover rate is higher than 3.3% is shown in table 5, and the test result when turnover rate is lower than 3.3% is shown in table 6.

According to table 5 and table 6, the two pair of canonical variables both satisfy the χ^2 test, which show that there is significant correlation between the canonical variables. That means, it is suitable for us to explain the independent variable with the influencing group variable.

Redundancy Analysis shows the explaining capability of the model. The result when the turnover rate is higher than 3.3% is shown in table 7, and the result when the turnover rate is lower than 3.3% is shown in table 8.

Table 7. Explaining capability of canonical variables (A)

Pair number	R^2	The first canonical variable	The second canonical variable
1	0.9872	72.1480	69.2384
2	0.9653	27.8520	30.7616

Table 8. Explaining capability of canonical variables (A)

Pair number	R^2	The first canonical variable	The second canonical variable
1	0.9244	55.9237	59.7943
2	0.9127	44.0763	40.2057

b. Analysis Results

Based on the work above, the canonical correlation models are provided: the model when the turnover rate is higher than 3.3% is shown table 9, and the model when the turnover rate is lower than 3.3% is shown table 10.

Table 9. Canonical model (A)

Pair number	Canonical model
1	$u_1 = 1.9052 y_1 - 0.3634 y_2$ $v_1 = -0.6642 x_1 - 0.2578 x_2$
2	$u_2 = 0.2108 y_1 + 0.9473 y_2$ $v_2 = -1.0743 x_1 + 0.5452 x_2$

Table 10. Canonical model (B)

Pair number	Canonical model
1	$u_1 = 0.2108\,y_1 + 1.7291\,y_2$ $v_1 = 0.3683\,x_1 + 1.3659\,x_2$
2	$u_2 = 0.8186\,y_1 + 0.3714\,y_2$ $v_2 = 0.9803\,x_1 + 0.7732\,x_2$

4.4. Discussion

According to the canonical correlation models established in this paper, we can describe the effect of college teachers' turnover on college performance as follows.

When the turnover rate is higher than 3.3%:

The first·canonical variable extracts scores on students education (Canonical load, 1.9052) from college performance, and the natural wastage of college teachers is negatively related with the scores on students education (Canonical load, -0.6642);

The second canonical variable extract scores on scientific research (Canonical load, 0.9743) from college performance, and the voluntary turnover is negatively related with the scores on scientific research (Canonical load, -1.0743).

When the turnover rate is lower than 3.3%:

The first canonical variable extract scores on scientific research (Canonical, load 1.7291) from college performance, and the voluntary turnover is positively related with the scores on scientific research (Canonical load, 1.3659).

The second canonical variable extracts scores on students education (Canonical load, 0.8186) from college performance, and the natural wastage of college teachers is positively related with the scores on students education (Canonical load, 0.9803).

Such a results on the effect of college teachers' turnover on college performance can be effectively explained by the theory of dissipative structure. The theory of dissipative structure is pioneered by the Brussels school of thought in the 1970s (Prigogine and Nicolis, 1977), this theory is firmly rooted in physics and chemistry. Nevertheless, it was later applied to urban spatial evolution, organizational change and transformation, changes in small groups and group dynamics, and political revolutions and change in political systems.

The most suitable example of the dissipative structure in the physical system should be convection in a liquid. If we heat the cooking oil in a shallow pan, the following changes will occur. First, while the temperature of the cooking oil is relatively uniform, heat is transmitted through the body of liquid by means of conduction in which the molecules' heat energy (molecular vibration) is transmitted to neighboring molecules via collision without major change of position. We can say that the system is still in a thermodynamic equilibrium. Next, as the pan is heated further, the temperature gradient between the upper and lower portion of the oil in the pan becomes more pronounced and thermal non-equilibrium increases. At a certain temperature gradient, convection starts and heat is then transferred by the bulk movement of molecules. Evidently, however, the surrounding environment at first suppresses the smaller convection streams, but beyond a certain temperature gradient, the fluctuations are reinforced rather than suppressed. The system moves into a dynamic regime, switching from conduction to convection, and a new macroscopic order called 'Benard cells' (i.e. a pattern of regular hexagonal cells that appear on the surface of liquid) emerges, caused by a macroscopic fluctuation and stabilized by an exchange of energy with the environment. Such a structure is called a hydrodynamic dissipative structure, and is a version of spatial structure.

Open systems make an effort to avoid a transition into thermodynamic equilibrium by a continuous exchange of materials and energy with the environment. By doing this, a negative entropy condition can be maintained. It has been understood for a long time that entropy is a quantification of randomness, uncertainty, and disorganization, and negative entropy therefore corresponds to (relative) order, certainty, and organization. However, the mechanics underlying this idea had not been clear until it was explained in the work of Prigogine and Nicolis(1977), Prigogine and Stengers (1984) in the theory of dissipative structure and order that exists in the non-equilibrium condition.

According to the theory of dissipative structure, an open system has a capability to continuously import free energy from the environment and, at the same time, export entropy. As a consequence, the entropy of an open system can either be maintained at the same level or decreased (negative entropy), unlike the entropy of an isolated system (i.e. one that is completely sealed off from its environment), which tends to increase toward a maximum at thermodynamic equilibrium. This phenomenon can be represented in quantitative terms as follows (Nicolis and Prigogine, 1977; Jantsch, 1980; Prigogine and Stengers, 1984). According to the second law of thermodynamics, in any open system, change in entropy dS in a certain time interval consists of entropy production due to an irreversible process in the system (an internal component) d_{iS} and entropy flow due to exchange with the environment (an external component) d_{eS}. Thus, a change in entropy in a certain time interval can be represented as $d_S = d_{eS} + d_{iS}$ (where $d_{iS} > 0$). However, unlike diS, the external component (d_{eS}) can be either positive or negative. Therefore, if deS is negative and as numerically large as, or larger than, diS, the total entropy may either be stationary ($d_S = 0$) or decrease ($d_S < 0$). In the former case, we can say that the internal production of entropy and entropy exported to the environment are in balance. It can be concluded that order in an open system can be maintained only in a non-equilibrium condition. In other words, an open system needs to maintain an exchange of energy and resources with the environment in order to be able to continuously renew itself.

The internal structure and development of dissipative systems, as well as the process by which they come into existence, evolve, and expire, are governed by the transfer of energy from the environment. Unlike isolated systems (or closed systems in a broader sense), which are always on the path to thermal equilibrium, dissipative systems have a potential to offset the increasing entropic trend by consuming energy and using it to export entropy to their environment, thus creating negative entropy or negentropy, which prevents the system from moving toward an equilibrium state. A negentropic process is, therefore, the foundation for growth and evolution in thermodynamic systems.

For dissipative systems to sustain their growth, they must not only increase their negentropic potential, but they must also eliminate the positive entropy that naturally accumulates over time as systems are trying to sustain themselves. The build up of the system's internal complexity as it grows is always accompanied by the production of positive entropy ($d_{iS} > 0$), which must be dissipated out of the system as waste or low-grade energy. Otherwise, the accumulation of positive entropy in the system will eventually bring it to thermodynamic equilibrium, a state in which the system cannot maintain its order and organization.

Although the argument so far is fundamentally based on chemical or biological systems, we argue it also applicable to the college as an open system. It is suggested that the net resource used by an college can be viewed as being divided into two parts. First is that concerned with the maintenance of the internal environment, and second, that which is transacted with the external environment. The former is treated as the change of entropy due to necessary maintenance and support processes (d_{iS}), which is always positive due to the nature of indirect costs, and the latter as the change of entropy in the input-transformation-output process (d_{eS}), which may be positive or negative (e.g. a college may experience poor performance or good performance). It is suggested, further, that d_{iS} refers to all the activities that are necessary to keep the college maintained and supported (e.g. management, administration, research and development, etc.) and d_{eS} refers to all the activities where there is interaction with the environment (e.g. recruit students, recruiting teachers, etc.) and production of products and services (Capable students). We further maintain that, in order for the college to remain viable, the flow component of entropy must be negative and greater in magnitude than that of the maintenance and support component since the support and maintenance activities always result in a net drain or loss to the college due to the exploitation of resources, but the input-transformation-output process (i.e. Education and students employment activities) may result in a net gain for the college if its earning is greater than its cost. In summary, we conclude, albeit perhaps at a metaphorical level, that in order for an college to maintain its order it must be in a non-equilibrium state.

5. Conclusion

With the reformation of management system of Chinese colleges, the human resource management and appraisal mechanism of Chinese colleges have changed greatly. And the pressure of teachers in colleges grows significantly, and the burnout and turnover appears greatly. The development of colleges depends on a relatively steady teachers team of high quality, so how to have charge of the turnover intention of teachers effectively is necessary for maximization the utility of human resource. Aiming at some studies and many practitioners think that the teachers' turnover rate influences college performance negatively, the paper makes investigation on the relationship between the performance of college which is represented by scores on students education and scores on scientific research and the turnover rate of college teachers which is represented by the natural wastage of teachers and the rate of voluntary turnover collected from "The statistical table of teachers in common college of China" and "Appraisal of Chinese colleges". The model shows that the relationship between turnover rate of teachers and the college performance is somewhat like an *inversed U-shaped curve*, and further the result shows that while the turnover rate is lower than 3.3%, there is positive relationship between them, otherwise turnover rate has negative effect on performance of college.

The result can be explained effectively by the theory of dissipative structure. According to the theory of dissipative structure, as an open system, when teachers' turnover rate is below a certain level, 3.3% in this research, a college can receive many new ideas, new methods and new behavior modes which will be very helpful to complement the traditional and stiff modes of the college. However, when the turnover rate is higher than a certain level, 3.3% according to this research, the college face the serious loss of critical teachers. In other words, college managers should assure that the higher-qualified teachers are very satisfied with the college, and the lower-qualified teachers have to improve their own capability or choose to leave. For college managers, the teachers' turnover rate should be controlled within a certain range in order to improve college performance; on the contrary, with the increase of teachers' turnover, college performance will collapse.

Though this paper contributes much to this topic, there are some limitations. First, the data we used are very limited, just 4 years, which will weaken the correctness of our conclusion; Second, the sample size is not large enough. Due to the limitation of data sources, we can only acquire the data of the top 100 colleges for each year in China. Third, the psychological process of an individual teacher who choose to leave has not been analyzed in detail. As we know, the decision-making process on turnover is a very complicated process which involves many psychological components and emotional processes needing to be noted. The future research should pay attention to the above three topics.

Acknowledgment

This research was supported by the Scientific Research Foundation of Xi'an University of Technology under Grant 107-210803.

Appendix 1. Code of Colleges in This Study

College code	College name	College code	College name	College code	College name
1	Tsinghua University	2	Peking University	3	Zhejiang University
4	Fudan University	5	Nanjing University	6	Huazhong University of Science and Technology
7	Wuhan University	8	Xian Jiaotong University	9	Jilin University
10	Shanghai Communications University	11	Zhongshan University	12	Sichuan University
13	Shandong University	14	University of Science and Technology of China	15	Harbin Institute of Technology
16	Southeast China University	17	Central-South University	18	Tianjin University
19	Tongji University	20	Institutes Of Technology Of South China	21	Nankai University
22	Beijing University of Aeronautics and Astronautics	23	Northeastern University	24	Xiamen University

Table. Continued

College code	College name	College code	College name	College code	College name
25	China Mining University	26	jing Normal University	27	Shanghai Second Medical University
28	Dalian Univ Technol	29	University of Science & Technology Beijing	30	Chongqing University
31	ina Agricultural University	32	Wuhan University of Technology	33	Zhengzhou University
34	Northwestern Polytechnical University	35	Suzhou University	36	East China University of Science and Technology
37	Lanzhou University	38	East China Normal University	39	China University of Geosciences
40	Nanjing University of Science & Technology	41	The China Petroleum University	42	Shanghai University
43	Hunan University	44	China Renmin University	45	Beijing Institute of Technology
46	Yangzhou University	47	Southwest Jiaotong University	48	University of Electronic Science and Technology of China
49	Nanjing Normal University	50	Agricultural University Of Nanjing	51	Nanjing University of Aeronautics and Astronautics
52	Northwestern University	53	Northeast Normal University	54	Nanchang University
55	Jinan University	56	Xidian University	57	Beijing University of Technology
58	Central China Normal University	59	Central China University of Agriculture	60	Chinese Medical Sciences University
61	Capital University of Medical Sciences	62	Northwest A & F University	63	North Jiaotong University
64	Qingdao University	65	Hohai University	66	Fuzhou University
67	Jiangsu University	68	Hunan Normal University	69	Guangdong University of Technology
70	University Guangxi	71	Yunnan University	72	HeFei University of Technology
73	South China Normal University	74	Zhongnan University Of Economics & Law	75	Hebei University
76	Nanjing Forestry University	77	Hebei Normal University	78	Institutes Of Technology Of Taiyuan
79	Shandong Agriculture University	80	Nanjing University of Technology	81	Kunming University of Science and Technology
82	Shaanxi Normal University	83	Fujian Normal University	84	Ocean University of Qingdao
85	Donghua University	86	Agricultural University Of South China	87	Yanshan University

Table. Continued

College code	College name	College code	College name	College code	College name
88	Shandong University of Science and Technology	89	Xiangtan University	90	Beijing Forestry University
91	Shandong Normal University	92	Beijing University of Chemical Technology	93	Southwestern Normal University
94	Chengdu University of Technology	95	Shanxi University	96	Hebei University of Technology
97	ChangAn University	98	Henan University	99	University Of Agriculture and Forestry In Fujian
100	Anhui University				

Appendix 2. Data on Teachers' Turnover and College Performance

Code	2002				2003				2004			
	y_1	y_2	x_1	x_2	y_1	y_2	x_1	x_2	y_1	y_2	x_1	x_2
1	7.46	9.57	1.42	2.54	7.46	9.06	1.23	2.25	7.16	3.93	1.32	1.98
2	18.1	5.74	1.39	4.38	11.7	23.8	0.70	1.94	4.28	6.81	1.37	1.57
3	9.58	14.4	1.01	2.49	33.2	10.7	1.03	1.81	5.93	-0.58	0.63	0.81
4	7.77	22.8	0.94	4.70	16.4	16.9	1.90	4.19	0.98	6.27	0.75	1.77
5	14.3	21.0	0.39	2.45	12.9	-7.7	0.35	1.45	0.46	2.03	0.03	2.92
6	8.71	15.9	2.03	3.11	9.46	5.87	1.62	2.60	3.21	3.69	2.55	3.54
7	-5.76	7.99	1.38	3.79	7.36	8.46	1.73	3.50	-0.11	4.14	1.08	1.28
8	10.1	6.95	1.55	2.56	8.57	9.53	1.58	1.97	6.19	8.10	1.10	2.67
9	9.54	16.6	0.11	0.70	7.31	6.43	0.11	1.81	3.52	15.1	0.66	0.66
10	7.83	28.3	1.38	1.60	10.6	-6.3	0.85	2.28	-2.77	8.92	0.62	1.36
11	-5.21	7.96	1.66	3.26	12.7	6.57	1.51	1.88	0.37	8.57	0.73	0.73
12	8.62	8.47	0.84	1.27	-6.9	11.8	3.29	4.29	-1.27	19.1	0.55	0.97
13	-6.37	8.48	1.07	1.64	21.0	12,5	0.69	1.01	7.21	13.9	0.00	0.78
14	8.03	9.70	1.44	2.23	15.6	12.8	0.57	4.05	3.13	9.44	0.95	2.32
15	23.3	11.8	0.60	1.45	-9.0	14.8	0.71	0.71	1.70	22.1	0.90	0.90
16	16.4	19.6	1.02	4.25	12.9	11.7	0.26	1.57	11.4	17.2	0.00	1.49
17	1.59	14.4	0.30	1.54	16.8	11.8	0.31	0.93	-0.92	8.43	0.90	1.51
18	8.48	8.06	1.35	1.46	-19	3.68	2.09	3.08	3.52	8.41	1.02	2.04
19	15.8	10.0	0.56	0.75	0.57	-3.6	0.17	1.04	8.72	22.50	0.42	1.65
20	12.0	5.79	1.30	0.76	4.58	-9.4	1.16	4.06	5.38	17.88	1.27	1.34
21	4.38	7.43	0.08	0.15	-12	16.1	0.06	0.13	-2.04	20.2	0.26	0.40
22	-6.83	8.79	0.30	1.63	6.47	11.8	0.29	1.19	1.51	7.52	0.49	6.29
23	7.38	1.85	0.58	0.94	5.47	8.41	1.10	7.20	-1.23	39.4	0.36	0.58
24	9.70	0.53	3.52	4.68	3.63	-6.0	3.38	3.38	-5.85	1.92	1.72	1.72
25	8.23	16.6	0.74	1.80	3.68	7.43	1.60	2.38	4.93	5.54	1.60	2.40
26	10.5	0.99	0.65	0.87	4.66	5.74	0.00	4.34	-4.79	11.0	0.00	1.60

Table. Continued

Code	2002				2003				2004			
	y_1	y_2	x_1	x_2	y_1	y_2	x_1	x_2	y_1	y_2	x_1	x_2
27	12.6	21.6	0.82	1.80	7.52	4.67	1.10	2.07	1.80	5.05	1.01	1.96
28	-10.6	-0.6	2.07	3.06	9.32	3.45	1.90	3.28	3.16	28.2	0.42	1.38
29	-6.08	12.6	2.71	3.23	7.66	3.86	0.36	0.36	0.88	22.2	1.37	1.80
30	3.14	-7.4	0.82	0.96	7.54	-8.3	0.91	2.03	5.39	5.01	1.49	2.30
31	6.85	9.11	1.51	1.72	6.23	3.45	0.52	0.73	2.91	3.76	2.07	3.20
32	7.85	7.47	0.54	0.87	0.53	-11	0.92	1.25	-17.1	6.16	0.74	1.15
33	9.12	0.21	0.22	2.98	5.63	9.35	0.90	8.33	1.83	13.5	1.86	1.86
34	8.63	6.58	1.07	4.24	4.45	1.65	0.89	1.01	-0.35	16.0	0.96	1.08
35	13.5	7.47	0.25	2.04	6.23	8.64	1.80	2.57	-1.02	1.47	0.00	0.25
36	0.87	8.64	1.54	1.92	3.52	7.63	0.23	0.23	-2.00	0.70	0.31	0.31
37	13.8	6.43	2.39	3.18	13.6	16.9	0.00	0.99	1.86	-4.74	2.21	2.41
38	6.57	3.21	0.36	0.36	22.7	10.6	1.20	2.28	6.52	20.9	0.70	1.53
39	8.44	8.58	2.09	2.09	-4.7	0.73	1.14	3.20	2.01	16.9	0.88	0.88
40	14.0	6.94	1.00	5.79	6.43	3.63	1.02	1.02	3.19	16.4	0.00	0.00
41	8.11	7.58	0.00	0.00	4.54	7.64	0.00	1.47	9.39	7.21	0.64	1.92
42	9.05	17.6	1.31	5.75	8.63	9.05	1.23	1.54	17.05	8.83	2.44	5.19
43	18.5	7.04	1.08	1.08	-2.4	12.7	0.52	0.52	3.52	20.1	1.33	1.33
44	16.3	11.7	0.37	0.37	7.95	7.07	0.94	1.50	-0.18	36.6	0.73	0.92
45	8.06	10.8	0.81	4.59	7.43	-5.9	0.51	1.28	5.40	14.9	0.50	0.75
46	4.59	1.94	1.10	1.43	3.66	9.65	0.26	1.53	-2.27	27.0	0.06	2.19
47	7.91	14.6	0.39	0.59	7.54	0.75	2.01	2.21	-1.32	-0.14	1.79	2.04
48	11.4	-5.4	0.09	2.58	5.53	8.06	0.04	3.57	12.9	4.41	0.02	0.71
49	-4.85	5.07	1.39	5.39	10.8	0.49	1.37	1.96	2.99	7.43	0.53	2.28
50	1.02	0.69	2.23	3.20	1.85	3.97	0.43	1.37	3.20	6.70	1.19	1.75
51	8.34	-9.7	0.89	1.36	24.7	12.7	0.41	9.44	0.17	10.4	0.84	1.32
52	0.56	6.46	2.34	3.02	4.07	1.75	0.82	1.54	7.02	11.7	0.48	0.64
53	-3.58	8.63	1.65	3.20	2.67	8.64	1.02	1.94	4.88	7.68	1.73	2.82
54	11.0	7.25	2.52	2.94	3.87	4.76	2.69	2.66	4.19	45.4	0.38	0.51
55	22.4	8.62	3.96	2.28	9.64	-7.9	2.48	1.10	5.76	9.24	0.63	0.70
56	6.65	19.4	1.62	2.71	4.78	3.86	2.29	2.67	4.86	34.8	0.51	1.030
57	4.58	22.5	1.51	2.46	5.87	5.80	1.98	2.31	8.64	13.9	3.00	4.60
58	4.72	13.5	0.90	1.24	3.45	2.14	1.45	1.45	4.63	19.6	0.40	0.40
59	4.05	14.6	3.49	7.85	7.64	9.06	0.48	4.98	4.80	23.9	0.29	2.35
60	6.47	2.36	0.00	1.50	4.34	7.86	0.77	1.26	17.3	29.1	0.97	1.79
61	8.28	-6.3	0.32	1.21	-6.6	-2.9	0.24	2.67	2.30	0.55	0.08	2.18
62	7.39	6.37	4.58	6.19	-15	6.95	0.54	0.50	4.06	6.82	1.78	6.07
63	14.3	3.65	4.68	6.35	1.55	4.65	0.89	2.67	0.20	4.62	1.39	1.39

Table. Continued

Code	2002				2003				2004			
	y_1	y_2	x_1	x_2	y_1	y_2	x_1	x_2	y_1	y_2	x_1	x_2
64	16.8	5.37	1.63	2.45	4.79	0.76	0.26	0.78	-5.24	8.77	0.46	0.46
65	2.79	6.37	0.46	0.89	7.54	6.85	0.64	11.6	0.14	6.80	0.84	1.50
66	0.74	9.36	0.28	1.13	4.67	7.85	1.52	3.22	1.13	-3.74	0.74	3.47
67	5.49	11.3	0.07	0.07	6.64	8.75	0.21	2.32	8.55	-5.59	0.13	2.29
68	14.5	10.5	1.31	2.63	4.36	8.43	1.78	3.80	13.1	3.43	0.00	0.00
69	27.7	20.7	2.78	1.65	0.34	5.64	0.77	1.46	0.16	9.58	0.571	1.29
70	-13.5	0.44	0.49	2.01	7.73	4.23	121	10.89	35.3	5.08	0.719	1.49
71	6.69	6.48	0.20	0.20	7.84	1.07	0.23	8.90	12.3	2.97	0.00	0.00
72	2.04	0.87	2.03	1.26	4.96	12.7	0.38	2.53	4.35	3.84	0.89	1.63
73	0.47	5.36	0.03	1.26	6.85	9.63	0.15	0.31	-3.37	8.93	0.00	0.00
74	5.89	13.6	2.60	3.23	16.7	7.74	0.65	8.70	95.94	-6.02	0.22	0.64
75	13.5	8.36	1.52	2.56	3.76	1.07	1.09	1.97	9.14	3.71	0.48	1.01
76	21.8	1.36	0.11	0.69	1.85	4.78	0.22	2.78	0.71	-7.94	1.13	1.13
77	7.38	1.07	0.39	1.77	8.45	13.7	0.14	0.56	1.32	30.3	0.00	0.00
78	5.36	8.96	0.00	1.41	11.4	15.7	0.28	2.00	-13.9	5.39	0.15	0.75
79	2.66	5.79	0.88	1.68	23.5	12.6	0.78	3.89	-13.1	9.11	0.65	0.71
80	15.4	4.47	0.59	0.59	7.44	8.40	0.69	1.38	2.89	7.36	1.18	1.31
81	5.47	4.32	1.46	4.14	6.54	12.0	1.29	1.53	—	—	1.63	2.22
82	0.48	1.87	2.83	3.77	0.64	5.84	2.26	14.7	5.05	4.78	0.87	4.88
83	6.27	1.60	0.21	1.39	4.68	9.43	0.00	0.28	7.31	0.36	0.56	0.75
84	12.7	0.86	0.27	1.67	4.08	5.57	2.08	2.16	-5.77	9.08	0.72	1.20
85	-0.57	12.9	0.08	1.15	0.07	6.94	0.73	0.97	-6.76	13.4	0.11	0.11
86	7.58	13.9	1.19	0.46	0.85	12.7	0.19	0.58	11.6	13.0	0.00	0.89
87	0.42	8.44	0.04	0.85	2.45	7.12	0.35	2.08	8.37	-6.42	0.06	0.78
88	9.07	13.2	0.51	0.83	9.05	4.56	0.13	1.43	—	—	3.54	7.86
89	2.84	9.56	0.00	0.90	3.76	5.67	0.00	0.28	7.36	7.31	1.32	0.50
90	-8.00	7.90	0.12	0.12	0.46	7.34	0.50	1.13	-4.37	8.36	1.49	1.68
91	11.8	14.7	0.26	0.35	—	—	0.38	0.85	—	—	0.06	0.73
92	5.48	12.3	0.06	0.76	23.7	6.66	1.36	2.46	6.36	-3.67	1.00	2.11
93	8.47	11.7	0.00	0.59	8.53	5.45	0.15	0.92	6.46	5.07	0.10	1.31
94	0.96	15.0	0.14	0.88	5.95	0.56	0.72	1.91	-8.22	7.23	0.22	16.4
95	4.26	0.50	1.24	1.55	3.79	11.6	0.43	0.69	—	—	2.38	1.16
96	7.83	-7.2	0.28	0.64	6.76	4.36	1.48	2.76	—	—	0.18	0.18
97	9.75	7.38	0.34	1.74	8.73	0.54	1.53	2.08	8.35	5.35	0.37	0.46
98	6.04	8.04	1.01	1.89	0.74	5.53	4.55	5.17	0.34	3.27	0.50	1.52
99	4.35	1.15	0.37	0.98	—	—	1.09	1.46	—	—	0.08	0.08
100	9.05	-4.2	1.23	2.44	4.77	6.79	1.93	0.23	9.35	12.8	1.43	0.92

References

Alexander, Jeffrey, A., Bloom, Joan, R. & Beverley, A. Nuchols (1994). Nursing turnover and hospital efficiency: and organization level analysis. *Industrial Relations*, **33**(4), 505- 520.

Baron, James, N., Hannan, Michael, T. & Diane Burton, M. (2001) Labor pains: Change in organizational models and employee turnover in young high-tech firms. *American Journal of Sociology*, **106**, 960-1012.

Batt, Rosemary. (2002). Managing customer services: human resource practices, quit rates, and sales growth. *Academy of Management Journal*, **45**(3), 587-597.

Baster Weel. *"Does Manager Turnover Improve Firm Performance? New Evidence Using Information from Dutch Soccer, 1986-2004,"* ftp://repec.iza.org/RePEc/Discussionpaper/ dp2483.pdf.

Bingley, Paul and Niels Westergaard-Nielsen (2004) Personnel Policy and Profit. *Journal of Business Research*, **57**, 557-563.

By McElroy, James, C., Morrow, Paula, C. & Rude, Scott, N. (2001). "Turnover and organizational performance: A comparative analysis of the effects of voluntary, involuntary, and reduction-in-force turnover," *Journal of Applied Psychology.*, Vol 86(6), Dec 2001, 1294-1299.

Carroll, Glenn, R. & Richard Harrison, J. (1998) Organizational Demography and Culture: Insights from a Formal Model and Simulation. *Administrative Science Quarterly*, **43**, 637-67.

Dalton, D. R. & Todor, W. D (1979). "Turnover turned over: an expanded and positive perspective", *Academy of Management Review*, Vol. 4, No.2, 225-35.

De Paola, Maria and Scoppa, Vincenzo. "The Effects of Managerial Turnover: Evidence from Coach Dismissals in Italian Soccer Teams," *MPRA Paper,* 11030, 2008.

Dess, Gregory, G. & Jason, D. Shaw (2001) Voluntary turnover, social capital, and organizational performance. *Academy of Management Review*, **26**(3), 446-456.

Huselid, Mark, A. (1995). The impact of human resource management practices on turnover, productivity, and corporate financial performance. *Academy of Management Journal*, **38**, 635-672.

Ilmakunnas, Pekka, Maliranta, Mika and Jari Vainiomäki (2005) Worker turnover and productivity growth. *Applied Economics Letters*, **12**(7), 395-399.

John, M. Levine & Richard, L. Moreland. "Personnel Turnover and Team Performance," United States Army Research Institute for the Behavioral and Social Science. *Technical Report* 1157.

Jovanovic, Boyan (1979) Job matching and the theory of turnover. *The Journal of Political Economy*, **87**(5), 972-990.

Kersley, Barbara & Christopher Martin (1997). Productivity growth, participation and communication. *Scottish Journal of Political Economy*, **44**(5), 485-510.

Lazear, Edward, P. (1979). " Why is there mandatory retirement?" *Journal of Political* Economy, *December*, **87**, 1261-64.

Loretta, A. Terry William Allan Kritsonis. (2008). "A National Issue: Whether the Teacher Turnover Effects Students' Academic Performance?" *National Journal for Publishing and Mentoring Doctoral Student Research*, Volume 5 Number 1, 1-5.

Mark, J. & Roberts and James R. (1997). Tybout. "Producer Turnover And Productivity Growth In Developing Countries, "*World Bank Research Observer,* Volume 12, Number 1, 1-18.

McEvoy, Glenn & Wayne Cascio (1987). Do good or poor performers leave? A metaanalysis of the relationship between performance and turnover. *Academy of Management Journal,* **30**(4), 744-762.

McElroy, James C., Morrow, Paula, C. & Scott, N. Rude (2001) Turnover and Organisational performance: a comparative analysis of the effects of voluntary, involuntary and reduction-in-force turnover. *Journal of Applied Psychology,* **86**(6), 1294-1299.

Mefford, Robert N. (1986) The effect of unions on productivity in a multinational manufacturing firm. *Industrial and Labor Relations Review,* **40**(1), 105-114.

Miller, E. M.. (1987). "A Comparison of large and small firm productivity, labor compensation, and investment rates. *Review of Business & Economic, Research,* **23**, 26-37.

Prigogine, Ilya; Nicolis, G. (1977). *Self-Organization in Non-Equilibrium Systems.* Wiley. ISBN 0471024015.

Prigogine, Ilya; Stengers, Isabelle (1984). *Order out of Chaos: Man's new dialogue with nature.* Flamingo. ISBN 0006541151.

Robert Hussey, (2005). Quadrature-Based Methods for Solving Heterogeneous Agent Models with Discontinuous Distributions," *Computational Economics, Springer,* vol. 26(1), pages 1-17, August.

Takao Kato & Cheryl Long, (2006). "CEO Turnover, Firm Performance and Enterprise Reform in China: Evidence from New Micro Data," *IZA Discussion Papers 1914,* Institute for the Study of Labor (IZA).

Williams, Charles R. & Linda Parrack Livingstone (1994). Another look at the relationship between performance and voluntary turnover. *Academy of Management Journal,* **37**(2), 269-298.

W. Stanley Siebert, Nikolay Zubanov, Arnaud Chevalier, Tarja Viitanen. "Labour Turnover and Labour Productivity in a Retail Organization," Discussion Paper Series, Institute for the Study of Labor, September 2006, IZA DP No. 2322.

In: Progress in Education, Volume 21
Editor: Robert V. Nata, pp. 55-76

ISBN: 978-1-61728-115-0
© 2011 Nova Science Publishers, Inc.

Chapter 3

"CAPITAL" IZING ON CULTURE: A SOCIO-HISTORICAL AND CURRENT PERSPECTIVE OF THE PARENTAL INVOLVEMENT PATTERNS OF AFRICAN AMERICANS

*Roni M. Ellington[1] and Rona Frederick-Taylor[2],***
[1]Morgan State University
[2]The Catholic University of America

Abstract

Conversations regarding the "achievement gap" fail to consider the historical, economic, sociopolitical and moral backdrop that created the "education debt" experienced by African-Americans. These conversations around the "achievement gap" do not take into consideration the systemic inequities that have accumulated over centuries, resulting in African Americans' cumulative denial of quality learning opportunities (Ladson-Billings, 2006). As a result, many African American students are not afforded access to adequate resources to achieve at the levels comparable to their white counterparts. Despite the legacy of the systematic inequity, many African American parents, historically and presently, continue to successfully pursue quality formal learning opportunities for their children. Using qualitative data from high achieving African American mathematics students matriculating through undergraduate mathematics programs, we argue that African-Americans have both historically and currently utilized social and cultural capital to produce high academic achievers, in spite of the "educational debt". The central question guiding this research is how have African American parents of urban public school students empowered themselves in ways that address the educational debt? Results suggest that African-American parents instilled values, advocated for their children and mobilized various resources to positively impact their children's achievement.

* E-mail address: roni.ellington@morgan.edu. Corresponding author: Roni M. Ellington, Department of Advanced Studies Leadership and Policy, Morgan State University, Baltimore, Maryland, 21251.

Introduction

There has been much discussion in the media, in both academic and political domains about the No Child Left Behind Act (NCLB), and particularly its intention to close the achievement gap between poor, non-Asian minority children and their white middle class counterparts, particularly in urban environments. There has been little agreement among scholars, government officials and community leaders concerning the causes, consequences and solutions of this gap. The achievement gap is particularly alarming when it comes to the performance of African American students. Research suggests that African-American students lag behind their White counterparts on nearly all measures of achievement including performance on standardized tests (Livingston & Wirt, 2004), college admissions and completion rates (NCES, 2002), SAT performance (NCES, 2007), and advanced placement course taking (The College Board, 2003).

Nowhere is the achievement gap between Black and White students more prevalent than in the discipline of mathematics. When examining the mathematics achievement of African-American students, one finds a pervasive history of underachievement, lack of persistence and overall disenfranchisement; especially post Brown v. Board of Education. Because of a history of low performance, cultural insensitivity, and negative experiences in mathematics classrooms, there are relatively few African-American students pursuing rigorous mathematics or completing degrees in mathematics related disciplines (Bailey, 1990; Bentz, 1990; Cooper, 2000; Kenschaft, 1993). This reality is disheartening given the importance of mathematics to future educational and labor markets in the technological age. Furthermore, several scholars argue that the pervasiveness of the "mathematics achievement gap" is a particular concern because it limits the educational and career options of students, and there is little evidence that this gap is significantly decreasing (Davison, Davenport, Butterbaugh, & Davison, 2004; Kao & Thompson, 2003; Townsend, 2002).

Although there has been much discussion about the causes and consequences of the achievement gap between African-Americans and white students (Townsend, 2002), these discussions have failed to examine how African-Americans have individually and collectively addressed this gap. Specifically, one of the key questions that has not been adequately answered is what are some of the ways that African American parents have empowered themselves currently to compensate for this achievement gap? As educators, researchers and parents, this current research was shaped by our desire to answer the above question. In particular, we examined the participation patterns of African-American parents and how they prepared and navigated the educational process for their children throughout their educational careers. Thus, this study provides the necessary qualitative insights into how African American parents have participated in their children's education in ways that lead to academic success and achievement in urban public schools, particularly in the field of mathematics. We begin by reviewing the literature on African American parental participation and the achievement gap. We couch our methods section in a discussion about social and cultural capital. As we discuss social and cultural capital, we infuse examples from the literature that illustrate patterns of African American parental participation from the past. This section is followed by the current ways African American parents impact their children's success in mathematics by examining qualitative interview data from eight high achieving mathematics students and their perspectives on how their parents participated as they matriculated through U.S. public schools. We discuss how these parents used social networks to help propel their students towards academic achievement. We conclude with implications about how African American parents can participate in their children's education, specifically their mathematics education to increase the likelihood of their children's achievement.

This study is important because little is known about successful parental participation in the field of mathematics in urban public schools. Although much has been written about strategies for participation, a comprehensive study of how parents used their social and cultural capital toward their children's success has been scantly examined (Harowboski, Manton, & Greif, 1998; 2002). Specifically absent from the literature are studies that investigate the role of parental involvement from high achieving African-American students' point of view with the intention to understand the types of parental participation that made a difference in the minds of the student. This study is especially important given conversations in the larger media that continue to focus on what parents can do to make a difference in their children's education (Cosby, Poussaint & Nelson 2009). In fact, in President Barack Obama's acceptance speech for the democratic nomination, he stated the importance of individual and collective responsibility among parents. This paper responds to the desire of parents, policy makers and other stakeholders who care deeply about the educational outcomes of African American children by sharing authentic examples of how African American parents have successfully participated in their high achieving children's education.

Participation Patterns of African Americans

When African American parental participation is discussed in the literature (Dornbusch, Ritter, Leiderman, Roberts & Fraleigh 1987; Darling, Mounts, & Dornburch 1994; Spera 2005), it is, in many cases, inaccurate (Mandara, 2006); or limited (McKay, Atkins, Hawkins, Brown & Lynn, 2003). Unfortunately, in much of the literature, parental participation in schools is assumed to look exactly the same across cultures (Mandara, 2006). As a result, conversations around parental styles and academic achievement have largely ignored the cultural perspective (Mandara, 2006). Hence, a comprehensive understanding of African American participation must take into account how they participate from their perspectives. This could, in turn, shed light on how African American parents may shift their modes of participation in the current educational environment in order to insure academic engagement and success for their children, especially in the area of mathematics.

African American parents, in some arenas, are perceived as non-caring with regard to their children's academic lives (Chavkin, 1993). In many cases, "care" is viewed as visibility in the school, participation in the PTA, attending school events (Epstein & Daubar, 1991; Stone & McKay, 2000) and discourse that matches the language and cultural norms of the teachers, which has been posited as not reflecting the ways parents of color are involved in their children's academic process. This disconnect is a result of a limited understanding of the varied ways that African Americans perceive schooling and how these perceptions shape how parents engage in their children's schooling. For example, Lareau (2000) has found that many working class African Americans intentionally turn the responsibility for education to the school and teachers. This action, by African Americans, does not demonstrate a lack of care, but moreover, a way of relating to the educational system that may be embedded in a cultural style. As we discuss later, this cultural style may be a function of how the schools and community have historically functioned as partners in educating African American students; however, as the data in this study reveals, African-American parents may need to adopt other ways of participating under the current climate of NCLB in order to ensure their children's academic success.

Framing the So-Called Achievement Gap

Researchers offer numerous explanations for disparities in academic achievement for African American students attending public schools. Some argue that there is a widespread problem of low expectations by many white, female pre-service teachers with regard to the academic achievement of children of color (Ladson Billings, 1999; Ziechner, 1993, Ziechner & Melnick, 1995). Others believe that there is a lack of cultural congruency among teachers and students (Irvine, 2000), while other scholars see structural inequalities reinforcing racism, classism, and sexism in educational institutions (Darling-Hammond, 1995).

Ladson Billings in her 2005 Annual Education Research Association (AERA) presidential address offered a different explanation for understanding the achievement gap. The explanation she provides has the most potential to shift the conversation in ways that communities can respond in meaningful ways. She argued that explanations of the achievement gap fail to consider the historical, economic, sociopolitical and moral backdrop that laid the foundation for the current crises in education. Ladson-Billings, suggested that rather than viewing the ongoing underperformance of African-American students as an achievement gap, it can be viewed as an "education debt." The "achievement gap," or rather the "education debt," is the result of systemic inequities that have accumulated over hundreds of years which denied access to quality education to African Americans. As a result, African-American students were not given the appropriate resources to achieve at the levels of white students and so they were systematically left behind. She contends that even if the "achievement gap" is closed for any given period of time, this would not abolish the "education debt" that has accumulated over the past 400 years.

We agree with Ladson-Billings argument which shifts the academic language of achievement gap to one of "educational debt." By couching the achievement argument in the language of "debt" we can now respond to paying down the debt with "capital". By capital, we mean resources that can be leveraged for goods, services or other resources that yield social profit (i.e. access to knowledge, networking etc.) (Lareau, 2000). We argue that in spite of the systemic inequality that has historically impeded full access to knowledge and resources for members of the African American community, there are examples in which members, both historically and currently, utilized various forms of capital to close the "educational debt". Based on our review of the literature, we found that prior to integration, many members of the African American community utilized their money and resources to build and maintain schools in their neighborhood. By the close of the 19th century, people of African descent relied upon each other to develop and control their own schools (Anderson, 1988; Butchart, 1980). For instance, Fortress Monroe (founded in 1866) was one of the first Black schools created by Africans, and its teachers were educated southern African Americans. In another case, Savannah Education Association, founded in Georgia in 1865 organized and sustained its own Aid society. As Butchart (1980) notes, the Association schools were entirely self sufficient, relying exclusively on the local Black community for their support and [housed] all Black faculty. As evidenced, there was no separation of parent and community. Many members of the community worked together with the charge of self-education. As of 1865, only 10% of Blacks in the South were literate. By 1940, the black literacy rate had increased to 89% (Blum 2007), demonstrating the desire to self educate in the face of systemic racism and oppression.

Siddle Walker (1993) evidences one striking example of how Black self-help efforts led to the closing of the "educational debt" during the Rosenwald era in her examination of the Caswell Training School, which opened in 1906. In this case, African Americans pooled their resources to hire twenty-two teachers who taught 735 students. The financial commitment and support of the parents and the larger community ensured the schools' existence despite the lack of support from the all White school board. As Siddle-Walker notes, the Parent Teacher Association meetings focused not only on financial issues and mission statements, but also on specific issues concerning the students. Walker shares that the principal used a portion of the meeting to report to parents the educational objectives, current happenings in the schools or ways in which the parents could help their children improve academically (p. 168). During this period, forms of social capital were marked by self help, monetary sacrifice, and community responsibility. In addition, parents played "advocacy roles by soliciting funds and providing a home-based support for the principal and teachers (Siddle-Walker 1993). Parents and the school worked together as socializing units for the children. As Walker conveys, one student commented that, "my mommy and daddy are pushing me and my teachers are pushing me...oh well, I got to do good." Although the Rosenwald movement ended in the 1930's, it became a living testament to the ways in which African Americans and the overall community utilize their resources in spite of the system working against them to develop culturally appropriate, community-based schools for their children.

Although we highlight examples of how African-Americans have used their social and cultural capital as a way to respond to the educational debt, we understand that the educational debt is a result of social and cultural inequities that exist in society. In order to fully eradicate the educational debt, social and cultural institutions must be transformed. However, until then we must continue to showcase how African-American parents have empowered themselves to address these inequities as a way to empower and educate our people. In what follows, we describe social and cultural capital theory as it was used to frame the current study and use data from this study to illustrate current examples of how African-American parents used their social and cultural capital to foster an atmosphere of high achievement for their children.

Social and Cultural Capital Theory

The theoretical lens used in this study was grounded in social and cultural capital theory. Although there are various conceptualizations of cultural capital (Lin, 2001; Bourdieu, 1986, Coleman, 1988: Franklin, 2004), researchers contend that social and cultural capital, just as economic capital, can be invested and mobilized by a group or individual to yield positive outcomes in society such as wealth, power or reputation (Lin, 2001). According to Bourdieu (1986), cultural capital refers to the system of attributes, dispositions, language skills, cultural beliefs, values and knowledge derived by one's parents that indicate class status; thus the more these values reflect the dominant culture the more cultural capital the person or group possesses.

These cultural values, knowledge and beliefs are held by the dominant culture and are legitimized as the "objective" culture and values of the society. Hence those who have values, beliefs and dispositions of the dominant cultural group have "capital" that they can use to profit from social and cultural institutions such as educational systems. Bourdieu (1986) defines social capital as

> the aggregate of actual or potential resources which are linked to possession of a durable network of more or less institutionalized relationships of mutual acquaintance and recognition--or in other words, to membership in a group-which provides each of its members with the backing of collectively-owned capital, a 'credential' which entitles them to credit, in the various senses of the word. (Bourdieu, 1986, p. 248-249)

In other words, social capital is the social resources available to a group or individual that can be accessed and used to promote positive outcomes. Forms of social capital include an understanding of "the system," using social and community networks to help facilitate academic and social success, and drawing on social contacts and community resources to help gain access to educational systems and successfully navigating these systems (Yosso, 2005).

In the same vein, Franklin defines social capital as "the network of social organizations, cultural institutions, voluntary civic associations, family and kinship groups in the community that assist in the development of an economic enterprise (Franklin, 2004: pg 36). Although Bourdieu and Franklin's conceptions of social capital differ, each recognizes that social capital consists of resources embedded in the social relations and social structures to which a person has access. These resources can be mobilized when one wishes to increase the likelihood of success in an institutional or social setting (Lin, 2001). "Collective" cultural capital, defined by V. P. Franklin, is the sense of group consciousness and collective identity that serves as an economic resource for the financial and material support of business enterprises that are aimed at the advancement of an entire group (Franklin, 2004: pg. xiv).

A growing body of research is applying social capital theory to understanding educational outcomes, particularly of African-American youth (Perna & Titus 2005; Yan 1999, Yosso, 2005). Results of this research reveal that social capital, as measured by family structure, parental education, and parents' aspirations, had a positive impact on educational achievement and attainment (Dinka & Singh 2002). This current study draws on the notion that parental involvement and values are vehicles of both cultural and social capital because it is the parents who instill beliefs, attitudes and values into their children that can be used in ways to benefit them in academic and social institutions. In addition, parents have access to various social and community networks that can be garnered to help their children successfully maneuver systems that were, in many cases, not designed for their success (Yosso, 2005). Hence, African Americans have a distinct way of wielding their resources in order to navigate the larger U.S. society. As evident in our findings, students possessed several forms of social and cultural capital that they accumulated and mobilized that were critical to their success and persistence in mathematics.

In the following section we will present findings on how parents of successful college mathematics students used forms of social capital (i.e., advocacy, and social networks) to foster high academic achievement in their children in urban public schools. These findings reflect current ways that parents participate in the success of their children, particularly in mathematics.

Methods

To understand parental participation in the current context, we used interpretive case study methods framed by social and cultural capital theory. Interview data from a sample of eight high achieving African-American mathematics majors was collected, transcribed verbatim and analyzed using a start list of codes and open and axial coding. In order to select participants, purposeful sampling was employed, since it allows the researcher to select people for a study based on the belief that this sample can contribute to or expand the knowledge base (Schloss & Smith, 1999). The following four criteria were used to select the participants for this study:

1. Multi-generational African-Americans born in the United States and received their pre-college education in the United States
2. Current junior or senior students in a four-year college or university
3. Cumulative GPA of 3.0 or better and have declared majors in mathematics
4. Taken or are taking mathematics courses above the Calculus sequence

After participants were selected, they were interviewed twice over the course of six months. Each student was considered a case and data was reported by cross-case analysis. During the first one hour interview, participants were asked questions about the social and cultural factors that impacted their success in mathematics. After initial data collection and analysis, a second one hour interview was conducted to further explore emerging themes. We also utilized QSR NVivo software to assist in coding and compiling the data into categories. Categorical data was grouped to identify relationships among and between them and develop preliminary themes. After the second interview, case study portraits were created and each participant was given a case analysis to review and provide their corrections, additions and any other input that they saw as relevant. In addition, a final group interview was conducted and data from this group interview was analyzed to further confirm and in some cases disconfirm emerging themes. This methodology was used in order to capture the essence of the groups' experiences and to foster a space that would give voice to these students who have been successful in mathematics. In what follows, we present our theoretical lens.

Findings

Eight high-achieving African American students were interviewed in order to understand the social and cultural factors that shaped their success and persistence in mathematics. All of the students were multi-generational African-Americans born in the United States, received their pre-college education in the United States, and had cumulative GPA of 3.0 or better as mathematics majors. Six of the eight participants were female and the remaining two participants were males.

Participants

Anita James was a 20 year old junior mathematics major attending a predominately white mid-sized public university on the east coast with a cumulative GPA of 3.5. She was a Sterling Scholar.

Karen Johnson was a 20-year old mathematics major from a predominately white mid-sized public university on the east coast and working a cumulative GPA of 3.6. She was also a Sterling Scholar.

Michael Brown was a 21 year-old senior mathematics major at a mid-size public university on the east coast with a cumulative GPA of 3.8. He was also a Sterling Scholar.

Tina Jones was a 22 year-old senior mathematics major at a mid-size public university on the east coast with a cumulative GPA of 3.4. She was also a Sterling Scholar.

Tennille Smith was a 21 year old senior mathematics major at a mid-sized Historically Black University on the east coast with a cumulative GPA of 3.8. She received a full scholarship to pursue graduate studies in mathematics.

Joyce Michaels was a 19 year-old junior mathematics major from a large predominately white research university with a cumulative GPA of 4.0.

David Simmons was a 24 year old junior mathematics major at a large predominately white research university on the east coast with a cumulative GPA of 3.2.

Shanice Jackson was a 20-year old junior mathematics major who attended a large predominately white research university on the east coast with a cumulative GPA of 3.6.

Although the researchers acknowledge that the experiences of these students, who fit the criteria of the study, were from middle-class, two-parent homes do not reflect the experiences of many African-American students, we assert that much can be gleaned from the family and community efforts that shaped their success in mathematics. Particularly, these students' parents can be viewed as "caring adults," who were invested in their success which is often reflected in the experiences of other African American high achievers with various family structures (Moody 2004; Walker 2006). By caring, we mean that the adults in their lives exhibited concern for them and therefore encouraged and supported them in their personal as well as academic pursuits.

Participants highlighted several key roles that their parents played in their success in mathematics, particularly in their early years. The roles that their parents played were multi-dimensional and spanned their entire educational careers. However, their parents' influence was most prominent in their early years up until their entry into accelerated programs in elementary school. In this section, we discuss the primary ways that these students perceived the role of their parents in their success and persistence in mathematics.

All of the students in this study began their formative years in a two-parent household, and the values and structures of these households provided a firm foundation for their entry into school and into formal mathematics learning. In these households, their mothers and fathers had important and distinct functions. However, both parents presence in the household had a positive impact on their preparation for school, initial interest in mathematics and science, and early mathematics-related experiences. In many of these cases, being from a two-parent home allowed one-caretaker, primarily the mother, to take an active role early in their child's education.

The Nurturing Mother

The mothers provided essential pre-school experiences and supervision that created a nurturing environment that helped foster an initial interest in learning and provided an academic structure that was essential to these students' later success in school. For example, Karen Johnson recalls a conversation she had with her mother about her infancy years. Her mother shared with Karen how she taught her the alphabet as an infant and how she was an early talker. Also her mother exposed her to mathematical concepts before she entered pre-school. Karen credits these early experiences with giving her a head start over many of her peers.

> Well, with my mom- when we were little, she sat in the crib and she used to do letters and stuff like that, and different things where we'd learn the alphabet and stuff like that, at 11 to 12 months. We all talked early. I know I started talking, she said 9-10 months or whatever. ... My mom taught us how to count and everything like that. And every time we went someplace, oh, what's $1 + 2$? And what's $2 + 2$? ... But I know before 5, I know I could add and stuff like that.

By giving Karen this attention as a young child, she received the skills to be an early talker and reader, which gave her a head start in her preparation for formal schooling. In addition, she specifically recalls her mom providing early mathematical experiences. Because of her family structure, her mom was available to provide these experiences and take an active role in her child's learning.

David's mother also provided a nurturing and academically focused home environment that helped to cultivate his early interest in learning. In his early years, David's mother was a stay at home mom and was able to give David considerable attention. He asserts that this early supervision was important to his initial interest in learning and readiness for school. Like Karen, David was also an early talker and reader and his mother taught him to count at an early age. Having these early educational experiences had a positive impact on his school success, and he attributes this to the fact that his mom was available.

> My mother really didn't work for the first several years of my life, and her just being there to watch Sesame Street with me. I think I had an advantage over a lot of kids because my mother actually took us to the library...She had nothing else to do but to just take care of us. And watch out for us, and take us to the library... watching Sesame Street with us, making sure I learned how to tie my shoes before I went to kindergarten. I was just ahead of the game early on... In kindergarten I was way ahead of those kids. I probably should've gone straight to first grade. I knew how to count, I knew how to add....My mom was a beast, like Mom can you leave us alone? Like, can I watch cartoons? No, I want to see you write your name twenty times. So, that helped me.

His mother being available to engage him in educational experiences early in his life helped to prepare him for school. Thus, his mother was able to transfer skills and develop values that would be integral when he began school, which by definition is a form of cultural capital. Later in David's academic career he drew on these early experiences to enable him to succeed in the field of mathematics.

In Joyce's narrative, we see similar experiences. Joyce recalls that her mom being home to monitor her socially and academically was a key component to her early success in school. Because Joyce's mom was home, she was able to provide needed supervision and pre-school experiences that influenced Joyce in positive ways. Although, Joyce could not recall any particular kinds of activities she engaged in with her mother, she perceived her mothers' presence in the home as very influential in her later success in school.

> She [my mother] always wanted me to be an engineer, so I think she was supportive of me being within a technical field. I think her presence in the house when I was younger contributed to the way I grew up. Like, my mom was always home so I never had to do after-school programs. I know her presence has had a huge influence on how I turned out. When we were out of school, a lot of people's parents are at work, so you know they're running amok in the streets. My mom was home.

We see from the above vignettes that these participants' mothers played a major role in providing early educational experiences that shaped their interest in learning and readiness for school. Although not all of these early educational experiences were mathematics and science specific, they were positive experiences that cultivated a love of learning, problem solving skills, and key reading skills. Having these skills helped these students place in Gifted and Talented and Accelerated programs in early elementary school. Clearly, these skills and values served as forms of capital that gave them access to educational opportunities that very few African American students are afforded. Once these students had access to these accelerated programs, they were able to further develop the human capital needed to be successful in school, particularly mathematics.

Fathers Cultivating an Early Interest in Mathematics

In these two parent families, the fathers also played an important role in their children's educational lives, particularly in their mathematics learning. Many of the fathers, five out of eight, had technical or science based careers; therefore, they were proficient in mathematics and science and helped cultivate an early interest in science and mathematics. This interest later grew into a love for the subject that was essential to their persistence.

Joyce Michaels, whose father was a civil engineer, admits that her dad influenced her to be interested in mathematics. Being the only girl in a male-dominated household, Joyce was exposed to mechanical things her entire life. Her earliest recollections of being interested in mathematics began when she was in the first grade. Her dad bought home a computer game with multiplication and other mathematics related activities. She became intrigued with trying to figure out how it worked. She admits that she liked mathematics because it made sense and was straightforward. When asked if her father's occupation influenced her choice to become a mathematics major, Joyce recalls:

> I definitely think that my father influenced me to be interested in math and science. I was never interested in engineering but I always did like math...I think my earliest exposure to being interested in mathematics- it had to be when I was younger and my dad bought me this computer game. ..I guess ever since then I always liked math because it always made sense,

and it was just very straightforward I thought. We [Joyce and her dad] used to sit there and like put the circuit together so the train could work.

We see from the above excerpt that Joyce's dad provided her with early mathematics related experiences that cultivated her initial interest in the subject. She perceived these early experiences with her father as key to her interest and subsequent success in mathematics. She notes that these experiences were "more advanced" than what she was learning in school, which reflects the idea that she began school with a head start over her peers.

Tina, Karen, Anita and Michael, whose fathers were also in technical fields, shared similar experiences. Tina's father worked a variety of positions including working as a technician on a fighter jet. Although Tina admits that she was not certain of her father's occupation, she knew it was science and technology related. Tina describes how he was able to relate the science and mathematics concepts she was learning in school to the real world, which she found helpful in her own studies:

He [her father] uses math every day. He'll tell me stories of him growing up, how engineers-he had to explain to them what to do, even though he doesn't have an engineering degree, he knew more about stuff and he had to show engineers how their blueprints were wrong. So, to me, my dad [could] relate what I'm learning about, to the real world. [Since he was] adding numbers and electrons, this is what my dad does! You know, he has to use this stuff [mathematics].

Anita, whose father was a computer scientist, gave her general encouragement and supported her decision to persist in mathematics. Although she does not recall any mathematics specific encouragement, she contends that her father valued mathematics and served as a positive role model.

Michael's father received his undergraduate degree in physical science and worked for the Pentagon in a science-based field; however, Michael was not sure what he did for the organization. His father insisted that he participate in science and mathematics related programs. This insistence may have been a result of his father's own background in science and mathematics, although Michael did not say this specifically.

Well when I was younger, they (his parents) tried to put me in summer programs, just to, like NASA summer programs or space camp, nothing that's solely based on mathematics...The summer program wasn't geared toward mathematics, they're more geared towards life science type stuff. And like aerospace stuff.

Although Karen's father's occupation was not directly related to mathematics and science, his job required him to interact with people in mathematics and science related fields. Through these interactions, he came to believe that mathematics and science were important in establishing a financially lucrative career and articulated these beliefs to his daughter. He stressed the importance of mathematics and science and encouraged her to excel in these subjects. He also facilitated her exposure to science and mathematics related activities in order to extend her understanding of concepts discussed in class. Karen recalls in our second interview:

My parents, they weren't into math and science. But, they knew where the jobs were, and my dad hires people a lot for his company, and he works for an aluminum company in their like public affairs position. And he's like, all the money is here. … If we were reading something in science and I'm really interested, I'm going to ask my dad about it. You know, he's going to tell me what he knows about it. Or we'll watch the Discovery Channel program about it.

As evident from the above data, the father's occupation and/or interest in mathematics had an impact on the participants' early interests in science and mathematics and provided them with related support, encouragement and values that developed their interest in mathematics. Their fathers helped them learn to value mathematics and developed positive beliefs about mathematics, while the mothers provided early educational experiences and created a nurturing and academically rich environment. All of these experiences can be seen as forms of cultural capital, which were essential components to their success and persistence in mathematics.

Once these students entered formal schooling, their parents continued to play a significant role in their children's success in school. One of the major ways that the parents impacted their success was by instilling in their children a variety of academic and social values that were necessary for their later success in school mathematics. Some of these values included an emphasis on hard work, discipline, the value of education, and giving back to the community- all of which later contributed to these students specific success in mathematics.

Success-Related Values

The parents of these high achievers instilled various success related values that served as a source of cultural capital that helped shape their success in mathematics. The values that these parents imparted proved useful throughout their mathematics educational pursuits because it helped them cultivate what Bourdieu refers to as embodied cultural capital (Bourdieu 1986). This capital reflects the dispositions, attitudes and ways of being embedded in the individual through socialization. In the case of these high achievers, their parents instilled values such as discipline that requires hard work, and strong prior knowledge that translated into dispositions and habits that were imperative for their success in mathematics. This influence began before these students entered school and became more pronounced when they entered formal academic settings. In general, these students' parents' valued education, believed in hard work and discipline, and saw giving back to the community as fundamental values that were instilled in their children. Hence, they communicated these values to their children in a variety of ways, and these values supported their children's academic advancement.

Karen recalls her parent's commitment to education and its impact on her success in school. Her parents' experiences in segregated schools shaped their beliefs about the importance of school and giving back to the community. These values stayed with Karen and provided a degree of motivation for her. She recalls:

My parents were gonna find a way so that we could do things to be successful because they wanted more for us. They wanted more for the community… My dad always says if you don't take responsibility for your people, even though you don't want to claim them all the time, nobody else will. So I think that's why all of us feel like we have to do stuff for the black community, even though they might shut out my parents some of the time.

Knowing that her parents "wanted more for her," and encouraged her to "take responsibility for her community," Karen did not want to let her parents down and was willing to "comply" with her parents' expectations. Karen saw her success as a way to give back to the community. As we will see later, this need to give back to the community was an important personal motivator for several of the participants' success in mathematics.

Karen also revealed how her parents modeled hard work and perseverance which were traits that she adopted in her own academic pursuits. Her parents instilled in her that her "job" was to do well in school. When asked what the pay was for this "job," Karen replied:

> When we got good grades, we got you know money and stuff like that. ... And my parents worked very hard so that their kids get what they wanted and they saw that we worked hard. Because they asked us to do well in school, that's what we did. Because we saw our parents work hard every day, and I guess that's what helped me work hard. Because I know how hard my parents have worked, and how many jobs they worked.

In Karen's case, her parents modeled working hard and encouraged her and her siblings to do the same. By modeling the success-related value of hard work, Karen's parents instilled this characteristic in her. As the above vignette reveals, even though she was rewarded with money for doing well in school, this was not the only reason she chose to succeed in school. She chose to do her best because she saw it as a "payback" to her parents for being a source of motivation and inspiration for her.

In David's case, he describes his mother as a go-getter. She instilled in him the importance of going after what was important and seizing every opportunity presented to him. Therefore, his mother served as a role model for David because he took on similar characteristics that helped shape his academic character. He credits his mother with helping him cultivate this character trait of going after what he wants, an attitude that helped him in his persistence in mathematics.

> [My mother would say] do whatever you can do, because you may not get this opportunity again. So she's very much a go-getter. And now, you know, I kind of have that attitude now. You know. Where, I'll apply for everything. You know, I show up for everything. I try to participate in everything.

David's mother planted seeds that encouraged him to take risks and go after opportunities that were presented to him. This characteristic was a key component to his success in mathematics since he admits that mathematics requires him to be willing to make mistakes and try various approaches in order to arrive at ultimate success.

When asked how she developed a strong commitment to doing well in school, Shanice credits her parents with instilling this commitment in her. Because of her upbringing, she perceived average performance as unacceptable, and would therefore do what was required to achieve at a higher level. While discussing what experiences had a memorable impact on her drive to be successful in school and in mathematics, Shanice credits her parents with instilling important values in her as a young child:

> My parents [instilled a desire to be the best] from the beginning and when [I] started to get older, [I] realized for myself that it's [being successful in school] important to my future to do well in school. So, it's just important for me to do well. I don't want to get a C. I would be

really upset if I got a C in a class. So, I guess like I just won't allow myself not to do well. If I feel like I'm starting to slip, then like I won't allow it to happen. You know?

Shanice's parents, just like several other parents of these high achievers, instilled a variety of success-related values that were perceived as having a positive impact on their success and persistence in mathematics. Values such as giving back to the community, valuing education, working hard and pursuing what was important to them were fostered in their children from an early age; therefore providing an additional layer of parental influences that shaped their success in mathematics. These students adapted these beliefs and values and they were key ingredients to their academic achievement, particularly in mathematics.

Parental Advocacy

The most intrusive way in which these students perceived their parents impacting their success and persistence in school mathematics is through parental advocacy. Parental advocacy is distinct from support and encouragement. Parental advocacy, which can be viewed as a form of social capital, is defined in this study as parents taking intrusive actions to navigate their child's educational paths to ensure their success in school. This advocacy was most pronounced in the early elementary school years where major educational decisions were made that set the course for the participants' entire school experience. Actions that reflect this behavior include parents being active in the school, making recommendations about the child's academic track, demanding that their child take particular mathematics courses, and advising them about ways to navigate educational and social institutions for their benefit.

In general, it was the mothers who advocated for their children. Mothers not only provided important pre-school educational experiences, as mentioned earlier, but many students recall how their mothers pushed them once they were in school to be successful. Four out of eight of these mothers were educators and the other four mothers had education beyond high school. Therefore, they knew how to navigate the educational system to ensure their children's success. Shanice explains how her mother insisted that her daughter be placed in the appropriate classes to ensure that she receive maximum benefit from her educational experience.

> ...My mom worked in a school system, so she knows what's up. Like the [gifted and talented] GT kids get all these best attention, and if you're in GT to begin with, that's the track for the rest of your life. ... She knew that it was important to get me in the GT classes and stuff. If you want to be successful, if you want your kid to be successful, then you should try to get them in the GT classes. Because if they start in GT in elementary school, they'll be in GT in middle school and high school, and those are the kids that are successful and, you know, you can get into good colleges and get scholarships and things like that.

Shanice's mother continued to advocate for her daughter even when she failed to meet the GT admissions score on the placement test. She further explains in a second interview:

> Everybody takes a [placement] test; I think it in third or fourth grade you take a test to get into GT classes. ... Depending on how well you do on the test, you're placed in either GT or [regular] classes. I don't know if they had honors or what... I didn't do well on the math part

of the test actually when I was in third grade. And I wasn't supposed to be in GT math, but my mom *made* them put me in GT math.

Although Shanice did not test into the program, her mom interceded and persuaded the school to place her in the most advanced mathematics track. In a follow-up interview, she explains how her mother knew that by placing her in the advanced track in elementary school it would positively impact the rest of her educational career.

Yeah, she knew that it was important to get me in the GT classes and stuff if you want to be successful. If you want your kid to be successful, then you should try to get them in the GT classes. Because if they start in GT in elementary school, they'll be in GT in middle school and high school, and those are the kids that are successful and, you know, you can get into good colleges and get scholarships and things like that.

This type of intentional interference on the part of the parent, particularly the mother, can also be seen in Karen Johnson's story.

My parents *made sure* that I was on the accelerated track in elementary school. I was in Gifted and Talented, so I started from first grade on, and I always took honors courses...and I graduated from middle school at the top.

Both Karen and Shanice's mothers insisted that their daughters be placed in accelerated programs in early elementary school. The advocacy of Karen's mother did not stop with having her placed in the accelerated track in elementary school. Karen's mother, who was a teacher and guidance counselor, purposely enrolled her in certain courses that would challenge her academically as well as socially. While discussing her experiences in elementary school, Karen explains the advantages of having a mother who understood the educational system.

[One of] the advantages of having your mother as head of guidance is she tried to make the schedule so it'd be conducive for me. And that's what most people who work in guidance [would do] if their children were there; they [would] try to make the schedule such that their kids wouldn't have to have teachers who they knew that they would struggle with. But sometimes my mother went ahead and put me in those classes with teachers that I would struggle with, because she [knew] I needed to experience that.

Elaborating on what she meant by having teachers that she would 'struggle with,' Karen admits that her mother wanted her to experience teachers who would challenge her socially and academically in order to teach her how to overcome these challenges.

...A lot of these teachers didn't have the social skills when working with her, so she knew that they weren't going to have the social skills with me. She was like, you're not always gonna get the teacher that you want to get. If you can't do well in a teacher's class who doesn't like you, and you don't like them, how are you gonna do well in any other course? Once you can do that [do well with these challenging teachers], you can do that with anybody.

Similar experiences were shared by other participants who had mothers who were educators. Tina, like Karen, went to a school where her mother taught; hence, she also understood the system and navigated the system on her daughter's behalf. When asked what experiences in elementary school influenced her most on her mathematics journey, she comments on how mom placed her in the most challenging classes.

> In elementary school I went to the school my mother taught at. She was a third grade teacher, and I went there from pre-K to fifth grade. And so she had a role in picking the hardest teachers for me to take. She made sure I was in the hardest classes. She made sure that I did not always have the teacher who's the nicest, but they wanted the most from the experience. So, from the beginning, I knew I had to put [out] more. I had to do more than, I wouldn't say anyone else, but my mother expected me to push myself more, and I came to expect it in myself, you know, to push myself more.

We see from the above comments that both Karen and Tina had mothers who were intentional about placing their daughters in challenging classes with demanding teachers. In these classrooms, their daughters could gain the academic and social skills to help them in the future and to learn how to deal with and overcome challenges. This type of intentional placement is a form of social capital in two ways. Firstly, these parents understood "the system" because many of them were employed by the school system, mainly as teachers. As a result, they mobilized their social resources, through parental advocacy, to increase their children's potential for success in school (Lin, 2001). Secondly, as a result of their social networks, these parents enabled their children to access resources such as matriculating through an honors program so that they could, in turn, establish their own institutionalized relationships that they could utilize to help them "profit" from the educational establishment.

What is common in all of the above students' experiences was that these mothers took intrusive actions that directly impacted their children's academic trajectories. These mothers did more than simply tell their children that they could overcome challenges. They placed them in situations that required them to overcome challenges and build their academic and social character. This act of intrusion on behalf of their children is a key component of parental advocacy and the participants acknowledge that these acts of advocacy impacted their success and persistence in accelerated programs, which includes mathematics courses.

The Church and Spirituality

Another commonality among these high achieving students was their accountability to a higher power. Parents instilled spiritual values early in their children's lives and required them to attend church on a consistent basis. When these students got older, they continued to participate in church related activities and cultivate their growing spiritual identity. They also began to rely on their spiritual base at times when they struggled through school. Discussion from David, Karen and Joyce best exemplifies how they had a desire to give back to their community through their activities in the church. For example, Karen demonstrates how being a part of a church family allowed her to be a positive role model for children in her church. In turn, she was able to use her math skills to serve the community. She believes that it was her responsibility as a person who has been blessed with gifts and advantages.

> 'Cause when I go back home to church, I try to help out my friends who've graduated from college, to set up other tutoring programs at our church. To let kids know, don't be scared of math you can do it. And if things are hard, I'll help you, you know. You can have my email address; you can have this, as long as you work hard and try. A lot of kids looked up to me at

church because they see me as all right because I did sports. I wasn't just a nerd or whatever. I was popular when I was in school.

Joyce also expressed how the church supported her during youth. Joyce recalls:

...I've had huge support from my church, like from my youth group. ...I was very active in my church's youth groups, so I built friends through it. And I just think that any opportunity that allows you to make friends with people, like it helps your self-esteem, you know, you feel more confident, um, you just feel more comfortable with yourself. So, in that sense, it probably helped my development.

David expressed similar sentiments:

...We always went to church on Sunday. You know, I couldn't- she [mother] did not allow me to stray away too far. You know, whatever I did on Saturday night, I had to go to church on Sunday. So even if I went out and hung out until 5 in the morning, I had to wake up and go to church. ...And church kind of gave me that foundation, where I knew what was right or wrong. Even when I was out in high school doing wrong, in the back of my head, I knew it was wrong. You know, even- you know, I was hanging out, lying to my mom, like Oh yeah, I'm at this place, and I'm at some other place. I knew it was wrong. And I had a conscience...It wasn't one of those things where I was a cold-blooded type person.

Being a part of a church community gave several of these participants a spiritual foundation and community structure that enhanced their overall self-esteem, provided them with a focus that kept them out of trouble, as in David's case, and allowed them to connect with the larger African-American community and their peers. This foundation was instrumental in giving them a sense of accountability to something outside of themselves. In many cases they shared that they began to rely more heavily on their spirituality to help them overcome various challenges they faced in and outside of the mathematics classroom. They credit their parents for instilling the spiritual base.

Discussion

We argue that African American parents, in the current atmosphere of accountability, have no choice but to be proactive in their children's education in very distinct ways. The deeply rooted historical, social-political, and economic inequities are responsible for the current crisis in African American education and calls for parenting styles that are proactive and self-reliant.

Although historically, pre-Brown, many African-American parents could rely on the schools, to intellectually, socially and emotionally nurture the power and potential of Black youth, today, the sole reliance on the schools to foster the aforementioned environment in the current context is a recipe for disaster (i.e., academic tracking, high dropout rate, mortality). African American parents must be made aware of the specific and practical parenting strategies that parents use to help their children navigate US public schools, especially in the area of mathematics.

We argue that both collective cultural capital and individual self-help efforts are needed to make change not only for the individual, but also for the community as a whole. In order to deal with the current challenges facing African American children, particularly in education, parents and communities must utilize collective and individual self-help efforts in order to insure positive educational outcomes for our children.

Secondly, we found that African American parents used their social networks, a form of social capital, and knowledge of "the system" to navigate their children through the educational pipeline (Coleman 1988; Yosso, 2005). In essence these parents understood that there was a school "game" to be played, and that they were going to make sure that their children would be "players" at an early age. Since many of the participants' mothers were educators or had experiences in educational settings, they understood and had access to the necessary social and human resources they needed to positively impact their children's educational trajectories. Specifically, parents of these high achievers had access to the various educational networks, built relationships with key educators, and accessed personal resources with the clear intention of building the human capital of their child. For example, all of the students in the study attended public schools. Although these students attended public schools, parents made sure that their children had access to "the best" programs available in these school by guiding their children to the appropriate schools and/or programs that they believed would best prepare their children academically. Many of these parents understood that they needed to personally advocate for their children to ensure that they would receive quality educational experiences. As demonstrated in the case of Shanice, when she failed to test in the gifted and talented program, her mom insisted that she be placed in the program because she believed that her daughter could handle a more rigorous academic curriculum. As this case and many of the other cases demonstrate, parents were unwilling to allow "the system" to make decisions in the best interest of their child. They drew upon their own social and cultural capital to facilitate their children's upward mobility in the educational system (Lamont & Lareau, 1988) and these efforts, although different in context, mirror the kinds of self-help efforts that African- American parents used historically to insure the academic success of their children.

Finally, we found that both parents played integral roles in the development of their children's academic skills. Mothers engaged their children in various pre-school learning experiences that prepared them for formal learning experiences. They provided the foundation for their placement in elite academic programs that, in turn, provided these high achievers with the mathematical knowledge needed for advanced study in college. In addition, the mothers provided these students with the social norms that they needed to adapt in order for them to succeed in the educational system and benefit from social networks. Fathers provided their children with these early learning experiences, particularly cultivating and early interest in mathematics.

To be clear, both fathers and mothers, worked collaboratively to provide the necessary foundational skills, beliefs and values to ensure that their children were successful in school. Moreover, parents relied on a spiritual base to instill in their children a value system and community that could be a support even when the parents were not present. We argue that even if children are not from two-parent households, as a community we must understand that key people play an integral role in the academic achievement of students. Thus, mentors that can provide these experiences must be garnered in order to provide students with the necessary resources they need to be successful.

Conclusion

Unlike the common rhetoric that purports that African-American parents are non-participatory in their children's education due to intimidation by school personnel (Anderson 1994), poor understanding of how to navigate the educational system (Rao 2000) or Black parents reporting negative school experiences (McCaleb 1994; Menacker, Hurwitz & Weldon 1988), the findings of this study illuminate not only that African-American parents have historically and currently participate, but the kind of participation necessary in order for their children to be successful in schools. We found that parents and significant others fostered nurturing pre-school learning environments that cultivated the kinds of values that instilled self reliance, perseverance and community consciousness which propelled these students to succeed, especially in mathematics. These values benefited the participants as mathematics students by helping them to cultivate their own human capital (Bourdieu, 1996) as mathematics learners.

Future research should include more case study research on African-American parents and their socialization patterns with regard to participation in schools. As mentioned earlier, many working class parents place the responsibility of education solely on the school. Understanding the reasons may lead to alternate constructions of parental involvement in schools by African Americans. Additionally, an examination of parents of high achievers may shed light on the strategies they use to maximize achievement in this current era of No Child Left Behind. In addition, more historical research on African-American parents' participation in schools is instructive in that it speaks against the deficit models of participation and underscores the ways in which Black parents wield their cultural capital. Cultural capital, in this case, must be understood by culturally appropriate standards rather than by the standards of the dominant culture in order to understand the essence of African American participation in the educational experiences of their children. Finally, comparative studies with parents of underachieving students alongside successful parents could reveal more insight into the way cultural capital is exercised in the African American community.

References

Anderson, J. (1988). *The Education of Blacks in the South, 1860-1935*. Chapel Hill: North Carolina Press.

Anderson, M. G. (1994). Perceptions about behavioral disorders in African American cultures and communities. In R.L. Peterson & S. I. Jordan (Eds.) *Multicultural issues in the education of students with behavioral disorders* (pp 93-104). Cambridge, MA: Brookline.

Bailey, R (1990). Mathematics for the millions, science for the people: Comments on black students and the mathematics, science and technology pipeline. *Journal of Negro Education,* **59**(3), 239- 245.

Bentz, N. (1997). What stops women and minorities from choosing and completing majors in science and engineering? In D. Johnson, D., Ed., *Minorities and Girls in School: Effects on Achievement and Performance* (pp. 105-140) Thousand Oaks: Sage.

Butchart, R. (1980). *Northern Schools, southern blacks, and reconstruction: freedmen's education, 1862-1875*. Westport: Greenwood Press.

Bourdieu, P. (1986). The forms of capital. In Richardson, J. (Ed.) *Handbook of Theory and Research for Sociology of Education*. New York: Greenwood Press.

Bourdieu, P & Wacquant. L. (1992). *An invitation to reflexive sociology*. Chicago: University of Chicago Press.

Brown, K. (2000). African-American immersion school: Paradoxes of race and public education. In Delgado, R. & Stefancic, J. (Eds.), *Critical Race Theory: The Cutting Edge* (pp. 415-238). Philadelphia: Temple University Press.

Coleman, J. S. (1988). Social capital in the creation of human capital. *American Journal of Sociology*, **94**, 95-120.

Chavkin, N.F. (Ed.) (1993). Families and schools in a pluralistic society. Albany, NY: State University of New York Press.

Clewell, B., Anderson, B. & Thorpe, M. (1992). Breaking the barriers: Helping female and minority students succeed in mathematics and science. San Francisco, CA: Jossey- Bass.

Cooper, D. (2000). Changing the faces of mathematics Ph.D's: What we are learning at the University of Maryland. In Strutchens, M. Tate, W., and Johnson, M. (Eds.).*Changing the faces of mathematics, volume 3: Perspectives on African Americans*. Reston: National Council of Teachers of Mathematics.

Cooper, R., Slavin. R., & Madden, N. (1998) Socio-cultural and within school factors that affect the quality of implementation of school-wide programs (Crespar Rep. #28). Baltimore: John's Hopkins University.

Coleman, J. (1992). Some points on choice in education. *Sociology of Education*, **65**(4), 260-262.

Cosby, B & Poussaint, A. (2007). Come on, people: On the path from victims to victors. Nashville, TN: Thomas Nelson, Inc.

Laurence Steinberg, Susie D. Lamborn, Nancy Darling, Nina S. Mounts and Sanford M. Dornbusch (1994). Over-Time changes in adjustment and competence among adolescents from authoritative, authoritarian, indulgent, and neglectful families *Child Development*, **65**, (3) 754-770.

Darling-Hammond, L. (1995).Inequality and access to knowledge (pp. 465-483) Banks, James A. and Cherry A. McGee Banks (Eds.). *Handbook of research on multicultural education*. Macmillan Publishing

Davison, M. L., Seo, Y. S., Davenport Jr., E. C., Butterbaugh, D., & Davison, L. J. (2004). When do children fall behind? what can be done?. *Phi Delta Kappan,* **85**(10), 752. Retrieved November 23, 2009, from Questia database: http://www.questia.com/ PM.qst?a =o&d=5006720299

Dinka, S. L. & Singh, K. (2002). Applications of social capital in educational literature: A critical synthesis. *Review of Educational Research,* **72**(1), 31- 60.

Dornbusch, S. M. Ritter, P. L, Leiderman, P. Roberts D. F. Fraleigh M.J. (1987) The relation of parenting stule to adolescent school performance. *Child Development*, (58) 5 1244-1257.

Epstein, J. &Dauber, S. (1991). School programs and teacher practices of parent involvement in inner-city elementary and middle schools. *The Elementary School Journal*, **91** 289-305.

Franklin, V.P (2004). Introduction. In Franklin V.P. & Savage C. (Eds). *Cultural Capital and Black Education: African American Communities and the Funding of Black Schooling*. Greenwich: Information Age Publishing.

Futrell, M. (2004).The teachers: The impact of the Brown Decision on African American educators in (Eds.) The unfinished agenda of Brown V. Board of Education (pp 79 – 96). Hoboken, NJ: John Wiley & Sons, Inc.

Goodwin, L. (2002). Resilient spirits: Disadvantaged students making it at an elite university. New York: Routledge Falmer

Haberman, M. (1991) The pedagogy of poverty versus good teaching, *Phi Delta Kappan,* **73** (4), 290-29.

Irvine, J. (2001). The critical elements of culturally responsive pedagogy: A synthesis of research in culturally responsive teaching. New York: McGraw.

Kenschaft P. (1993). Black women in mathematics. In Hine, D., Brown, E. & Terborg-Penn, R. (Eds.). *Black women in America: A historical encyclopedia.* New York: Carlson Publishing.

Kozol, J. (1995). *Amazing grace: The lives of children and the conscience of a nation.* New York: Crown.

Ladson-Billings, G. (1995b). But that's just good teaching!:The case for culturally relevant pedagogy. *Theory into Practice*, **43** (3), 159-165.

Ladson-Billings, G.J. (2006). From the achievement gap to the education debt: Understanding achievement in u.s. schools. Presidential address at the American Educational Research Association Annual Meeting, San Francisco, CA.

Lamont, M., & Lareau, J. (1988, Fall). Cultural capital: Allusions, gaps and glissandos in recent theoretical developments. *Sociological Theory*, **6**, 153-168.

Lareau, A. (2000). *Home Advantage: Social class and parental intervention in elementary education.* Rowman & Littlefield Publishers: Lanham.

Lin, N. (2001). *Social capital: A theory of social structure and action.* Cambridge, UK: Cambridge University Press.

Livingston, A., and Wirt, J. (2004). *The condition of education 2004 in brief (NCES 2004–076).* U.S. Department of Education, National Center for Education Statistics. Washington, DC: U.S. Government Printing Office.

Mandara, 2006. The impact of family functioning on African American Males' Academic Achievement: A review and clarification of the empirical literature. *The Teachers College Record.* **109** (2) 206-223.

McKay, M, Atkins, M., Hawkins, T. Brown, C. & Lynn, C. (2003). Inner-City African American parental involvement in children's schooling: Racial socialization and social support from the parent community. *American Journal of Community Psychology*, **32**, (1/2) 107-114.

McCaleb, S. P. (1994). Building a community of learners: A collaboration among teachers, students, families and community. Hillsdale, NJ: Lawrence Erlbaum Associates, Inc.

Menacker, J., Hurwitz, E., & Weldon, W. (1988). Parent-teacher cooperation in schools serving the urban poor. The Clearing House, **62**, 108-112.

Moody, V. (2004). Sociocultural orientations and the mathematics success of African American Students. *The Journal of Educational Research,* **97**(3), 135 – 142.

National Center for Education Statistics. (2007). Digest of Education Statistics, 2006 (NCES 2007-017), Chapter 2. National Center for Education Statistics. (2007). Digest of Education Statistics, 2006 (NCES 2007-017), Table 131.

National Center for Educational Statistics (2007). Status and trends in education of racial and ethnic minorities. Retreived on January 1, 2007 from http://nces.ed.gov/pubs2007/2007039.pdf.

National Center for Education Statistics. (2002). Coming *of age in the 1990s: The eighth-grade class of 1988 twelve years later.* Washington, DC: Author.

Oakes, J. (1985). *Keeping Track: How schools structure inequality.* New Haven, CT: Yale University Press.

Ogbu, J. (1991). Immigrant and involuntary minorities in comparative perspective. In M. Gibson & J. Ogbu (Eds.). *Minority status and schooling*, 3-33. New York, New York: Garland.

Purna, L. & Titus, M. (2005). The relationship between parental involvement as social capital and college enrollment: An examination of racial/ethnic differences. *The Journal of Higher Education,* **76**(5), 485 – 518. Press.

Rao, S.S. (2000). Perspectives of an African American mother on parent-professional relationships in special education. *Mental Retardation*, **38**(6), 475-488.

Savage, C. J. (2004). Our school in our community in Franklin, V.P. & Savage, C. (Eds.). *Cultural Capital and Black Education.* Greenwich, CN: Information Age Publishing.

Siddle-Walker, V. (1993). Caswell training school, 1933-1969: relationships between community and school. Harvard Educational Review, **63**(2), 161-182.

Siddle-Walker, V. (1996). *Their highest potential: An African American school community in the segregated south.* Chapel Hill: University of North Carolina

Siddle-Walker, V. (2001) African American teaching in the south 1940-1950. *American Educational Research Journal*, **39**(4), 751-779.

Spera, 2005. A review of the a review of the relationship among parenting practices, parenting styles, and adolescent school achievement. *Educational Psychology Review* **17**(2) 125-146

Stone, S. & McKay, M. (2003). Predictors of urban parent involvement. *School Social Work Journal*, **15**, 12-28.

Blum, E. (2007) *Reforging the white republic: Race, religion and American Nationalism.* Baton Rouge: LSU Press

Walker, E. N. (2006). Urban high school students' academic communities and their effects on mathematics success. *American Educational Research Journal*, **43**(1), 43-73.

Yan, W. (1999). Successful African American students: The role of parental involvement. *Journal of Negro Education*, **68**(10), 5 – 22.

Yosso, T. (2005). Whose culture has capital? A critical race theory discussion of community cultural wealth. Race, Ethnicity and Education **8**(1), pp. 69-91.

In: Progress in Education, Volume 21
Editor: Robert V. Nata, pp. 77-104

ISBN: 978-1-61728-115-0
© 2011 Nova Science Publishers, Inc.

Chapter 4

GRADE RETENTION AND POSTSECONDARY EDUCATION

Suh-Ruu Ou[*]

Institute of Child Development, University of Minnesota-Twin Cities

Abstract

Using data from the National Education Longitudinal Study of 1988 (NELS: 88/2000), this study investigated whether grade retention is associated with postsecondary education attendance and bachelor degree completion. Three questions are addressed in the present study: 1) Is grade retention associated with postsecondary education attendance and BA degree completion? 2) Is timing of retention associated with postsecondary education attendance and BA degree completion differently? and 3) Do students who were retained but persisted to graduate from high school differ in postsecondary education attendance and BA degree completion from continuously promoted students?

Findings indicated that the experience of grade retention was significantly associated with lower rates of postsecondary education attendance and BA degree completion when sociodemographic factors, academic achievement, and school factors in eighth grade were taken into account. Both early and late retention were significantly associated with lower rates of postsecondary education attendance and BA degree completion. However, late retention (between fourth and eighth grades) was more strongly linked to lower rates of postsecondary education and BA degree completion than early retention (between first and third grades). Among participants who have a high school diploma, retained participants have a lower rate of BA degree completion than those who were never retained. However, there is no significant difference in postsecondary education attendance between retained and never retained participants.

As President Obama has reiterated several times, higher education is critical to the national economic and social prosperity. Higher education has been shown to be beneficial both to individuals and the broader society. As institutions are forced to cope with tight budgets under the circumstance of economic crises all over the country, it has become more

---

[*] E-mail address: sou@umn.edu. Corresponding author: Suh-Ruu Ou, 204 Child Development, Institute of Child, Development, 51 East River Road, Minneapolis, MN 55455.

challenging than before to increase students' success in postsecondary education. The topic of college student retention has gained considerable attention over the past several decades, and numerous studies have been conducted. The majority of the studies have focused on developing and testing theories of student retention in the hope of explaining why some students leave and others persist. However, the rates of postsecondary education attendance have been stagnant in the U.S. over the past years. It might be important to explore other factors in addition to those that occur in college or are directly related to college persistence. Early experiences prior to college that are associated with college attendance and degree completion warrant examination. The present study examined one such early experience, grade retention.

As an approach to improve academic proficiency, grade retention has been implemented for decades. Although the effectiveness of grade retention on either academic or social-behavioral difficulties has not been consistently reported, somehow this practice is treated as effective and increasingly implemented over the years. In particular, the number of students who were retained has increased since the policy of "high-stakes testing" and "No child left behind (NCLB)" (Heubert & Hauser, 1999). Many studies have reported the positive relation between grade retention and school dropout. Given the well-known connection between school dropout and postsecondary education attendance, it is worth further exploring whether grade retention is associated with postsecondary education and degree completion. If grade retention is associated with lower rates of postsecondary education attendance and bachelor (BA) degree completion, then grade retention would be one risk factor that can be used to identify students who are at high-risk of not attending postsecondary education or completing a BA degree. By identifying at-risk students early on, intervention could be started as early as elementary school. Such intervention would provide different effects from the programs implemented in college to promote success. For example, the target population of the intervention would be broader unlike college programs, which can only reach students who are already enrolled in postsecondary institutions.

Grade Retention, Dropout, and Postsecondary Education

The intended purpose of grade retention is to promote better academic performance and school adjustment. Therefore, many studies have been conducted to examine the relations between grade retention and academic performance (e.g., Alexander, Entwisle, & Dauber, 2003; Bonvin, Bless, & Schuepbach, 2008; Lorence, Dworkin, Toenjes, & Hill, 2002). Most studies have shown that grade retention fails to achieve its intended effects. Findings indicate either that retained students did not perform better academically than low-achieving promoted peers (Beebe-Frankenberger, Bocian, MacMillan & Gresham, 2004; Hong & Raudenbush, 2005; Jimerson, Carlson, Rotert, Egeland & Sroufe, 1997; Silberglitt, Appleton, Burns & Jimerson, 2006) or that there were negative associations between grade retention and academic achievement (Hong & Yu, 2007; Reynolds, 1992). In addition, several meta-analyses show similar conclusions (Holmes, 1989; Holmes & Matthews, 1984; Jackson, 1975; Jimerson, 2001). Some findings show that, in comparison to the promoted students, retained students improved academic achievement one and two years after initial retention (Greene & Winters, 2004, 2006, 2007). However, recent findings show that the gains from retention did not last (Jacob & Lefgren, 2004; Roderick & Nagaoka, 2005) and that retention decreased the growth rate of mathematical skills and had no significant effect on reading skills (Wu, West & Hughes, 2008).

While many findings show that there is no association between grade retention and academic performance, findings on the relations between grade retention and school dropout are more consistent. The positive associations between grade retention and high school dropout have been reported in many studies (Alexander, Entwisle, Dauber, & Kabbani, 2004; Eide & Showalter, 2001; Jimerson, 1999; Guèvremont, Roos, Brownell, 2007; Jimerson, Anderson, & Whipple, 2002; Jimerson, Ferguson, Whipple, Anderson, & Dalton, 2002; Jimerson & Kaufman, 2003; McCoy & Reynolds, 1999; Rumberger, 1995; Temple, Reynolds & Ou, 2004). Grade retention is also identified as an important predictor of dropout (Alexander, Entwisle & Horsey, 1999; Alexander, Entwisle & Kabbani, 2001; Ensminger & Slusarick, 1992; Janosz, LeBlanc, Boulerice & Tremblay, 1997; Rumberger, 1987, 1995).

Although there are many studies on grade retention, the relation between grade retention and postsecondary education were only examined in two studies (Fine & Davis, 2003; Ou & Reynolds, 2010). Both studies found that grade retention was associated with lower rates of postsecondary education attendance. The relation between grade retention and degree completion has never been examined. Therefore, two outcomes of postsecondary education, attendance and BA degree completion, were examined in the present study.

Furthermore, because of the well established relation between grade retention and school dropout, it is worth exploring whether students who were retained but persisted to graduate from high school have similar rates of postsecondary education attendance and BA degree completion to those students who were promoted and graduated from high school. Some researchers might argue that the positive relation between grade retention and school dropout is the only reason driving the negative relation between grade retention and postsecondary education attendance. A separate analysis focusing on only students who graduated from high school will provide a rough idea on this issue.

Timing of Grade Retention

The effects of the timing of grade retention have been examined in a few studies. Findings related to academic achievement are mixed. One study found that the effects of early grade retention (grades 1–3) were similar to those of later grade retention (grades 4–7) (McCoy & Reynolds, 1999). One study found that retention increased achievement for third-grade students but had little effect on math achievement for sixth-grade students (Jacob & Lefgren, 2004). Another study showed that both early and late retention were associated with higher rates of school dropout, but the association between late retention and school dropout was larger than the relation between early retention and school dropout (Temple et al., 2004). Finally, Jacob & Lefgren (2009) found that grade retention led to a modest increase in the probability of dropping out for older students (eighth grade), but had no significant effect on younger students (6th grade). To sum up, late retention seems to have a larger association with negative academic outcomes than early retention.

The Present Study

Using data from the National Education Longitudinal Study of 1988 (NELS: 88/2000), three questions are addressed in the present study: 1) Is grade retention associated with postsecondary education attendance and BA degree completion? 2) Is timing of retention associated with postsecondary education attendance and BA degree completion differently? and 3) Do students who were retained but persisted to graduate from high school differ from continuously promoted students in postsecondary education attendance and BA degree completion?

The present study is unique in several respects. First, the study used data from a longitudinal data set (NELS:88/2000) including participants from all over the country. The study sample included over 10,000 participants, unlike the small sample sizes of previous studies of grade retention. Although recent studies evaluating the effects of "end social promotion" or "high-stakes testing" have larger sample sizes, many previous findings are based on sample sizes less than 800, some even less than 150. Second, although there are many studies which examine grade retention and college persistence separately, only two studies examined the relation between grade retention and postsecondary education attendance. Most studies on college persistence do not have data on grade retention, and few studies on grade retention have data for more than six years after the initial retention, which makes it difficult to examine the relation between grade retention and postsecondary education. NELS:88/2000 provides data up to age 26/27, and information on both grade retention and degree completion is available. Third, the present study examined the timing of retention, which is seldom examined as most studies of grade retention did not have sample sizes large enough or did not have longitudinal data that would allow such investigations.

Finally, the present study examined the relation between grade retention and BA degree completion, which has never been examined before. The nearly exclusive focus has been on the relations between grade retention and academic achievement, and between grade retention and school dropout. The relation between grade retention and other adult outcomes are under-investigated. Many studies have already showed that retention did not help students improve their academic performance. Moreover, retained students have much higher school dropout rates than other students. To expand our understanding of retention, it is essential to examine outcomes beyond academic achievement and dropout.

Method

Data and Study Sample

The study sample is drawn from the National Education Longitudinal Study of 1988 (NELS: 88/2000). The NELS:88 is a longitudinally study conducted by the U.S. Department of Education, which began in 1988 (base-year) with a nationally representative sample of eighth-graders. Follow-up data have been collected in 1990, 1992, 1994, and 2000 (the fourth follow-up study). Data have been collected from the students (participants), the students' parents, teachers, and schools (Curtin, Ingels, Wu & Heuer, 2002). The postsecondary education data used in the present study was collected in 2000, the year when most eighth-grade cohort members turned 26. The study sample included those who have information on experience of retention and postsecondary education (N=11,441). The weight variables were not used in the present study because the purpose of the present study was to examine grade retention as one of the school experiences and participants need to have information on both retention and postsecondary education to be included in the present study. The author does not intend to generalize the findings to national population.

Measures

Table 1 defines the variables in the present study. Postsecondary education by age 26/27 was measured through two dichotomous variables: any postsecondary education attendance and BA degree completion. In addition to outcome measures, explanatory variables were briefly described in the following categories: experience of grade retention, sociodemographic factors, characteristics of eighth grade school, and academic achievement at eighth grade and problem behavior by high school.

Grade retention was defined as any incidence of grade retention from first grade through eighth grade. Data were derived from a retrospective question "Has respondent ever been held back a grade in school?" in the second follow-up (1992), and then grades retained were identified by respondents: To better distinguish the retention groups, kindergarten retention was not examined in the present study. Timing of retention was measured by two dichotomous variables: early retention and late retention. Early retention indicates whether one had been retained between first and third grade. Late retention indicates whether one had been retained between fourth and eighth grade. One hundred and eight students were retained both early and late. When both early and late retention were examined in the regression model, the reference group was the promotion group. Figure 1 presents the numbers of students who were retained by grade in the study sample. Students retained multiple times were included.

Table 1. Definition of variables

Variables	Definition
Postsecondary education by age 26/27	
Postsecondary education attendance	Ever attended any postsecondary education by 2000. 1 = yes, 0 = no.
BA degree completion	Completed BA degree by 2000. 1 = yes, 0 = no.
Grade retention between 1st and 8th grade	
Retention between 1st and 8th grade	1 = yes, 0 = no
Retained more than once between 1st and 8th grade	1 = yes, 0 = no
Early retention (between 1st and 3rd grade)	1 = yes, 0 = no
Late retention (between 4th and 8th grade)	1 = yes, 0 = no
Both early and late retention	1 = yes, 0 = no

Table 1. Continued

Variables	Definition
Sociodemographic factors:	Measured at base-year (8th grade)
Female	Sex (1 = female, 0 = male)
Race/ethnicity	Race/ethnicity
White	1 = White, 0 = others
Black	1 = Black, 0 = others
Hispanic	1 = Hispanic, 0 = others
Asian/pacific islander	1 = Asian/pacific islander, 0 = others
American Indian/AK native	1 = American Indian/ Alaska Native, 0 = others
Parent highest education level at 8th grade	1 = didn't finish HS, 2= HS grad or GED, 3=Some college, 4= College graduate, 5= MA/equivalent, 6= Ph.D., MD., other.
Family structure at 8th grade	
Two-parent family	1=two-parent family, 0 = other
Single-parent family	1 = single-parent family, 0 = other
Other than two-parent or single-parent family	1=Other than two-parent or single-parent family, 0=other
Number of siblings in home at 8th grade	Range from 0 to 6
Mother's employment status at 8th grade	
Mother worked full-time	1 = yes, 0 = no.
Mother worked part-time	1 = yes, 0 = no.
Mother not worked	1 = yes, 0 = no.
Family SES quartile	Composite family socio-economic status was constructed using both parents educational level, occupation, and family income. 1 = quartile 1 low, 2 = quartile 2, 3 = quartile 3, 4 = quartile 4 high.
Age at August 1990	Min. 14.67, Max. 18.58, Mean=16.50
English is native language	1=yes, 0=no.
Ever reported handicap programs recipient	1=yes, 0=no.
Characteristics of 8th grade school	
Percent free lunch	Percentage of students had free or reduced price lunch at the school. 0 = none, 1 = 1-5%, 2 = 6-10%, 3 = 11-20%, 4 = 21-30%, 5 = 31-50%, 6 = 51-75%, 7 = 76-100%
Type of school	
Public school	1=yes, 0=no.
Private religious school	1=yes, 0=no.
Private non-religious school	1=yes, 0=no.
Total school enrollment	01 = 1-199 students, 02 = 200-399, 03 = 400-599, 04 = 600-799, 05 = 800-999, 06 = 1000-1199, 07 = 1200+

Table 1. Continued

Variables	Definition
Geographic region of school	
West	Mountain and Pacific states, 1 = yes, 0 = no
South	South Atlantic, East South Central, and West South Central states, 1 = yes, 0 = no
North central	East North Central and West North Central states, 1 = yes, 0 = no
Northeast	New England and Middle Atlantic states, 1 = yes, 0 = no
Urbanicity of school	
Urban	Central city, 1=yes, 0=no.
Suburban	Area surrounding a central city within a county constituting the MSA (Metropolitan Statistical Area), 1=yes, 0=no.
Rural	Outside MSA, 1=yes, 0=no.
Academic achievement at 8th grade	
Reading standardized scores	The test included 21 items, consists of five short passages followed by comprehension and interpretation questions (α = .84).
Math standardized scores	The test included 40 items, consists of quantitative comparisons and other questions assessing mathematical knowledge (α = .90).
Number of reported problem behaviors by 1992	Number of reported problem behaviors (been considered to have a behavior problem at school, been suspended from school, or been expelled from school) by parents. Ranges: 0-3.

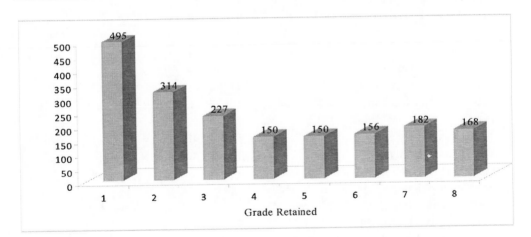

Figure 1. Numbers of students retained by grade.

All sociodemographic factors were measured at the base-year (eighth grade). Dichotomous variables were used for many sociodemographic factors because most of the characteristics were categorical, such as gender, race/ethnicity, family structure, and mother's employment status. Some variables include more than two categories, so they were coded into three or four dichotomous variables depending on number of categories.

Except for age, status of whether English is native language, family SES, and total school enrollment, missing values were imputed through multiple imputation procedures using the EM algorithm. Because missing values were imputed for various variables, a missing index was created and included in all analyses. If values were missing for five or more variables in a participants' record, that participant was coded 1. Otherwise, participants were coded as 0. Table 2 provides the valid sample sizes and means for key variables.

Table 3 presents the characteristics of the study sample by retention groups. Characteristics include sociodemographic factors (such as gender, race/ethnicity, parents' educational level, and family structure), characteristics of eighth grade school, eighth grade school achievement and problem behaviors at high school. There are significant differences between the retention and promotion groups in most characteristics except for number of siblings, mother worked full-time, urbanicity of school, and geographic region of school at northeast. For example, the retention group has lower rates of female, two-parent family, mother worked part-time, attended private school than the promotion group. The retention group has lower levels of parent education and family SES, a higher rate of attended handicap programs, and attended schools that have higher percentage of students received free or reduced-price lunch and schools that have more students enrolled than the promotion group. Those characteristics were used as covariates to ensure that the differences between the groups were not due to sociodemographic characteristics.

Table 2. Descriptive Statistics for Study Variables

Measures	N	Min.	Max.	Mean	SD
Sociodemographic factors					
Female	11446	0	1	.53	.50
Race/ethnicity					
White	11446	0	1	.70	.46
Black	11446	0	1	.09	.29
Hispanic	11446	0	1	.13	.34
Asian/pacific islander	11446	0	1	.07	.25
American Indian/AK native	11446	0	1	.01	.11
Parent highest education level at 8th grade	10803	1	6	3.10	1.26
Family structure at 8th grade					
Two-parent family	10745	0	1	.71	.46
Single-parent family	10745	0	1	.16	.37
Other than two-parent or single-parent family	10745	0	1	.14	.34
Number of siblings in home at 8th grade	9485	0	6	1.61	1.24
Mother's employment status at 8th grade					
Mother worked full-time	9868	0	1	.51	.50
Mother worked part-time	9868	0	1	.21	.41
Mother not worked	9868	0	1	.28	.45
Family SES (quintile)	10866	1	4	2.56	1.13
Age at August 1990	11197	14.67	18.58	16.50	.56
English is native language	11323	0	1	.88	.33
Ever reported handicap programs recipient	11446	0	1	.20	.40
If missing 5 or more measures	11446	0	1	.06	.23

Table 2. Continued

Measures	N	Min.	Max.	Mean	SD
Characteristics of 8th grade school					
Percent free lunch at 8th grade	10687	0	7	3.01	2.04
Type of school					
Public school	11266	0	1	.83	.38
Private religious school	11266	0	1	.13	.34
Private non-religious school	11266	0	1	.04	.21
Total school enrollment	10866	1	7	3.70	1.56
Geographic region of school					
West	10848	0	1	.20	.40
South	10848	0	1	.33	.47
North central	10848	0	1	.28	.45
Northeast	10848	0	1	.20	.40
Urbanicity of school					
Urban	10866	0	1	.25	.43
Suburban	10866	0	1	.44	.50
Rural	10866	0	1	.32	.47
Academic achievement at 8th grade					
Reading standardized scores	10494	31.92	70.55	51.67	10.05
Math standardized scores	10494	34.09	77.20	51.85	10.24
Number of reported problem behaviors by 1992	9987	0	3	.24	.61
Grade retention					
Retention between first and 8th grades	11446	0	1	.143	.350
Early retention (between first and third grades)	11446	0	1	.088	.284
Late retained (between 4th and 8th grades)	11446	0	1	.064	.245
Both early and late retention	11446	0	1	.010	.097
Retained more than once between 1st and 8th grades	11446	0	1	.017	.128
Postsecondary education by age 26/27					
Any postsecondary attendance	11441	0	1	.78	.41
BA degree completion	11441	0	1	.35	.48

Table 3. Descriptive Statistics of Study Sample

Measures	Mean	Ever Retained	Promotion	p-value
Sociodemographic factors				
Female	.53	.42	.55	.000
Race/ethnicity				
White	.70	.60	.71	.000
Black	.09	.16	.08	.000
Hispanic	.13	.19	.12	.000
Asian/pacific islander	.07	.04	.07	.000
American Indian/AK native	.01	.02	.01	.003
Parent highest education level at 8th grade	3.10	2.45	3.20	.000
Family structure at 8th grade				
Two-parent family	.71	.57	.73	.000

Table 3. Continued

Measures	Mean	Ever Retained	Promotion	p-value
Single-parent family	.16	.23	.15	.000
Other than two-parent or single-parent family	.14	.19	.13	.000
Number of siblings in home at 8th grade	1.61	1.58	1.61	.443
Mother's employment status at 8th grade				
Mother worked full-time	.51	.49	.51	.210
Mother worked part-time	.21	.17	.21	.000
Mother not worked	.28	.34	.27	.000
Family SES (quintile)	2.56	1.90	2.66	.000
Age at August 1990	16.50	17.36	16.36	.000
English is native language	.88	.84	.89	.000
Ever reported handicap programs recipient	.20	.34	.17	.000
Characteristics of 8th grade school				
Percent free lunch at 8th grade	3.01	3.62	2.91	.000
Type of school				
Public school	.83	.92	.81	.000
Private religious school	.13	.06	.14	.000
Private non-religious school	.04	.03	.05	.000
Total school enrollment	3.70	3.84	3.68	.000
Geographic region of school				
West	.20	.15	.20	.000
South	.33	.45	.31	.000
North central	.28	.23	.29	.000
Northeast	.20	.18	.20	.114
Urbanicity of school				
Urban	.25	.26	.25	.420
Suburban	.44	.41	.44	.059
Rural	.32	.33	.31	.196
Academic achievement at 8th grade				
Reading standardized scores	51.67	44.13	52.83	.000
Math standardized scores	51.85	43.93	53.08	.000
Number of reported problem behaviors by 1992	.24	.52	.20	.000

Data Analysis

Probit regression analysis was conducted to examine the differences in outcomes between the retention and promotion groups after adjusting for covariates. STATA 11 was used to conduct the analyses (StataCorp, 2009). Marginal effects of retention were reported. A marginal effect denotes the percentage change in the outcome associated with being retained (value of 1 versus 0, being promoted). For example, if the marginal effect of ever retained from first grade to eighth grade on college attendance was -19.4%, which indicates that students who were retained had a rate of college attendance that was19.4 percentage points lower than students who were continuously promoted.

Logistic regressions analyses were conducted as alternative analyses. Explanatory variables were entered in two steps. The first step included sociodemographic factors and grade retention variables. The second step included school characteristics, academic achievement and problem behaviors at high school. SPSS 17.0 was used to conduct the analyses. The coefficients for explanatory variables in logistic regression analysis were presented in odds ratios. An odds ratio is the odds of being in a group (outcome) for a particular value of the predictor, divided by the odds for the predictor value that is one unit lower. In other words, an odds ratio indicates the amount the odds of being in a group are multiplied when the predictor (independent variable) is incremented by a value of one unit (Cohen, Cohen, West & Aiken, 2003). Odds ratios greater than 1 indicate positive regression coefficients, and reflect the increase in odds of being in the group (outcome) associated with each unit increase in the predictor (independent variable). Odds ratios less than 1 indicate negative regression coefficients, and reflect the decrease in odds of being in the group (outcome) associated with each unit increase in the predictor (independent variable). For example, if the odds ratio on college attendance for whether students expecting to go to college or not (dichotomous variable) is 2.2, it indicates if students expected to go to college then they were 2.2 times more likely to attend college than those who did not expect to go to college.

Results

By age 26/27, 78% of the study sample reported postsecondary attendance, and 35% of the study sample reported BA degree completion. Table 4 presents the overall and unadjusted rates of outcomes by groups. The retention group had lower rates of participation in postsecondary education and BA degree completion than the promotion group ($p < .01$). Although members of the retention group had higher rates of postsecondary education attendance and BA degree completion if they had high school diplomas, they still had lower rates of participation in postsecondary education and BA degree completion than the promotion group ($p < .01$). See bottom part of Table 4.

Table 4. Unadjusted Rates of Outcomes by Groups

Outcomes	N	Study sample	Retention (grades 1-8)	Promotion	p-value
Study sample			n=1,633	n=9,808	
Any postsecondary education attendance, %	11441	78.4	51.6	82.9	.000
BA degree completion, %	11441	34.5	7.3	39.0	.000
High school diploma only			N=1,030	n=9,054	
Any postsecondary education attendance, %	10084	84.9	67.9	86.8	.000
BA degree completion, %	10084	39.0	11.4	42.2	.000

Table 5 presents the unadjusted rates of outcomes by early and late retention groups. Among the groups, the group of students who were retained both early and late had the lowest rates of postsecondary education attendance, followed by late retention group and the early retention group ($p < .01$, promotion group as the reference group). Although members of the retention groups had higher rates of postsecondary education attendance and BA degree completion if they had high school diplomas, they still had lower rates of participation in postsecondary education and BA degree completion than the promotion group ($p < .01$). See bottom part of Table 5.

Table 5. Unadjusted Rates of Outcomes by Groups

Outcomes	Study sample	Early Retention	Late Retention	Retained both early and late	Promotion
Study sample	N=11,441	n=898	n=627	n=108	n=9,808
Any postsecondary education attendance, %	78.4	56.1**	49.3**	26.9**	82.9
BA degree completion, %	34.5	9.5**	5.3**	0.9**	39.0
High school diploma only	N=10,084	N=654	N=341	N=35	N=9,054
Any postsecondary education attendance, %	84.9	69.3**	66.9**	51.4**	86.8
BA degree completion, %	39.0	12.8**	9.4**	2.9**	42.2

Note. Retention groups were compared with the promotion group. ** $p < .01$.

Table 6. Marginal Effects and Coefficients from Regression

Outcomes	Adjusted rate / mean		Retention	
	Ever retained (1-8)	Promotion	Marginal effects	P-value
Study sample				
Any postsecondary education attendance, %	83.1	87.3	-4.2	.001
BA degree completion, %	15.7	30.6	-14.9	.000
High school diploma only				
Any postsecondary education attendance, %	89.3	91.2	-1.9	.098
BA degree completion, %	21.2	37.4	-16.2	.000

Note. The marginal effects are shown in percentage change. Results are adjusted for covariates: sociodemographic factors, scholastic abilities, and school factors as described in the measures section. Retained more than once was included in the model, but it was never significant for any outcome.

Grade Retention, Postsecondary Education, and BA Degree Completion

The differences between the retention (grades 1-8) and promotion groups were examined after taking into account covariates (sociodemographic factors and other school factors). The top half of Table 6 shows the marginal effects and coefficients from probit regression analyses. There were significant differences between the retention and promotion groups in both postsecondary education attendance and BA degree completion. Relative to the promotion group, the retention group had lower rates of postsecondary education attendance (83.1% vs. 87.3%, marginal effect = -4.2%, $p < .01$), and BA degree completion (15.7% vs. 30.6%, marginal effect = -14.9%, $p < .01$). The marginal effect of retention was larger on BA degree completion than on postsecondary education attendance. See Appendix 1 for results from logistic regression.

Controlling for covariates, the timing of retention (early versus late retention) also was examined. The top half of Table 7 shows the marginal effects and coefficients from probit regression analyses for early retention and late retention. The reference group was the promotion group. Both early and late retention were significantly associated with lower rates of postsecondary education attendance and BA degree completion ($p < .05$). The late retention (grades 4 to 8) group had the lowest rates of both postsecondary education attendance and BA degree completion among the three groups, and had larger marginal effects on both postsecondary education attendance and BA degree completion than the early retention group. For example, the marginal effect of late retention on postsecondary education attendance was -6.8% while it was -2.8% for early retention. The marginal effect of late retention on BA degree completion was -20.3% while it was -12.2% for early retention. The marginal effects of retention on BA degree completion were larger than the effects of retention on postsecondary education attendance. See Appendix 2 for results from logistic regression.

Table 7. Marginal Effects and Coefficients from Regression

Outcomes	Adjusted rate / mean			Early retention (1-3) Marginal effects (p-value)	Late retention (4-8) Marginal effects (p-value)
	Early retention (1-3)	Late retention (4-8)	Promotion		
Study sample					
Any postsecondary education attendance, %	84.6	80.6	87.4	-2.8 (.043)	-6.8 (.000)
BA degree completion, %	18.6	10.5	30.8	-12.2 (.000)	-20.3 (.000)
High school diploma only					
Any postsecondary education attendance, %	90.1	87.5	91.2	-1.1 (.366)	-3.7 (.036)
BA degree completion, %	24.0	15.3	37.5	-13.5 (.000)	-22.2 (.000)

Note. Reference group is the promotion group. The marginal effects are shown in percentage change. Results are adjusted for covariates: sociodemographic factors, scholastic abilities, and school factors as described in the measures section. Retained both early and late was included in the model, but it was never significant for any outcome.

Retained Students Who Persisted to Graduate from High School versus Continuously Promoted Students

To answer the third question, "does it matter if retained students persisted to graduate from high school?" participants who had high school diploma were selected (N=10,084) to test if the associations between grade retention and outcomes of postsecondary education differ. The bottom half of Table 6 shows the marginal effects and coefficients from probit regression analyses. There was a significant difference between the retention and promotion groups in BA degree completion, but not in postsecondary education attendance. Relative to the promotion group, the retention group had a lower rate of BA degree completion (21.2% vs. 37.4%, marginal effect = -16.2%, $p < .01$). The marginal effect of retention on BA degree completion was larger (relative to the whole study sample) when only participants who had high school diplomas were included (-16.2% vs. -14.9%). See Appendix 3 for results from logistic regression.

Controlling for covariates, the timing of retention (early versus late retention) was also examined. The bottom half of Table 7 shows the marginal effects and coefficients from probit regression analyses for early retention and late retention. The reference group was the promotion group. Late retention remained significantly associated with lower rates of postsecondary education attendance and BA degree completion ($p < .05$). The late retention group had the lowest rates of postsecondary education attendance and BA degree completion among the three groups, and had larger marginal effects on outcomes than the early retention group. For example, the marginal effect of late retention on BA degree completion was -22.2% while it was -13.5% for early retention. However, there was no significant difference between early retention and promotion groups in postsecondary education attendance. The marginal effects of both early and late retention on BA degree completion were slightly larger when only participants who had high school diplomas were included. See Appendix 4 for results from logistic regression.

Discussion

Findings indicated that experience of grade retention was significantly associated with lower rates of postsecondary education attendance and BA degree completion when sociodemographic factors, academic achievement, and school factors were taken into account. In terms of timing of retention, both early and late retention were significantly associated with lower rates of postsecondary education attendance and BA degree completion when sociodemographic factors, academic achievement, and school factors were taken into account. However, late retention (between fourth and eighth grades) was more strongly linked to lower rates of postsecondary education and BA degree completion than early retention (between first and third grades).

When only participants who had high school diplomas were included, the significant difference between the retention and promotion groups in BA degree completion remained, but the difference in postsecondary education attendance between the groups was no longer statistically significant. The marginal effects of both early and late retention were slightly larger on BA degree completion when only participants who had high school diplomas were examined.

Grade Retention, Postsecondary Education Attendance, and BA Degree Completion

Findings on the negative relation between grade retention and postsecondary education attendance are consistent with previous findings (Fine & Davis, 2003; Ou & Reynolds, 2010). Retained students are also less likely to have completed BA degrees than students who had never been retained. Although the retention group has lower rates of postsecondary education attendance and BA degree completion, the marginal effect of retention on BA degree completion is much larger than the marginal effect of retention on postsecondary education attendance. Both postsecondary education attendance and BA degree completion are important indicators of adult well being. College degrees are found to be associated with higher income and lower rates of unemployment than high school completion without college degree (U.S. Department of Labor, 1999). In addition, having some college without a degree is associated with higher income than a high school diploma alone (Hecker, 1998). Due to the advantages and benefits associated with postsecondary education and BA degree over the course of life, it is important to understand why grade retention would be negatively associated with postsecondary education attendance and BA degree completion. Potential explanations through mediators are discussed.

First, the connection between retention and school dropout might explain such negative associations. As mentioned earlier, the relations between grade retention and school dropout are reported in many studies (Hauser, 2001; Jimerson, 1999; Jimerson, Anderson et al., 2002; Kaufman & Bradby, 1992; Rumberger & Larson, 1998; Temple et al., 2004). In 2004, 21.4% of youth ages 16-19 who had ever been retained dropped out of school (U.S. Department of Education, 2006). It is well known that dropouts are less likely to attend college. Some scholars argue that retained students are a select group whose members had poor academic performance before they were retained, and so, they argue, it is not surprising that retained students are more likely to drop out and are less likely to attend college. In this case, if the connection between grade retention and school dropout can fully explain the association between grade retention and postsecondary education attendance and BA degree completion, then as long as retained students persisted to graduate from high school, they should have similar rates of postsecondary education attendance and BA degree completion as their never retained peers. However, findings from the present study indicate that retained students who persisted to graduate from high school still had significantly lower rates of BA degree completion relative to students who were never retained. The connection between grade retention and dropout might partially explain the association between grade retention and BA degree completion, but cannot fully explain such an association.

Second, grade retention might have negative influence on socio-emotional development, such as social competence and adjustment. Recent studies show that non-cognitive abilities, such as competence of interactions with other people, might have the same or larger predictive power relative to cognitive abilities on college attendance or degree completion (Heckman & Rubinstein, 2001; Heckman, Stixrud & Urzua, 2006; Ou & Reynolds, 2009). The relations between grade retention and social-emotional and behavioral adjustment have been investigated, although findings on social development are inconsistent. For instance, some findings indicate that retention might have negative influence on social adjustment and behavior, such as low self-esteem, poor social adjustment, negative attitudes toward school, and problem behaviors (Jimerson et al., 1997; Jimerson & Ferguson, 2007; Nagin, Pagani,

Tremblay, & Vitaro, 2003). Some findings indicate that there was no evidence of negative effects of grade retention on problem behaviors (Gottfredson, Fink & Graham, 1994), delinquency (MaCoy & Reynolds, 1999), and social-emotional development (Hong & Yu, 2008). However, Reynolds (1992) found that retention had a significant, positive association with children's perceived school competence.

Finally, grade retention might be associated with postsecondary education through other mediators, such as school mobility and students' motivation. School mobility has been found to be significantly associated with lower educational attainment (Ou, 2005; Ou & Reynolds, 2008). Grade retention might be related to higher numbers of school moves, which then lead to lower rates of college attendance.

To summarize, the linkage between grade retention and postsecondary education and BA degree completion might be explained through various pathways. For example, if grade retention is a negative experience instead of a positive experience for individuals, it might have a snowball effect on students' development. Either of the pathways would start at the initial retention experience, and that small difference between retention and promotion groups in early years could grow into a large gap ten years later. The gap between certain groups in college attendance and persistence exists even before students enter college. Therefore, it is important to pay attention to early experiences in school in addition to experiences in college.

What about Retained Participants Who Persisted to Graduate from High School?

What if retained students persisted to graduate from high school? Would they have similar rates of college attendance and BA degree completion as students who were never retained? When only participants who had high school diplomas were examined, there was no significant difference in postsecondary education attendance between participants who were retained and those who had never been retained. This finding contradicts the finding that retained students who persisted to graduate from high school have a lower rate of postsecondary education participation than students who were never retained from another study (Fine & Davis, 2003). In that study, researchers also used the NELS:88 dataset, but the information of postsecondary education came from the follow-up in 1994 and school factors were not taking into account. The present study examined the final educational status in 2000. The contradicted findings indicate that in the long run, retained students who persisted to graduate from high school might have a similar rate of postsecondary education participation as never retained students, but the former might tend to delay their attendance of postsecondary education than the latter. Nevertheless, retained students who persisted to graduate from high school had a lower rate of BA degree completion than continuously promoted students.

Grade retention is considered as a risk factor of not attending postsecondary education because of its positive relation with school dropout (Horn, 1997; Horn & Chen, 1998; Kaufman & Bradby, 1992). However, even if retained students persisted to graduate from high school, they were still less likely to attend postsecondary education. A high school diploma is important because it opens the door to postsecondary education. As long as participants have a high school diploma, they are qualified to apply for postsecondary education even though they might decide not to do it immediately after high school graduation. Nevertheless, similar chances of applying for postsecondary education do not imply similar chances of BA degree completion. Postsecondary education attendance includes attendance in various degree programs, such as certificates, associate degrees, and belcher degrees. There are different requirements, accessibilities, length, and benefits associated with different programs. Among various degrees, a BA degree is associated with the largest benefits, such as income and employment opportunities. The retained students were more likely to attend postsecondary education to pursue degrees other than a BA degree. Fine and Davis (2003) reported that among high school graduates, students who had been retained were less likely to attend 4-year colleges than those who were never retained by age 20/21 when family SES, race/ethnicity, and achievement were taking into account. The findings of the present study concur that among participants who had a high school diploma, those who had been retained had a lower rate of BA degree completion than those who were never retained. The marginal effect is, in fact, slightly larger than the effect for the whole study sample.

Timing of Retention

Findings on timing of retention are consistent with previous studies: late retention is associated with much higher rates of dropout and lower rates of college attendance than is early retention (Fine & Davis, 2003; Ou & Reynolds, 2010; Roderick, 1994; Temple et al., 2004). In addition, Pomplui (1988) reported that the positive effects of retention decrease for students who were retained in higher grades. The findings from the present study suggest that grade retention in late grades also has larger detrimental associations with postsecondary education attendance and BA degree completion than retention in early grades.

Although the large association between late retention and BA degree completion might be due to the fact that late retention has a stronger connection with high school dropout than early retention, a similar pattern is found among participants who have a high school diploma. Thus, the explanation through the connection between late retention and school dropout is less plausible. Another potential explanation through the connection between grade retention and social emotional development seems more likely.

As mentioned earlier, the relations between grade retention and socio-emotional and behavioral adjustment have been investigated, although findings are not consistent. Other than socio-emotional and behavioral adjustment, it is important to consider the students' perspective. For example, how students perceive the experience of grade retention would have an important impact on the students as well. Studies show that grade retention was rated as one of the most stressful life events by students (Anderson, Jimerson, & Whipple, 2005; Yamamoto & Byrnes, 1987). Moreover, socio-emotional development varies by student's grade, because as students get older they become more attached to their peers and more self-conscious. Thus, the experience of grade retention might have a bigger impact on older students than younger students. This is a potential explanation for the larger association between late retention and postsecondary education attendance and BA degree completion relative to the association between early retention and postsecondary education outcomes. The associations between later retention and psychological development warrant further investigation.

Conclusion

There are some limitations of this study. First, the estimated associations of grade retention were based on regression-adjusted scores within a prospective longitudinal design. Study participants were not randomly assigned to groups. The correlational findings should be interpreted cautiously. Second, the focus of the present study was to examine the associations between grade retention and postsecondary education outcomes. Only a limited set of covariates were included in the analysis. For example, sociodemographic factors, such as maternal education, were used as covariates to control the differences resulted from family background. Limited factors on academic achievement, problem behaviors and school factors were included in the present study, but there might be other factors associated with grade retention which have not been included. It is important to note the limitation of omitted variables. Finally, information on grade retention came from self-report and was asked retrospectively. Although answers from different questions were cross-referenced, and extreme cases were removed from the study sample, measurement error of grade retention remains.

Implications

The negative associations between grade retention and both postsecondary education attendance and BA degree completion have important implications for promoting college attendance and degree completion. As large benefits and potential come with higher education, promoting higher education has become a priority in the society. Findings on the negative associations between grade retention and both postsecondary education attendance and BA degree completion suggest that grade retention can be viewed as a risk factor for not attending postsecondary education or not completing a BA degree. In other words, students who experienced grade retention were less likely to attend postsecondary education and less likely to complete a BA degree. This finding can be applied in two different ways.

First, it would be better to provide remedial services to help struggling students rather than to retain them. If students are retained, even if their performance might improve, the experience of retention might bring unintended harm in the long run. Second, colleges should provide additional attention to students who experienced grade retention, because they are at-risk of leaving college before degree completion. It would be challenging for colleges to try to identify students who have experienced grade retention. However, programs targeting those students who are at-risk of leaving college might be more cost-effective in promoting students' success in college than universal programs directed toward all college students.

Implications of the findings from the present study can be viewed from the perspective of the cost-effectiveness of grade retention as a practice in school. Eide and Showalter (2001) estimated that the cost of retention is approximately $2.6 billion per year and affects about 450,000 children when the annual retention rate is assumed to be 1%. The cost was estimated based on the annual cost of education only and did not take into account other costs related to retention, such as the cost related to increasing high school dropout rates. To calculate the costs and benefits of grade retention, it is necessary to know whether grade retention is associated with long-term outcomes, such as BA degree completion, beyond academic achievement (Eide & Goldhaber, 2005). If grade retention improves academic achievement one or two years after the initial retention but increases the risk of dropping out or ultimately decreases the possibility of BA degree completion, its overall effect would be negative, and the short-term improvement of academic achievement would not be worth the cost after all.

Appendix 1. Odds Ratio of the Models Any Retention

Variables	Postsecondary attendance		BA degree completion	
	Model 1	Model 2	Model 1	Model 2
Sociodemographic factors:				
Female	1.22**	1.184**	1.313**	1.296**
Race/ethnicity (White as reference group)				
Black	1.276*	1.912**	.955	1.686**
Hispanic	1.244*	1.554**	.544**	.831
Asian/pacific islander	2.166**	1.934**	1.336**	1.506**
American Indian/AK native	.541**	.783	.289**	.508*
Parent highest education level at 8th grade	1.445**	1.309**	1.455**	1.257**
Family structure at 8th grade (2-parent as reference group)				
Single-parent family	.889	.996	.659**	.720**
Other than two-parent or single-parent family	.703**	.773**	.426**	.461**
Number of siblings in home at 8th grade	.914**	.901**	.948*	.938**
Mother's employment status at 8th grade (not work as reference)				
Mother worked full-time	1.083	1.072	.959	.995
Mother worked part-time	1.078	1.037	.944	.915
Family SES (quintile)	1.753**	1.522**	1.772**	1.532**
Age at August 1990	.647**	.727**	.835**	.943
English is native language	.664**	.665**	.546**	.538**
Ever reported handicap programs recipient	.639**	.813**	.670**	.885
If missing 5 or more variables	.955	.805	.937	.745
Grade retention				
Retention between first and 8th grades	.558**	.753**	.270**	.397**
Retained more than once between 1st and 8th grades	.928	.798	.395	.393
Characteristics of 8th grade school				
Percent free lunch at 8th grade		.954**		.947**
Total school enrollment		.985		1.011
Type of school (Public as reference group)				
Private religious school		1.408**		1.555**
Private non-religious school		1.171		1.703**
Geographic region of school (West as reference)				
South		1.008		1.289**
North central		.876		1.228*
Northeast		1.133		1.675**
Urbanicity of school: (Suburban as reference)				

Table. Continued

Variables	Postsecondary attendance		BA degree completion	
	Model 1	Model 2	Model 1	Model 2
Urban		1.282**		1.032
Rural		.973		1.032
Academic achievement at 8th grade				
Reading standardized scores		1.027**		1.024**
Math standardized scores		1.056**		1.063**
Number of reported problem behaviors by 1992		.615**		.361**
-2 log likelihood	8650.093	7964.637	10544.172	9321.946
Cox and Snell R Square ^{2}	.178	.230	.258	.339
Observed rate				
Percent correct for those coded 1	95.9	94.4	56.2	64.0
Overall percent correct	81.4	82.4	75.5	78.8

Note. * p < .05 ** p < .01

Appendix 2. Odds Ratio of the Models Timing of Retention

Variables	Postsecondary attendance		BA degree completion	
	Model 1	Model 2	Model 1	Model 2
Sociodemographic factors:				
Female	1.222**	1.185**	1.307**	1.292**
Race/ethnicity (White as reference group)				
Black	1.298**	1.936**	.960	1.693**
Hispanic	1.261*	1.575**	.544**	.833
Asian/pacific islander	2.164**	1.940**	1.335**	1.507**
American Indian/AK native	.544**	.790	.290**	.510*
Parent highest education level at 8th grade	1.448**	1.312**	1.456**	1.258**
Family structure at 8th grade (2-parent as reference group)				
Single-parent family	.895	1.001	.661**	.722**
Other than two-parent or single-parent family	.705**	.774**	.425**	.460**
Number of siblings in home at 8th grade	.915**	.902**	.949*	.939**
Mother's employment status at 8th grade (not work as reference)				
Mother worked full-time	1.084	1.074	.960	.995
Mother worked part-time	1.081	1.042	.944	.915
Family SES (quintile)	1.753**	1.522**	1.776**	1.535**
Age at August 1990	.668**	.741**	.836**	.944
English is native language	.670**	.669**	.545**	.537**
Ever reported handicap programs recipient	.637**	.813**	.668**	.881
If missing 5 or more variables	.956	.807	.941	.752

Table. Continued

Variables	Postsecondary attendance		BA degree completion	
	Model 1	Model 2	Model 1	Model 2
Grade retention				
Early retention (between 1st and 3rd grades)	.624**	.832	.345**	.484**
Late retained (between 4th and 8th grades)	.461**	.636**	.156**	.245**
Both early and late retention	1.115	.739	1.493	.921
Characteristics of 8th grade school				
Percent free lunch at 8th grade		.953**		.947**
Total school enrollment		.984		1.011
Type of school (Public as reference group)				
Private religious school		1.397**		1.554**
Private non-religious school		1.160		1.716**
Geographic region of school (West as reference)				
South		1.018		1.293**
North central		.877		1.230*
Northeast		1.138		1.675**
Urbanicity of school: (Suburban as reference)				
Urban		1.293**		1.031
Rural		.977		1.033
Academic achievement at 8th grade				
Reading standardized scores		1.027**		1.024**
Math standardized scores		1.057**		1.063**
Number of reported problem behaviors by 1992		.618**		.363**
-2 log likelihood	8639.910	7955.552	10533.706	9315.238
Cox and Snell R Square [2]	.179	.231	.258	.340
Observed rate				
Percent correct for those coded 1	96.0	94.5	56.4	63.9
Overall percent correct	81.6	82.5	75.6	78.8

Note. * $p < .05$ ** $p < .01$

Appendix 3. Odds Ratio of the Models Any Retention (HS Diploma Only)

Variables	Postsecondary attendance		BA degree completion	
	Model 1	Model 2	Model 1	Model 2
Sociodemographic factors:				
Female	1.367**	1.342**	1.332**	1.325**
Race/ethnicity (White as reference group)				
Black	1.430**	2.034**	.962	1.641**
Hispanic	1.564**	1.823**	.560**	.830

Table. Continued

Variables	Postsecondary attendance		BA degree completion	
	Model 1	Model 2	Model 1	Model 2
Asian/pacific islander	2.002**	1.736**	1.304*	1.448**
American Indian/AK native	.586*	.797	.289**	.471*
Parent highest education level at 8th grade	1.459**	1.327**	1.450**	1.262**
Family structure at 8th grade (2-parent as reference group)				
Single-parent family	.944	1.036	.702**	.743**
Other than two-parent or single-parent family	.780**	.821*	.448**	.476**
Number of siblings in home at 8th grade	.891**	.884**	.948*	.940*
Mother's employment status at 8th grade (not work as reference)				
Mother worked full-time	1.121	1.121	.958	1.005
Mother worked part-time	1.169	1.141	.949	.925
Family SES (quintile)	1.734**	1.499**	1.728**	1.501**
Age at August 1990	.758**	.835*	.895	.991
English is native language	.599**	.591**	.539**	.529**
Ever reported handicap programs recipient	.652**	.821*	.691**	.898
If missing 5 or more variables	1.200	1.072	.896	.738
Grade retention				
Retention between first and 8th grades	.655**	.854	.307**	.423**
Retained more than once between 1st and 8th grades	.834	.670	.579	.534
Characteristics of 8th grade school				
Percent free lunch at 8th grade		.955*		.951**
Total school enrollment		.984		1.007
Type of school (Public as reference group)				
Private religious school		1.204		1.551**
Private non-religious school		1.051		1.757**
Geographic region of school (West as reference)				
South		.937		1.280**
North central		.793*		1.195*
Northeast		1.118		1.642**
Urbanicity of school: (Suburban as reference)				
Urban		1.274*		1.035
Rural		.885		1.016
Academic achievement at 8th grade				
Reading standardized scores		1.028**		1.024**
Math standardized scores		1.050**		1.061**
Number of reported problem behaviors by 1992		.675**		.416**

Table. Continued

Variables	Postsecondary attendance		BA degree completion	
	Model 1	Model 2	Model 1	Model 2
-2 log likelihood	6598.290	6195.731	10068.396	9022.247
Cox and Snell R Square [2]	.118	.155	.235	.316
Observed rate				
Percent correct for those coded 1	98.9	97.8	60.1	65.3
Overall percent correct	85.7	85.8	73.1	76.7

Note. * p < .05 ** p < .01

Appendix 4. Odds Ratio of the Models Timing of Retention (HS Diploma Only)

Variables . ·	Postsecondary attendance		BA degree completion	
	Model 1	Model 2	Model 1	Model 2
Sociodemographic factors:				
Female	1.364**	1.340**	1.327**	1.322**
Race/ethnicity (White as reference group)				
Black	1.448**	2.046**	.967	1.649**
Hispanic	1.580**	1.840**	.560**	.831
Asian/pacific islander	2.018**	1.752**	1.305*	1.451**
American Indian/AK native	.593*	.806	.291**	.472*
Parent highest education level at 8th grade	1.46**	1.328**	1.451**	1.263**
Family structure at 8th grade (2-parent as reference group)				
Single-parent family	.947	1.037	.703**	.744**
Other than two-parent or single-parent family	.780**	.819*	.447**	.475**
Number of siblings in home at 8th grade	.891**	.884**	.948*	.940*
Mother's employment status at 8th grade (not work as reference)				
Mother worked full-time	1.121	1.122	.958	1.005
Mother worked part-time	1.171	1.144	.948	.925
Family SES (quintile)	1.737**	1.501**	1.731**	1.505**
Age at August 1990	.765**	.836*	.895	.992
English is native language	.604**	.594**	.537**	.528**
Ever reported handicap programs recipient	.648**	.817*	.687**	.893
If missing 5 or more variables	1.207	1.073	.900	.742
Grade retention				
Early retention (between 1st and 3rd grades)	.714**	.915	.374**	.499**
Late retained (between 4th and 8th grades)	.543**	.734	.191**	.276**
Both early and late retention	.997	.633	2.00	1.167

Table. Continued

	Postsecondary attendance		BA degree completion	
Variables	**Model 1**	**Model 2**	**Model 1**	**Model 2**
Characteristics of 8th grade school				
Percent free lunch at 8th grade		.954*		.951**
Total school enrollment		.983		1.007
Type of school (Public as reference group)				
Private religious school		1.198		1.551**
Private non-religious school		1.046		1.770**
Geographic region of school (West as reference)				
South		.939		1.283**
North central		.793*		1.196*
Northeast		1.121		1.644**
Urbanicity of school: (Suburban as reference)				
Urban		1.280*		1.034
Rural		.890		1.016
Academic achievement at 8th grade				
Reading standardized scores		1.028**		1.024**
Math standardized scores		1.050**		1.061**
Number of reported problem behaviors by 1992		.678**		.418**
-2 log likelihood	6594.305	6192.841	10061.192	9017.277
Cox and Snell R Square [2]	.118	.155	.235	.316
Observed rate				
Percent correct for those coded 1	98.9	97.9	59.9	65.3
Overall percent correct	85.7	85.8	73.2	76.6

Note. * $p < .05$ ** $p < .01$

References

Alexander, K. L., Entwisle, D. R. & Dauber, S. L. (2003). *On the success of failure: a reassessment of the effects of retention in the primary grades* (2nd ed.). New York: Cambridge university press.

Alexander, K. L., Entwisle, D. R., Dauber, S. L. & Kabbani, N. (2004). Dropout in relation to grade retention: An accounting from the Beginning School Study. In: H. J. Walberg, A. J. Reynolds, & M. C. Wang (Eds), *Can unlike students learn together? Grade retention, tracking and grouping* (5-34). Greenwich, CT: Information Age.

Alexander, K. L., Entwisle, D. R. & Horsey, C. S. (1999, November). *Grade retention, social promotion and "third way" alternatives.* Paper presented at the National Invitational Conference on Early Childhood Learning: Programs for a new age. Alexandria, VA.

Alexander, K. L., Entwisle, D. R. & Kabbani, N. (2001). The dropout process in life course perspective: Early risk factors at home and school. *Teachers College Record, 103*(5), 760-822.

Anderson, G. E., Jimerson, S. R. & Whipple, A. D. (2005). Student ratings of stressful experiences at home and school: Loss of a parent and grade retention as superlative stressors. *Journal of Applied School Psychology, 21*(1), 1-20.

Beebe-Frankenberger, M., Bocian, K. M., MacMillan, D. L. & Gresham, F. M. (2004). Sorting second-grade students: Differentiating those retained from those promoted. *Journal of Educational Psychology, 96*(2), 204-215.

Bonvin, P., Bless, G. & Schuepbach, M. (2008). Grade retention: Decision-making and effects on learning as well as social and emotional development. *School Effectiveness and School Improvement, 19*(1), 1-19.

Cohen, P., Cohen, J., West, S. G. & Aiken, L. S. (2003). *Applied Multiple Regression: Correlation Analysis for the Behavioral Science.* Hillsdale, NJ: Lawrence Erlbaum Associates.

Curtin, T. R., Ingels, S. J., Wu, S. & Heuer, R. (2002). *National Education Longitudinal Study of 1988: Base-Year to Fourth Follow-up Data File User's Manual (NCES* 2002-323). Washington, DC: U.S. Department of Education, National Center for Education Statistics.

Eide, E. R. & Showalter, M. H. (2001). The effect of grade retention on educational and labor market outcomes. *Economics of Education Review, 20*, 563-576.

Eide, E. R. & Goldhaber, D. D. (2005). Grade retention: What are the costs and benefits? *Journal of Education Finance, 31*(2), 195-214.

Ensminger, M. E. & Slusarcick, A. L. (1992). Paths to high school graduation or dropout: A longitudinal study of a first-grade cohort. *Sociology of Education, 65*(2), 95-113.

Fine, J. G. & Davis, J. M. (2003). Grade retention and enrollment in post-secondary education. *Journal of School Psychology, 41*, 401-411.

Gottfredson, D. C., Fink, C. M. & Graham, N. (1994). Grade retention and problem behavior. *American Educational Research Journal, 31*(4), 761-784.

Greene, J. P. & Winters, M. A. (2004). An evaluation of Florida's program to end social promotion. *Education working paper, No. 7.* New York, NY: Center for Civic Innovation at the Manhattan Institute for Policy Research.

Greene, J. P. & Winters, M. A. (2006). Getting farther ahead by staying behind: A second-year evaluation of Florida's policy to end social promotion. Civic Report, No. 49. New York, NY: Center for Civic Innovation at the Manhattan Institute for Policy Research.

Greene, J. P. & Winters, M. A. (2007). Revisiting grade retention: An evaluation of Florida's test-based promotion policy. *Education Finance and Policy, 2*(4), 319-340.

Guèvremont, A., Roos, N. P. Brownell, M. (2007). Predictors and consequences of grade retention: Examining data from Manitoba, Canada. *Canadian Journal of School Psychology, 22*(1), 50-67.

Hauser, R. M. (2001). *Should We End Social Promotion? Truth and Consequences. In G. Orfield & M. Kornhaber (Eds.), Raising the standards or raising barriers? Inequality and high stakes testing in public education* (151-178). New York: Century Foundation.

Hecker, D. (1998). Occupations and earnings of workers with some college but no degree. *Occupational Outlook Quarterly, 42*(2), 28-40.

Heckman, J. J. & Rubinstein, Y. (2001). The importance of noncognitive skills: Lessons from the GED testing program. *American Economic Review, 91*(2), 145-149.

Heckman, J. J., Stixrud, J. & Urzua, S. (2006). The effects of cognitive and noncognitive abilities on labor market outcomes and social behavior. *Journal of Labor Economics, 24*(3), 411-482.

Heubert, J. P. & Hauser, R. M. (1999) (eds). *High stakes: Testing for tracking, promotion, and graduation.* Washington, DC: National Academy Press.

Holmes, C. T. (1989). Grade-level retention effects: A meta-analysis of research studies. In L. A. Shepard & M. L. Smith (Eds.), *Flunking grades: Research and policies on retention* (16-33). London: Falmer Press.

Holmes, C. T. & Matthews, K. M. (1984). The effects of nonpromotion on elementary and junior high school pupils: A meta-analysis. *Reviews of Educational Research, 54*, 225-236.

Hong, G. & Raudenbush, S. W. (2005). Effects of kindergarten retention policy on children's cognitive growth in reading and mathematics. *Educational Evaluation and Policy Analysis, 27*(3), 205-224.

Hong, G. & Yu, B. (2007). Early-grade retention and children's reading and math learning in elementary years, *Educational Evaluation and Policy Analysis, 29*(4), 239-261.

Hong, G. & Yu, B. (2008). Effects of kindergarten retention on children's social-emotional development: An application of propensity score method to multivariate, multilevel data. *Developmental Psychology, 44* (2), 407-421.

Horn, L. J. (1997). *Confronting the odds: Students at risk and the pipeline to higher education* (Report No. NCES 98-094). Washington, DC: U.S. Department of Education, National Center for Education Statistics.

Horn, L. J. & Chen, X. (1998). *Toward resiliency: At-risk students who make it to college* (Report No. PLLI 98-8056). Washington, DC: U.S. Department of Education, Office of Educational Research and Improvement.

Jackson, G. (1975). The research evidence on the effects of grade retention. *Review of Education Research, 45,* 613-635.

Jacob, B. A. & Lefgren, L. (2004). Remedial education and student achievement: A regression-discontinuity analysis. *Review of Economics and Statistics, 86*(1), 226-244.

Jacob, B. A. & Lefgren, L. (2009). The effect of grade retention on high school completion. *American Economic Journal: Applied Economics, 1*(3), 33-58.

Janosz, M., LeBlanc, M., Boulerice, B. & Tremblay, R. E. (1997). Disentangling the weight of school dropout predictors: A test on two longitudinal samples. *Journal of Youth and Adolescence, 26*(6), 733-762.

Jimerson, S. R. (1999). On the failure of failure: Examining the association between early grade retention and education and employment outcomes during late adolescence. *Journal of School Psychology, 37*, 243-272.

Jimerson, S. R. (2001). Meta-analysis of grade retention research: implications for practice in the 21st century. *School Psychology Review, 30*(3), 420-437.

Jimerson, S. R. & Ferguson, P. (2007). A longitudinal study of grade retention: Academic and behavioral outcomes of retained students through adolescence. *School Psychology Quarterly, 22*(3), 314-339.

Jimerson, S. R., Anderson, G. E. & Whipple, A. D. (2002). Winning the battle and losing the war: examining the relation between grade retention and dropping out of high school. *Psychology in the Schools, 39*(4), 441-457.

Jimerson, S. R., Carlson, E., Robert, M., Egeland, B. & Sroufe, L. A. (1997). A prospective longitudinal study of high school dropouts: Examining multiple predictors across development. *Journal of School Psychology,* **36**(1), 3-25.

Jimerson, S. R., Ferguson, P., Whipple, A. D., Anderson, G. E. & Dalton, M. J. (2002). Exploring the association between grade retention and dropout: A longitudinal study examining socio-emotional, behavioral, and achievement characteristics of retained students. *The California School Psychologist,* **7**, 51-62.

Jimerson, S. R. & Kaufman, A. M. (2003). Reading, writing, and retention: a primer on grade retention research. *The Reading Teacher,* **56**(7), 622-635.

Kaufman, P. & Bradby, D. (1992). *Characteristics of at-risk students in NELS:* **88** (Report No. NCES 92-042). Washington, DC: U.S. Department of Education, National Center for Education Statistics.

Lorence, J., Dworkin, A. G., Toenjes, L. A. & Hill, A. N. (2002). Grade retention and social promotion in Texas, 1994-99: Academic achievement among elementary school students (pp. 13-67). In D. Ravitch (ed.), *Brookings Papers on Education Policy*, Brookings Institution Press.

McCoy, A. R. & Reynolds, A. J. (1999). Grade retention and school performance: an extended investigation. *Journal of School Psychology,* **37**(3), 273-298.

Nagin, D. S., Pagani, L., Tremblay, R. E. & Vitaro, F. (2003). Life course turning points: The effect of grade retention on physical aggression. *Development and Psychopathology,* **15**, 343-361.

Ou, S. (2005). Pathways of Effects of an Early Intervention Program on Educational Attainment: Findings from the Chicago Longitudinal Study. *Journal of Applied Developmental psychology,* **26**(5), 578-611.

Ou, S. & Reynolds, A. J. (2008). Predictors of Educational Attainment in the Chicago Longitudinal Study. *School Psychology Quarterly,* **23**(2), 199-229.

Ou, S. & Reynolds, A. J. (2009, April). *Early Determinants of Postsecondary Education Participation and Degree attainment: Findings from an Inner-City Minority Cohort.* Paper presented at the Biennial Meeting of Society for Research in Child Development in Denver, CO, April 2009.

Ou, S & Reynolds, A. J. (2010). Grade Retention, Postsecondary Education, and Public Aid Receipt. *Educational Evaluation and Policy Analysis,* **32**(1), 118-139.

Pomplun, M. (1988). Retention: The earlier, the better? *Journal of Educational Research,* **81**(5), 281-287.

Reynolds, A. J. (1992). Grade retention and school adjustment: An explanatory analysis. *Educational Evaluation and Policy Analysis,* **14**(2), 101-121.

Roderick, M. (1994). Grade retention and school dropout: investigating the association. *American Educational Research journal,* **31**(4), 729-759.

Roderick, M. & Nagaoka, J. (2005). Retention under Chicago's high-stakes testing program: Helpful, harmful, or harmless? *Educational Evaluation and Policy Analysis,* **27**(4), 309-40.

Rumberger, R. W. (1987). High School Dropouts: A Review of Issues and Evidence. *Review of Educational Research,* **57**(2), 101-121.

Rumberger, R. W. (1995). Dropping out of middle school: A multilevel analysis of students and schools. *American Educational Research Journal,* **32**(3), 583-625.

Rumberger, R. & Larson, K. (1998). Student mobility and the increased risk of high school dropout. *American Journal of Education,* **107**(1), 1-35.

Silberglitt, B. Appleton, J. J., Burns, M. K. & Jimerson, S. R. (2006). Examining the effects of grade retention on student reading performance: A longitudinal study. *Journal of School Psychology.* **44**, 255-270.

StataCorp. (2009). *Stata Statistical Software: Release 11.* College Station, TX: StataCorp Lp.

Temple, J. A. Reynolds, A. J. & Ou, S. (2004). Grade retention and school dropout: Another look at the evidence. In H.J. Walberg, A. J. Reynolds, & M.C. Wang (Eds), *Can unlike students learn together? Grade retention, tracking and grouping* (pp. 35-64). Greenwich, CT: Information Age.

U.S. Department of Education, National Center for Education Statistics (2006). The c*ondition of education, 2006.* Washington, DC: U.S. Department of Education.

U.S. Department of Labor (1999), *Report on the American workforce.* Washington, DC: U.S. Department of Labor.

Wu, W. West, S. G. & Hughes, J. N. (2008). Short-term effects of grade retention on the growth rate of Woodcock-Johnson III broad math and reading scores. *Journal of School Psychology,* **46**, 85-105.

Yamamoto. K. & Byrnes, D. A. (1987). Primary children's ratings of the stressfulness of experiences. *Journal of Research in Childhood Education,* **2**, 117-121.

In: Progress in Education, Volume 21
Editor: Robert V. Nata, pp. 105-125

ISBN: 978-1-61728-115-0
© 2011 Nova Science Publishers, Inc.

Chapter 5

CONNECTING SCHOOLS-COMMUNITIES-UNIVERSITIES TO TRANSFORM URBAN EDUCATION

Jana Noel
California State University, Sacramento

Abstract

Urban poverty; high mobility and displacement in and out of neighborhoods; inadequate funding to adequately cover the educational, social, and health needs of children and their families; and high teacher turnover are just some of the vital challenges of urban schools and communities. Too often, schools and teachers are inadequately prepared for the social, political, and economic conditions impacting the lives of their urban students, families, and communities. To be a meaningful part of the commitment to the struggle toward social, economic, cultural, and racial justice, schools must respond by transforming their focus and strategies to work more intimately with their urban communities, community-based organizations, and if applicable, nearby colleges and universities.

In so doing, urban education can move toward a more democratic form of education with input from all involved. Schools can build trust and collaboration with local community members, community organizations, and higher education. The transformation of not only urban education but also of communities toward a more clear form of social justice and equity underlies this approach.

This chapter begins by discussing theories of community strengths and community oriented pedagogy that underlie this approach. The chapter describes the values that develop in collaboration and that frame the work of such urban education strategies. It illustrates school-community-university connections by giving brief descriptions of several such programs, and describes more fully three exemplary models. And finally, the chapter synthesizes the key outcomes of utilizing this school-community-university collaborative approach to urban education.

The chapter mainly serves as a review of literature and of successful programs, but will also include the study of three exemplary programs which will be featured as models of successful school-community-university collaborations.

Introduction

Urban poverty; high mobility and displacement in and out of neighborhoods; inadequate funding to adequately cover the educational, social, and health needs of children and their families; and high teacher turnover are just some of the vital challenges of urban schools and communities. As Kincheloe, hayes, Rose, and Anderson (2006) explain, "The sociopolitical, cultural dynamics that frame urban education, to say the least, are not conducive to personal and social transformation" (p. xxx)

Too often, schools and teachers are inadequately prepared for the social, political, and economic conditions impacting the lives of their urban students, families, and communities. This is because, as Keyes and Gregg (2001) explain, "while an urban school is located *in* a community, it is not often *of the community*. Employees are rarely neighborhood residents. Many do not share the culture or race of their students" (p. 32). A deficit orientation toward urban students is often the result, in which teachers believe that the students have a home and community life that is deficient in the knowledge, skills, and attitudes presumably needed for success in school.

> To address this concern, Murrell (2001) documented that a key component of the new national agenda is collaboration among institutions of higher education, the K-12 schools they work with, and a broad community constituency. The success of urban school reform will depend, in part, on how the new national agenda makes good on its enthusiasm for creating new 'communities of learning,' embracing diversity, and preparing teachers through community and collaborative partnership. (p. 2)

Utilizing this approach, schools must respond by transforming their focus and strategies to work more intimately with their urban communities, community-based organizations, and if applicable, nearby colleges and universities. In so doing, urban education can move toward a more democratic form of education with input from all involved. Schools can build trust and collaboration with local community members, community organizations, and higher education. The transformation of not only urban education but also of communities toward a more clear form of social, economic, cultural, and racial justice and equity underlies this approach.

This chapter begins by discussing theories of community strengths and community oriented pedagogy that underlie this approach. The chapter describes the values that develop in collaboration and that frame the work of such urban education strategies. It illustrates school-community-university connections by giving brief descriptions of several such programs, and describes more fully three exemplary models. And finally, the chapter synthesizes the key outcomes of utilizing this school-community-university collaborative approach to urban education. The chapter does not include an exhaustive literature review on school-community-university connections, but rather lays a framework for understanding the value of creating such connections.

Theories of Community Strengths

The overarching principle for transforming urban education in this chapter is the need for educators to connect with community. In traditional forms of education at k-12 schools and at the university, students come to the institution to learn; educators do not go into the community to learn. This chapter hopes to instigate the practice of educators, both school teachers and university faculty, learning from community to enhance their own teaching and their students' learning. What can educators learn from the community? There are several theories of community strengths, strengths that can be learned and then put into practice in community oriented pedagogies. Theories of community strengths to be discussed here are cultural capital, funds of knowledge, and community cultural wealth.

Cultural Capital

Many theories of community strengths and community oriented pedagogy are variations on the term "cultural capital." Cultural capital can be seen in two basic yet quite opposed ways. The standard usage of the term comes from Bourdieu (Bourdieu & Passeron, 1977). According to Bourdieu, "cultural capital refers to an accumulation of cultural knowledge, skills and abilities possessed and inherited by privileged groups in society" (Yosso, 2005, p. 76), the skills and abilities valued most in society. This would include the abilities and skills needed to succeed in school, go to college, gain and maintain employment, and sustain a high level of socio-economic status. This definition of cultural capital has come to be interpreted that individuals and groups who possess this cultural capital will have a better chance to succeed, while less privileged groups, who do not have access to the same cultural capital, will lack the ability to succeed.

Noguera (2003) describes several strategies for connecting schools-communities-universities to increase cultural capital in low income, urban communities:

1. Community and university volunteers serve as tutors to help increase academic achievement among students who are lagging in academic achievement.
2. School-community partnerships are developed to create work-related internships that help students see the connections between schoolwork and work and community life.
3. Professional development is offered for school personnel in the areas of academic and community-based strategies.
4. Comprehensive, city-wide initiatives provide health and social services for urban children and their families (pp. 99-100)

However, as a number of authors write, a cultural capital perspective that sees communities as deficient in cultural capital, and in need of assistance to develop that privileged cultural capital, overlooks the point that cultural capital can be found within every group (Franklin, 2002; Oakes, 2009; Rodriguez, 2009; Yosso, 2005; Zipin, 2009; among others). Each cultural group has a set of beliefs, values, traditions, skills, and abilities that allow them to navigate through life. The problem is that society at-large does not always value these particular sets of skills. As will be seen below, several theories of community strengths have proposed that educators learn about and highlight the cultural capital held within non-privileged groups, including "funds of knowledge" and "community cultural wealth."

Funds of Knowledge

The concept "funds of knowledge," introduced by Moll, Amanti, Neff, and González (1992), refers to the sets of knowledge and skills found within a particular community. While these may sometimes be the types of knowledge valued in the educational system, the funds of knowledge often also include the knowledge community members need in order to live their daily lives. These types of knowledge are both cultural and strategic. Funds of knowledge can include such cultural components as language and traditions, or can include the network of relationships created to help get through life, for example the knowledge of which community members can help with child care, or who can help with automotive issues.

Important to the funds of knowledge perspective is that once educators have learned from community members, and have come to recognize the valuable household, relational, and community based knowledge into which children are immersed, those educators can better teach to the strengths of the child. Rather than seeing low income, culturally diverse children as being deficient of the cultural capital needed to succeed in society, Moll et al. (1992), founders of the educational movement toward funds of knowledge, write that "Our analysis of funds of knowledge represents a positive (and, we argue, realistic) view of households as containing ample cultural and cognitive resources with great potential utility for classroom instruction" (p. 134). With much work on funds of knowledge coming through work in Mexican-American communities, Vélez-Ibáñez and Greenberg (2005) write that:

> Our position is that public schools often ignore the strategic and cultural resources, which we have termed *funds of knowledge*, that households contain. We argue that these funds not only provide the basis for understanding the cultural systems from which U.S.-Mexican children emerge, but that they also are important and useful assets in the classroom. (p. 46)

Using an ethnographic approach, in which university faculty and k-12 teachers visited households in a k-12 school's community, researchers have identified several categories of funds of knowledge. These are all pieces and sets of knowledge and skills used by families to navigate their daily lives.

- Household Management: budgets, childcare, cooking, appliance repairs
- Material and Scientific Knowledge: construction, design and architecture, repair, maintenance
- Business: accounting, sales, loans, labor laws
- Medicine: first aid procedures, medicines, anatomy, herbal knowledge (Moll et al., 1992)

Moll et al. (1992) also reported in their study in Tucson, AZ on "how members of households use their funds of knowledge in dealing with changing, and often difficult, social and economic circumstances" (p. 133). They were especially interested in "how families develop social networks…and how these social relationships facilitate the development and exchange of resources – including knowledge, skills, and labor – that enhance the households' ability to survive or thrive" (p. 73). What they discovered was that these household funds of knowledge differ substantially from the typical classroom environment, which can result in students' difficulty in negotiating through the school system. In particular, the researchers found that the household funds of knowledge and social relationship networks are flexible and adaptive, with many relationships with persons from outside the home serving as key roles within household life. An uncle, for instance, may be the child's caregiver at some points, and the family's auto mechanic at others. He may be the family's connection to other family members in Mexico, and he also may be the one to help the child learn English. When teaching with funds of knowledge in mind, a teacher recognizes the important role of all of these types of knowledge as well as the types of relationships with various family and community members, and draws on those in teaching.

González, Moll, and Amanti (2005) point out the spirit of teachers who will be willing and able to learn about the community's funds of knowledge for the sake of their children. As they write, the funds of knowledge approach is "for educators who are willing to venture beyond the walls of the classroom. It is for those teachers and teachers-to-be who are willing to learn from their students and their communities" (p. ix).

Community Cultural Wealth

Yosso (2005) developed the concept of "community cultural wealth," which "focuses on and learns from the array of cultural knowledge, skills, abilities, and contacts possessed by socially marginalized groups that often go unrecognized and unacknowledged" (Yosso, 2005, p. 69). In that this concept urges educators to recognize the strengths of the communities of the students they serve, this is similar to other theories of community strengths. As such, Yosso uses the term community cultural wealth to describe the assets and resources, such as abilities and knowledge, held within marginalized communities.

Yosso (2005) details six types of "capital" held by members of marginalized communities.

1. "Aspirational capital" – "the ability to maintain hopes and dreams for the future, even in the face of real and perceived barriers" (Yosso, 2005, p. 77), also known as resiliency.
2. "Linguistic capital" – "the intellectual and social skills attained through communication experiences in more than one language and/or style" (Yosso, 2005, p. 78).
3. "Familial capital" – "those cultural knowledges nurtured among *familia* (kin) that carry a sense of community history, memory and cultural intuition" (Yosso, p. 79).
4. "Social capital" – "networks of people and community resources. These peer and other social contacts can provide both instrumental and emotional support to navigate through society's institutions" (Yosso, p. 79).
5. "Navigational capital" – "skills maneuvering through social institutions" (Yosso, p. 80).
6. "Resistant capital" – "knowledges and skills fostered through oppositional behavior that challenges inequality" (Yosso, p. 80).

Gaining and maintaining community cultural wealth, through any of these six types of capital, is difficult in the trying economic conditions commonly experienced by urban residents. At the same time, not all children will come from equal amounts or types of capital. However, when urban educators come to realize that many children and their families maintain these forms of community cultural wealth, even through difficult times, educators can learn to build upon and share that spirit with their students. When a teacher seeks and recognizes these forms of capital held by students, she will recognize the multiple knowledges, skills, supports, and networks within the children's lives. The next section discusses the ways that teachers can utilize the community's strengths through community-oriented pedagogy.

Theories of Community Oriented Pedagogy

Once teachers have gained an understanding of community strengths, several theories of community oriented pedagogy describe how teachers can draw on those community strengths within the classroom. These theories include culturally relevant pedagogy and the community teacher. In each of these, the emphasis is on urban school teachers and university educators becoming learners in their surrounding communities, learning about community strengths and then utilizing them to teach children in urban schools.

Culturally Relevant Pedagogy

Much of the community oriented pedagogical theory revolves around the concept of culturally relevant pedagogy. As discussed earlier, most teachers in urban schools do not live in the school's neighborhood (keyes & Gregg, 2001). Additionally, a 2005 study by the National Center for Education Information found that 85% of teachers in the United States are White. Urban teachers, in general, will not share the community's or ethnic or racial group's cultural background. In the absence of authentic sharing of culture through shared geographic or racial similarities, teachers will have little knowledge of how to create meaningful curriculum and pedagogy. Therefore, teachers need to learn to connect with the students' communities and cultures in order to better connect with the students. In other words, teachers need to become "culturally relevant."

Put simply, "Culturally relevant teachers utilize students' culture as a vehicle for learning" (Ladson-Billings, 1995, p. 161). By engaging with community to learn the strengths of the community, cultural relevant pedagogy "empowers students intellectually, socially, emotionally, and politically by using cultural referents to impart knowledge, skills, and attitudes" (Ladson-Billings, 1994, p. 18). In other words, instead of merely depositing the cultural capital of society's dominant culture into the children (a la Freire's "banking education," 1970), the culturally relevant teacher actively seeks to learn, understand, and incorporate the community's cultural wealth (Yosso, 2005) and funds of knowledge (Moll et al., 1992).

What characteristics of a teacher would enable a move toward becoming a culturally relevant teacher? Most importantly, the teacher would need to see her or himself as an active participant in the community, encouraging students to do the same. A culturally relevant teacher would learn as much as possible from the community, and draw on that in his or her classroom. The teacher helps students make the connections between their home and community life and the school's curriculum and activities. As Ladson-Billings (1994) explains, the "teacher-student relationship is fluid, humanely equitable, extends to interactions beyond the classroom and into the community" (p. 55). In her study of successful teachers of African American children, Ladson-Billings (1994) notes that "culturally relevant teaching involves cultivation of the relationship beyond the boundaries of the classroom" (p. 62). She relays the stories of teachers who take part in community events such as Girl Scouts, local religious services, and "lunch bunch" with the preparation of culturally-specific foods.

Community Teacher

Similarly, Murrell (2001) proposes a framework for urban education based on the idea of a "community teacher." As he writes, "A community teacher is one who possesses contextualized knowledge of the culture, community, and identity of the children and families he or she serves and draws on this knowledge to create the core teaching practices necessary for effectiveness in diverse setting" (Murrell, 2001, p. 52). Similar to the above discussion of culturally relevant teaching, this will take active participation on the part of the teacher in learning about the community. Murrell's suggested community teacher "is aware of and, when necessary, actively researches the knowledge traditions of the cultures represented among the children, families, ad communities he or she serves" (Murrell, 2001, p. 54).

Murrell (2001) moves beyond the individual teacher's involvement in community, and discusses the creation of "communities of practice." In this concept, all adults who work to improve the lives of children and their families, be it through school, community organizations, or university teacher education programs, take part in shared activities designed at improving lives. Murrell proposes three qualities of a community practice.

1. Collaborative engagement in joint activities, such as curriculum development.
2. A "shared repertoire of practices that are continuously revised in light of experience and inquiry."
3. A commitment to developing structural components to the collaboration, the development of systems that will allow for continuous exchange of shared ideas and shared practices to improve urban education. (p. 42)

Once they have participated in a of community of practice, community teachers can then "draw on a richly contextualized knowledge of culture, community, and identity in their professional work with children and families in diverse urban communities" (p. 4).

A community teacher can be found at the university level as well. In some examples, university faculty and k-12 teachers take part jointly in community events. Examples include university faculty who, along with a school's teachers, take part in "back-to-school" events in the school's neighborhood (Noel, 2010). Another example includes faculty, teachers, community members, and students of all ages and across several educational institutions who participate in the creation and maintenance of cultural community gardens (Hammond et al., 2009).

Connecting: Being There and Developing Trust

The practical educator may now be asking, how can the theories of community strengths and community oriented pedagogy become valued and important part of the functioning of the school's, community's, and university's work? How can these connections across disparate institutions and groups be achieved? What characteristics of the school, community, and university can facilitate the development of these connections?

"Being There" and the "Humility of Practice"

Due to differing levels of real and perceived authority and voice, communities may not readily accept efforts of schools and universities to take a community learning approach to their lives. As Reed (2004) describes:

> Low-income neighborhoods are jaded by the comings and goings of organizations that have no grassroots base in the community…Local residents are weary of seeing new initiatives come and go. They are tired of the disruptions caused by those who live outside the neighborhood who try to offer solutions that, no matter how well intentioned, are not grounded in the realities of the street. (p. 81)

Recognizing this very real possibility, Murrell (2001) introduces the term "humility of practice," with which he reminds us that educators "have to avoid the fatal assumption that they know all they need to know about the culture, values, traditions, and heritages of the people they purportedly serve" (p. 31). When working to connect with a community, teachers, administrators, and faculty must come to recognize that they will be working with organizations, groups, and individuals whose lives are different than their own.

These efforts take not only effort, but also simply time. Murrell's (1991, 2001) concept of teacher education programs "being there" in schools and communities comes into play here. As Murrell (2001) and Reed (2004) both describe, communities ask that teacher education be physically present in schools in order to learn, to show commitment, and to build trust with community members. Community members need to realize that community oriented educators are there, in the community, for the long term.

Rosenberg's (1997) sense of "dwelling" is another way to describe the importance of "being there," of spending time in the community. As Rosenberg describes, "We need to think about what it means for us to 'dwell' in the institution. To ask our students and ourselves to 'dwell' is to ask ourselves to exist in a given place, to fasten our attention, to tarry, to look again. We take root, day after day" (p. 88). With time, commitment, and humility of practice, urban educators can build trust with the community while learning with community members.

Developing Trust

The most important requirement for the development of school-community-university connections is the development of trust. Such disparate organizations and groups need to feel both that they can trust the other, and that the other trusts them.

Hoy and Tschannen-Moran (1999) have identified five facets of trust involved in developing and establishing trust between people and organizations: benevolence, honesty, openness, reliability, and competence. A key thread weaving through these facets of trust is the confidence that one person or organization has in the partner's intentions toward the people and project. As Tschannen-Moran (2004) writes, "Perhaps the most essential ingredient and commonly recognized facet of trust is a sense of caring or benevolence; the confidence that one's well-being or something one cares about will be protected and not harmed by the trusted party" (p. 19).

However, collaborative relationships do not begin with all five facets of trust already in place. Rather, trust builds over time. "Trust is a dynamic phenomenon that takes on a different character at different stages of a relationship. As a relationship develops, trust 'thickens' (Gambetta, 1988)" (Tschannen-Moran & Hoy 2000, p. 570). Several authors describe the stages in developing trust between two institutional partners. First, when partners do not have a professional or personal relationship, they will make a calculation about the worthiness of a potential collaborative partner based on factors such as the amount of risk connected with the collaboration and whether the activities and partners can be monitored (Gambetta, 1988). This calculation of possible trust may be based in part on a trust in the profession; schools and community organizations trust universities in the institutional sense, and vice versa. Since there often are both regulatory and ethical characteristics attached to institutions, these characteristics may be used as part of the determination of trust at this initial level (Bottery, 2003).

Second, as the collaboration begins and activities commence, partners can gauge the repeated activities and level of commitment of their partners. At this stage trust moves beyond speculative calculation and reaches a new level based on knowledge of practice in a common realm (Bottery, 2003; Tschannen-Moran and Hoy, 2000). This is a developing knowledge of individuals' work, commitment, and trustworthiness.

Third, as partners spend time working together, and repeated collaborative activities have been effective, partners come to recognize that they have developed relationships based on shared goals, procedures, and beliefs (Stefkovich & Shapiro, 2002). They come to realize that they can act on behalf of each other, comfortable and confident in the decisions, activities, and outcomes of the partnership.

Once these stages of partnership development have been reached, a nearly authentic partnership can be claimed. Flexibility is a hallmark of the mature partnership that has gone through this process of trust development (Hands, 2005). As challenges inevitably occur when individuals and organizations that may be of a fundamentally different nature interact, a more authentic partnership can expect partners to be able to act with flexibility, to enact change when needed, and to incorporate new community needs and institutional demands.

Types of Programs that Connect
Schools-Communities-Universities

Schools have long utilized organized structures for involving parents in a school's functioning. Parent Teacher Associations (PTAs) were first developed in 1897, founded by the National Congress of Mothers, for the purpose of providing support, information, and resources focused on the education of children. Now variantly called Parent Teacher Organizations (PTOs), this is a well-established and popular mechanism for involving parents in their children's education.

In a more structural format that allows for greater community input into how schools operate, schools now have a variety of options for connecting with families and community members. School Site Councils and English Language Advisory Committees, for instance, serve as a mechanism to bring community feedback into school decision-making. In these structures, either the school administration or the parents or community can propose an idea for school change, and the council or committee, which must include representation from both school and community, must give approval. In this sense, parents have a voice in decision-making at the school. Epstein, Coates, Salinas, Sanders, and Simon (1997) address these differing levels of parent involvement in schools. In their Six Types of Involvement, Epstein et al. layout a continuum that begins with the school serving as the expert, providing information for parents, to the school taking a more community-wide approach, collaborating with community agencies and organizations. The Six Types of Involvement include

1. Parenting: Help all families establish home environments to support children as students.
2. Communicating: Design effective forms of school-to-home and home-to-school communications about school programs and children's progress.
3. Volunteering: Recruit and organize parent help and support.
4. Learning at Home: Provide information and ideas to families about how to help students at home with homework and other curriculum-related activities, decisions, and planning.
5. Decision Making: Include parents in school decisions, developing parent leaders and representatives.
6. Collaborating with Community: Identify and integrate resources and services from the community to strengthen school programs, family practices, and student learning and development.

However, PTAs, School Site Councils, English Language Advisory Committees, and Epstein et al.'s (1997) framework for involvement all tend to operate with the perspective that parents must become more connected with the school, in order for their children to increase their academic and general educational achievement. None of these require that the school's personnel – teachers, staff, administration – take the time to learn about the community's strengths, its "funds of knowledge" and "community cultural wealth." They don't ask teachers to work toward becoming a part of the community, only that parents work toward becoming a part of the school. What this chapter proposes, rather, is that the school's teachers, staff, and administration become more connected with the community to increase children's general educational achievement. And extending this further, this chapter proposes that a nearby university should be partnered in this collaborative effort to connect more strongly with the school and its community.

Service Learning

A goal of urban universities in recent years has been to make stronger connections to the urban communities in which they are located (e.g. Coalition of Urban and Metropolitan Universities, Great City Universities, Urban Education Service Corps). One approach to developing connections has been through service learning, "which integrates meaningful community service with instruction and reflection to enrich the learning experience, teach civic responsibility, and strengthen communities" (Learn and Serve America's National Service-Learning Clearinghouse, http://www.servicelearning.org). University students may be assigned to provide service to a school, a community organization, a social service agency, a health provider, or a non-profit business. The key that differentiates service learning from other forms of service, such as volunteering, is that in a university model, university students undertake a service project not only to participate in helping community and becoming civic-minded, but also to gain experiences directly related to their coursework. Students are expected to provide some analysis of their service experience, through reflective journals, through completing a survey about their experiences, and sometimes through presenting their new understandings at a conference. Important to service learning is that there is a mutual agreement between the university and the school or community partner regarding the purpose and experiences for both the university students and the people served.

Service learning has been repeatedly shown to generate positive outcomes for university students as well as communities (Astin , Vogelgesang, Ikeda, & Yee 2000; Boyle-Baise & Sleeter, 2000; Eyler and Giles 1999; Moely, McFarland, Miron, Mercer, & Ilustre 2002).

Professional Development Schools

Service learning has the goal of connecting university students with schools or communities, and has resulted in positive outcomes for both students and communities. Another type of program, designed not only to connect schools-communities-universities but also to develop collaborative structures resulting in professional development opportunities, curriculum development, and community engagement is called the Professional Development School (PDS). The PDS model aims to transform entire schools. The goals of a PDS are:

1. Enhance k-12 student learning.
2. Improve field experiences for pre-service teachers.
3. Engage K-16 educators in continuous and targeted professional development.
4. Use action research to inform teaching and learning in schools. (Wong & Glass, 2009, p. 8)

In urban Professional Development Schools, where the vision tends to revolve around social justice and equity for the underrepresented (Abdal-Haqq, 1998), there may be a fifth goal: "to draw heavily on the expertise, experience, and knowledge of the local learning community – pupils, teachers, administrators, and community members – while purposefully integrating university actors (student teachers and instructors) into this learning community" (p. 11). And finally, as Wong and Glass (2009) add, "Advanced PDSs also tend to include participation from legislative/political bodies, community organizations, and teachers' associations" (p. 8). The Professional Development School initiative is one that attempts to fully connect schools-communities-universities in a transformation of the educational system at-large.

Community Organizing

The ultimate purpose of connecting urban schools-communities-universities is to transform the lives and education of children who reside in urban communities. As discussed previously in this chapter, this process can involves building trust among disparate groups, and can thus take time to develop. There are some basic activities that must take place for change to occur. Oakes, Rogers, and Lipton (2006) explain that there are three different levels involved in creating change: "building relationships, developing common understandings, and taking action" (p. 98). An excellent strategy for putting relationships and understandings into action is through collaborative community organizing.

In his chapter "Why Should Urban Educators Care about Community Organizing to Reform Schools?", Giles (2006) lays out the basics of community organizing. "In organizing approaches to improve schools, a local community organization brings together parents, members of congregations, community residents, youth, and educators, for the purpose of identifying and taking action on issues that interfere with teaching and learning in their schools" (p. 36). However, community organizing is not a simple affair. Due to differential access to equitable systems of education, health care, and political participation, not all participants in a school-community-university partnership will have equal position, power, or status. Daniel (2007) recommends a new definition of community that addresses these more critical aspects of the school-community-university relationship:

> the community to which I refer is a group of persons wherein the members remain aware of the intersections of oppressions, the multiple relational dynamics inherent in that space, and are continually working at making the community a comprehensive learning space for all of its members" (p. 32).

Although there may be both real and perceived differences in equity, all members of the school-community-university partnership can work together to create a newly revived urban education. As Giles (2006) writes, a critical approach to transformation is needed to guide these efforts. In making connections, not only is trust developed, but differential access to power structures and equitable systems need to be addressed for meaningful change to occur. "Through these relationships of greater trust, people also develop the *power*, or "ability to act" together to transform their schools and communities, and often, their sense as individuals that 'they count' in their neighborhoods and work-places" (Giles, p. 36). Finally, then,

> Community organizing initiatives offer an antidote to educators' sense of powerlessness and alienation through their strategy of creating a relational culture – as opposed to a bureaucratic culture – in the public schools in which they are involved. Through their individual and small-group meetings with educators, parents, youth, and community leaders, these organizations both seek participants' ideas about their schools, and build relationships of trust and reciprocity among participants, which they eventually can draw upon to make positive changes in their schools. (Giles, p. 41)

Three Exemplary Programs

Three exemplary programs at Sacramento State (California State University, Sacramento), will help to illustrate what connecting schools-communities-universities looks like in practice. In these three examples, the best of the previously discussed philosophies and practices can be found.

UTEC

The Sacramento State Urban Teacher Education Center (UTEC), created in 2004 in response to the call for universities to be better connected to their local schools and communities, is a community-oriented, field-based program for teacher preparation designed to prepare future educators for urban schools and communities. To better achieve this goal, UTEC moved off the university campus and into the very low income, very diverse urban Jedediah Smith Elementary School (94% free-and-reduced lunch, 56% African American, 94% children of color) that serves children from two public housing complexes. By locating itself in, and slowly becoming integrated into, the urban school and community, students and faculty have been able to gain a better understanding of the realities of urban education, including the social, political, and economic conditions impacting the lives and education of urban children and their families (Noel, 2006). As part of this work, both teacher education students and faculty get an in-depth understanding of the community agencies, community groups, and neighborhood efforts to provide support for children, their families, and their schools, as well as take part in the important work of these groups. Concurrently, students and faculty also learn about the community strengths within racially, ethnically, and linguistically diverse families and communities and learn how to draw on that within their own work as educators. And finally, community members, and school faculty and staff are able to serve as co-educators with the university faculty, with community members sometimes participating in university class sessions, and sometimes leading after-school programs, co-coordinating the efforts of the university students.

Following here are some of the activities undertaken by UTEC, activities that connect school-community-university.

Family Resource Center. In collaboration with J School's assistant principal, the UTEC coordinator and student teachers created the Family Resource Center in spring of 2006. UTEC students served coffee to parents, assisted with computer access, and operated the children's book give-away section and the parent book exchange. This center now serves as a classroom for a parenting workshop offered by the university and a G.E.D. course offered by the school district. It also serves as the after-school home to the community-run community/UTEC collaborative tutoring/mentoring program.

J School Library. J School did not have a librarian in 2005-2006, so the library could not be utilized by students. UTEC student teachers opened and operated the library during three lunchtime periods each week during the spring of 2006. Now that the school has a part-time librarian, UTEC student teachers currently assist in the library, re-shelving books and creating bulletin boards.

University Field Trip for 6th graders. Consistent with J School's focus on making students aware of the importance of attending college, the UTEC coordinator and student teachers helped organize and lead a field trip of 5th and 6th graders to the university in the spring of 2007.

Family Literacy Night. UTEC student teachers helped J School's Reading Coach and several classroom teachers plan, prepare, and facilitate a Family Literacy Night in the spring of 2007 and 2008.

Panthers Tutoring Center. This after school tutoring/mentoring program is a collaborative between the community and the UTEC program. Originally located within the adjacent public housing complex, the tutoring center was created and is operated by two men who grew up in the neighborhood, moved out to get their college degrees, and now give back to their former community by running this center. UTEC student teachers assisted as tutors/mentors for this program. Currently, the program has moved onto the school's campus, with UTEC students serving as tutors/mentors for the community-led Polynesian Dance Troupe.

"Community Liaison". UTEC's coordinator took a sabbatical during the fall 2006 semester to serve as an unofficial "community liaison." She spent time meeting with families, learning more about life in the neighborhoods, sitting in on social service agency meetings, and working to build closer connections between J School, UTEC, and the neighboring housing complexes – connecting school-community-university.

Statistics from surveys of student teachers in the traditional teacher education programs at Sacramento State, compared to student teachers in the school-community based UTEC, show evidence of increased motivation in UTEC students to teach in urban schools (35% vs 67%). Twice the number of students in UTEC desire to teach in areas of poverty (33% vs 65%). And in a pre- and post-program survey, UTEC student teachers increased their desire to work with families and communities when they become teachers as a result of their participation in UTEC (increased from 54% to 95%). Thus UTEC appears to be an effective program for developing within students the desire to create school-community-connections (Noel, 2006).

In an evaluation of the first five years of the UTEC program, teachers, staff members, administrators, and community members took part in surveys, interviews, and focus groups regarding their level of comfort with UTEC becoming a part of the school and community. Ninety-five percent of all participants in all evaluation instruments agreed that having UTEC at the school benefits both the school's children and the university UTEC students (Noel, 2010).

The Sacramento State Urban Teacher Education has won both state and local recognition. UTEC was the recipient of the 2008 California Quality Education Partnership Award for Distinguished Service to Children and the Preparation of Teachers. It also received a 2007 Special Recognition from the Sacramento City Unified School District for Dedication and Commitment to Educating Teachers in an Urban School District. UTEC was nominated for these awards and recognition by both school administration and by the neighborhood community organization, demonstrating how a positive collaboration between school-community-university can be valued by each group of participants.

65th Street Corridor

The 65th Street Corridor Community Collaborative Project (the "Project") is a high-impact and multi-component community mobilization effort aimed at increasing student academic achievement, fostering student leadership, and improving parent participation for immigrant children living in neighborhoods where gang violence, a lack of access to resources and low civic engagement create a need for innovative, culturally competent strategies (Sobredo, Kim-Ju, Figueroa, Mark, & Fabionar, 2008). The Project serves 7th-12th grade schools in Sacramento's 65th Street corridor, a low-income and diverse community adjacent to the University campus. Sacramento State faculty and students are actively engaged in the Project, working with administrators, teachers, students, and parents from these schools to build a more healthy, engaged and vibrant community. This ongoing interaction between Sacramento State and the 65th Street corridor creates a venue for community concerns to be voiced at the grassroots level. Furthermore, the Project's strong partnership with the Sacramento City Unified School District and its Student and Family Support Center Healthy Start program allow for ongoing educational and social issues, such as academic success, emotional health, violence prevention, and family strength, to be addressed in a continuous and effective manner in a rapidly changing community.

The Project, through its many programs, has developed into a comprehensive model of change for local residents and students in the 65th Street corridor. Its focus on creating educational pathways, developing student leadership, and building local communities corresponds to the Sacramento State's *Destination 2010* initiative, particularly the goal of "Recognizing diversity as vital to developing the New California."

The Project consists of four programmatic components, (a) the Tutoring and Mentoring Program, (b) the Student Bridge Program, (c) the Parent Partnership Program, and (d) the Action Research Program conducted at two "at-risk" schools, Will C. Wood Middle School (WW) and Hiram Johnson High School (HJ), in the 65th Street corridor. The Tutoring and Mentoring Program allows university tutors/mentors to serve as a resource in classrooms to increase the standardized test scores of 7th-12th grade students in Math and English classes. The Student Bridge Program is a series of individual field trips for 7th-12th grade students to build a "college-going culture" at each school and conduct workshops that provide them with college information and skills (e.g., financial aid, application process, student life, and academic expectations). The goals are to increase the number of students who apply for and receive acceptance in higher education. The Parent Partnership Program consists of field trips and workshops that provide opportunities for parents to not only learn about college preparation and higher education, but also to communicate their concerns about college preparation for their children. The goal is to provide support for parents to assist their children to have greater academic success. The Action Research Program involves a cadre of university service-learners who gather basic information about WW and HJ and the Project and disseminate this information to various individual and organizational stakeholders. These students serve as advocates on behalf of the schools and the Project to individuals outside of the specific targeted groups, e.g., community members, businesses, and politicians residing or serving in those areas. They are also able to more directly link their actions to public issues such as those that impact underrepresented and disadvantaged schools and groups.

The Project has been extremely successful in past years, providing effective outreach and service-learning efforts that promote tolerance and inclusion to a culturally and linguistically diverse urban population (Sobredo et al., 2008).

Science for Social Responsibility Program

The Science for Social Responsibility Program developed as a result of the high-level school-community-university collaborative of the Spanish-English Developmental Bilingual Department (SEDBED) at Bowling Green Charter Complex (elementary school) and the Sacramento State Bilingual/Multicultural Education Department (BMED) (Lum, Aguirre, Martinez, Campa-Rodriguez, & Ultreras, 2009). Developed as part of a Professional Development School model, the purpose was for k-12 teachers, university teacher educators, and university pre-service teachers earning their teaching credential

> to develop a social justice-oriented science curriculum that would engage pupils in high-quality science education, candidates and teachers in 'best practices' science teaching, university faculty members in authentic integration of theory and practice, and community members in supporting the pupils, their school, and their own community. (Lum et al., p. 69).

As the participants explain, "We believed that social justice-oriented curriculum, positive relationships with the community, and quality teaching can all occur interconnectedly" (Lum et al., p. 75).

In an effort to make the science curriculum more directly reflect both the local neighborhood issues and the approach of Cesar Chavez, the SEDBED learned that nearly 90% of the Latino families within the program had one or more family member with diabetes. Armed with this socially relevant knowledge, the elementary school (SEDBED) and the university (BMED) "began to construct the building blocks of our partnership for science for social responsibility" (Lum et al., 2009, p. 76). The first step was discovering community and culturally relevant science issues. The second step involved university faculty and SEDBED teachers developing a science curriculum that involved students at all grade levels in socially relevant health issues.

- Kindergarten and 1st grade curriculum focuses on fitness.
- 2nd grade emphasizes dental hygiene.
- 3rd grade examines nutrition.
- 4th grade focuses on diabetes and diabetes prevention. Students tied their learning to community by interviewing members of the community affected by diabetes and then conducting inquiry-based science lessons. As a final product, 4th graders produced a brochure that could be disseminated to the community.
- 5th graders focused on heart disease awareness, conducting research on the heart and heart disease. They developed a PowerPoint presentation as their final project.
- 6th graders focused on the human brain, and particularly the effects of drugs. Students in the 6th grade demonstrated their learning by writing and producing a play that they then video recorded and edited into a final, polished piece. (Lum et al., p. 76)

At the same time, pre-service teachers in the university's BMED program studied with classroom teachers at the school, learning the science and the methods for connecting with community around meaningful science issues. The resulting event each year is a heath fair, which is a collaboration among teachers, elementary school students, university professors, university students, community members, and various community agencies and organizations. Held at Bowling Green Charter Complex, a number of learning and screening stations are available for community members to get health information. Some of the learning stations are staffed by community health groups, in multiple languages represented within the community. During the health fair, university students, 6th grade students, and community members, supervised by a community medical doctor, screen for cholesterol, blood pressure, and diabetes. Community members learn about heart disease from 5th graders' PowerPoint presentations, and about diabetes from the 4th graders' brochures. Participants also watch a drug awareness play presented by the 6th graders, and watch K-3 students singing and dancing to tunes about health and nutrition. Additional activities include nutrition and physical fitness games, a tour of an ambulance, and nutritious snacks. Approximately 300-400 people are served annually by the health fair.

Students in this very diverse, urban elementary school have expressed an increased awareness of the possibility of science in their futures. In 2003, fourth grade students who were in their first year of this science for social responsibility program were surveyed about their feelings about science and science careers. Surveyed again two years later, in the 6th grade, students showed a change in their beliefs. In 9 out of the 10 survey questions, students increased their interest and self-confidence in science. Examples include:

Question #1: I can see myself as a scientist when I become a grown up. Scores increased from 12% to 24%

Question #4: I can see myself as a science teacher when I become a group up. Scores increased from 35% to 49%.

Question #9: I feel comfortable presenting science information to grown ups. Scores increased from 12% to 81%. (Lum et al., 2009, p. 80).

Conclusion

Pedro Noguera (2003) relates the story of working with teachers in a very wealthy Northern California county, whose school had experienced a shift in demographics from a largely White, wealthy population to one of 90% recent immigrants. Simultaneously, the school's test scores had dropped, there was a higher drop-out rate, with a lowered rate of college attendance. As he probed to learn how teachers explained these changes, Noguera documents that the teachers believed "the students came from a culture that did not value education. They believed that their students simply were conforming to the low expectations they had learned at home" (p. 47). Questioning further, Noguera discovered that

> As it turned out, most of the teachers knew very little about the lives of their students outside of school, and no one present could even say where most of the students lived…Several of the teachers said that they had heard their students talk about a 'zone' located near a canal, and they believed that was where most of the students lived. However, not one of the teachers present had ever visited the area. (p. 48)

This chapter has provided a discussion of theories, strategies, and initiatives designed to change the perspectives and practices of teachers like those described by Noguera. By proposing more authentic connections between schools-communities-universities, this paper encourages urban educators to both learn about and incorporate the community's daily and cultural experiences into both k-12 and university education of children.

This approach is not easy, and it takes time. To begin, by simply being there, taking root within the community, trust can begin to develop. Understanding theories of community strengths, including cultural capital, funds of knowledge, and community cultural wealth, gives a starting point for interacting with community members and organizations. Once an understanding of community strengths is gained, utilizing a community oriented pedagogy such as culturally relevant teaching and serving as a community teacher can improve students' experiences in schools. In joining together in collaborative efforts such as Professional Development Schools or community organizing, some of the political and social inequities, such as differential access to power and to change opportunities, can be altered at the individual, community, and structural levels. With this understanding of community strengths, utilization of community-oriented pedagogy, and collaborative large-scale initiatives connecting schools-communities-universities, schools and universities can gain validity within the communities where they do their work. All partners can move toward more authentic connections and collaborations.

Urban education is difficult, but it is full of possibilities. As Kincheloe et al. (2006) write, "Philosophically, urban education presents an enormous challenge to our imaginations and suggests that we have a moral responsibility not only to transform but also to be hopeful about the possibility for transformation" (p. xix).

References

Abdal-Haqq, I. (1998). *Professional Development Schools: Weighing the evidence.* Thousand Oaks, CA: Corwin Press.

Astin, A., Vogelgesang, L, Ikeda, E. & Yee, J. (2000). *How service-learning affects students.* Los Angeles: University of California, Los Angeles, Higher Education Research Institute.

Bottery, M. (2003). The management and mismanagement of trust. *Educational Management & Administration,* **32**(3), 245-261.

Bourdieu, P. & Passeron, J. (1977). *Reproduction in education, society and culture.* London: Sage.

Boyle-Baise, M. & Sleeter, C. E. (2000, Spring). Community service learning for multicultural education. *Educational Foundations,* 1-18.

Brooks, K. & Karathanos, K. (2009). Building on the cultural and linguistic capital of English Learner (EL) students. *Multicultural Education,* **16**(4), 47-51.

Daniel, B. J. (2007). Developing educational collectives and networks: Moving beyond the boundaries of "community in urban education. In: R. P. Solomon, & D. N. R. Sekayi, (Eds.), *Urban teacher education and teaching: Innovative practices for diversity and social justice* (31-47). Mahwah, NJ: Lawrence Erlbaum Associates.

Epstein, J. L., Coates, L., Salinas, K. C., Sanders, M. G. & Simon, B. S. (1997). *School, family, and community partnerships: Your handbook for action.* Thousand Oaks, CA: Corwin Press.

Eyler, J. & Giles, D. E. Jr. (1999). *Where's the learning in service-learning?* San Francisco, CA: Jossey-Bass.

Franklin, V. P. (2002). Introduction: Cultural capital and African-American education. *Journal of African-American History*, **87**, 175-181.

Freire, P. (1970). *Pedagogy of the oppressed.* New York: Continuum Publishing Company.

Gambetta, D. (1988). Can we trust trust? In D. Gambetta (Ed.), *Trust: Making and breaking cooperative relations* (213-219). Oxford: Basil Blackwell.

Giles, H. C. (2006). Why should urban educators care about community organizing to reform schools? In J. L. Kincheloe, k. hayes, K. Rose, & P. M. Anderson (Eds.), *The Praeger handbook of urban education: Vol. 1* (35-46). Westport, CT: Greenwood Press.

González, N., Moll, L. C. & Amanti, C.. (2005). *Funds of knowledge: Theorizing practices in households, communities, and classrooms.* Mahway, NJ: Lawrence Erlbaum Associates.

Hammond, L., Lambating, J. G., Beus, M., Winckel, P., Camm, J. F. & Ferlazzo, L. (2009). Floating boats and solar ovens: Involving candidates in science, mathematics, and technology learning communities. In P. L. Wong & R. D. Glass (Eds.), *Prioritizing urban children, teachers and schools through Professional Development Schools* (43-67). Albany, NY: SUNY Press.

Hands, C. (2005). It's who you know and what you know: The process of creating partnerships between schools and communities. *The School Community Journal*, **15**(2), 63-84.

Hoy, W. K. & Tchannen-Moran, M. (1999). Five facets of trust: An empirical confirmation in urban elementary schools. *Journal of School Leadership*, **9**, 184-208.

Keyes, M. C. & Gregg, S. (2001). *School-community connections: A literature review.* Charleston, SC: AEL Inc.

Kincheloe, J. L., hayes, k., Rose, K. & Anderson, P. M. (2006). Introduction: The power of hope in the trenches. In J. L. Kincheloe, k. hayes, K. Rose, & P. M. Anderson (Eds.). *The Praeger handbook of urban education (vol. 1, xvii-xliii).* Westport, CT: Greenwood Press.

Ladson-Billings, G. (1994). *The dreamkeepers: Successful teachers of African American children.* San Francisco: Jossey Bass.

Ladson-Billings, G. (1995). Toward a theory of culturally relevant pedagogy. *American Educational Research Journal*, **32**(3), 465-491.

Lum, C. A., Aguirre, E. M., Martinez, R., Campa-Rodriguez, M. & Ultreras, R. (2009). Science for social responsibility. In P. L. Wong & R. D. Glass (Eds.), *Prioritizing urban children, teachers and schools through Professional Development Schools* (69-85). Albany, NY: SUNY Press.

Moely, B. E., McFarland, M., Miron, D., Mercer, S. & Ilustre, V. (2002). Changes in college students' attitudes and intentions for civic involvement as a function of service-learning experiences. *Michigan Journal of Community Service Learning*, **8**(2), 15-26.

Moll, L. C., Amanti, C., Neff, D. & González, N. (1992). Funds of knowledge for teaching: Using a qualitative approach to connect homes and classrooms. *Theory into Practice*, **31**(2), 132-41.

Murrell, P. C., Jr. (1991). Cultural politics in education: What's missing in the preparation of African-American teachers? In M. Foster (Ed.), *Qualitative investigations into schools and schooling: Readings on equal education* (*Vol. 11*, 205-225). New York: AMS Press.

Murrell, P. C., Jr. (2001). *The community teacher: A new framework for effective urban teaching.* New York: Teachers College Press.

National Center for Education Information. (2005). *Profile of teachers in the U.S. 2005.* Washington, DC: Author.

Noel, J. (2006). Integrating a new teacher education center into a school and its community. *Journal of Urban Learning, Teaching, and Research, 2*, 197-205.

Noel, J. (2010, April). *Evaluating a school-community based urban teacher education center: Impact, integration, and trust.* Paper presented at the Annual Conference of the American Educational Research Association, Denver, CO.

Noguera, P. (2003). *City schools and the American dream: Reclaiming the promise of public education.* New York: Teachers College Press.

Oakes, G. L. St. C. (2009). An empirical test of five prominent explanations for the Black-White academic performance gap. *Social Psychology of Education: An International Journal, 12*(4), 415-441.

Oakes, J., Rogers, J. & Lipton, M. (2006). *Learning power: Organizing for education and justice.* New York: Teachers College Press.

Reed, W. A. (2004). A tree grows in Brooklyn: Schools of education as brokers of social capital in low-income neighborhoods. In J. L. Kincheloe, A. Bursztyn, & S. R. Steinberg (Eds.), *Teaching teachers: Building a quality school of urban education* (65-90). New York: Peter Lang.

Rodriguez, L. F. (2009). Dialoguing, cultural capital, and student engagement: Toward a hip hop pedagogy in the high school and university classroom. *Equity & Excellence in Education, 42*(1), 20-35.

Sobredo, J., Kim-Ju, G., Figueroa, J., Mark, G. & Fabionar, J. (2008). An ethnic studies model of community mobilization: Collaborative partnership with a high risk public high school. *American Journal of Preventive Medicine, 34*(Suppl. 2), S82-S88.

Stefkovich, J. & Shapiro, J. P. (2002). Deconstructing communities: Educational leaders and their ethical decision-making processes. In P. T. Begley & O. Johansson (Eds.), *The ethical dimensions of school leadership* (77-87). Dordrecht, The Netherlands: Kluwer Academic Publishers.

Tschannen-Moran, M. (2004). *Trust matters: Leadership for successful schools.* San Francisco: Jossey-Bass.

Tschannen-Moran, M. & W. K. Hoy. 2000. A multidisciplinary analysis of the nature, meaning, and measurement of trust. *Review of Educational Research, 71*, 547-593.

Vélez-Ibáñez, C. & Greenberg, J. (2005). Formation and transformation of funds of knowledge. In N. González, L. C. Moll, & C. Amanti (Eds.), *Funds of knowledge: Theorizing practices in households, communities, and classrooms* (47-69). Mahway, NJ: Lawrence Erlbaum Associates.

Wong, P. L. & Glass, R. D. (2009). The Equity Network: The contextual and theoretical frameworks for urban Professional Development Schools. In Pia L. Wong & Ronald D. Glass (Eds.), *Prioritizing urban children, teachers and schools through Professional Development Schools* (1-25). Albany, NY: SUNY Press.

Yosso, T. J. (2005). Whose culture has capital? A critical race theory discussion of community cultural wealth. *Race, Ethnicity and Education*, **8**(1), 69-91.

Zipin, L. (2009). Dark funds of knowledge, deep funds of pedagogy: Exploring boundaries between lifeworlds and schools. *Discourse: Studies in the Cultural Politics of Education*, **30**(3), 317-331.

In: Progress in Education, Volume 21
Editor: Robert V. Nata, pp. 127-143

ISBN: 978-1-61728-115-0
© 2011 Nova Science Publishers, Inc.

Chapter 6

GETTING OUT OF THE FIELD AND INTO THE FOREST: SUSTAINABLE MANAGEMENT PRACTICES FOR CAMPUS LANDSCAPES AND OTHER URBAN SITES

Linda Chalker-Scott

WSU Puyallup Research
and Extension Center, 2606 W Pioneer, Puyallup, WA 98371, USA

Abstract

Best management practices (BMPs) for urban landscapes, including school grounds and college campuses, are often based on production agriculture methods rather than current research in the field of urban horticulture. In particular, the overuse of organic amendments in landscape situations results in soil subsidence, poor plant health, and nutrient overload, which in turn can impact aquatic systems downstream. Instead of using a crop production model for managing urban soils, we should mimic natural processes seen in forest ecosystems. This chapter will outline the problems inherent in short-term (crop production model) management practices in urban landscapes that contribute to the shortened life span of landscape trees and shrubs. A new paradigm for sustainable landscape management will be presented based on the relatively young science of urban horticulture. The application of these site-appropriate methods to school and college landscapes provides ideal educational opportunities for school children, college students, and neighborhood volunteers. Not only will these BMPs improve the health and sustainability of soil and plant systems, they will also increase landscape resistance to invasive species and opportunistic pests. The result – a community-managed landscape requiring less fertilizer, fewer pesticides, and less labor – represents a truly sustainable model.

Introduction

Sustainably-managed landscapes have a number of environmental, economic, and human benefits that far outweigh the costs associated with installing and managing them. These benefits can be sustained for many decades if landscapes are installed and managed properly, but are quickly lost in improperly managed systems.

Environmental. Though most would accept on face value that sustainable landscapes have environmental benefits, it is useful to review them. Organically-mulched soils are protected from erosion, runoff, and compaction and boast increased fertility, improved aeration, and enhanced biodiversity of beneficial soil organisms. Healthy soils support equally healthy landscapes, whose presence can be used to improve microclimate (e.g., heat and wind reduction), reduce air and noise pollution, and support a diverse community of insects, birds and other animals. Sustainably-managed landscape trees and shrubs also require fewer pesticides and fertilizers, and their roots serve to reduce stormwater runoff and thus protect aquatic habitats from soil-borne contaminants. These environmental services, if converted to an economic value, would likely be worth hundreds of thousands (if not millions) of dollars to the typical college or school.

Economic. In addition to the environmental services provided by healthy, functional landscapes, there are other economic values to consider. These include reduced heating and cooling bills, reduced labor costs associated with pest and fertility management, and reduced costs for environmental cleanup. Like the environmental services provided by plants, these economic advantages are unquestioned, but their absolute dollar value is rarely determined and the cost savings remain unclear.

Human. Increasingly, the sociological benefits of sustainable landscapes are recognized, from the individual to community level [e.g., 1]. Diverse, healthy landscapes hold great aesthetic appeal, and physical activity within these landscapes improves personal health and well-being. Furthermore, such landscapes encourage individuals to interact with their neighbors and the larger community, which can often include schools and higher education institutions. [2 Thomas, 2005]

Thus, universities and nearby K-12 schools are ideal settings for demonstrating sustainable landscapes [3 Calhoun and Cortese, 2006]. Capstone courses can be combined with service learning to create practical, problem-solving experiences for highly trained, multi-disciplinary teams of students [4 Cahill and Chalker-Scott, 2002; 5 Chalker-Scott and Cahill, 2002]. Not only do these projects serve as significant portfolio additions for students searching for employment, they are also cost-effective ways of enhancing the aesthetics and ecological functionality of campus and school grounds. University and outside community members are more likely to perceive institutions as truly committed to sustainability when the evidence is literally in front of their feet.

Though the desire for sustainable landscapes has permeated educational institutions, the *successful* implementation of these landscapes has not. There are three principal reasons for this:

1. Schools, colleges and universities, both public and private, routinely accept the low-bid estimate from outside contractors on new landscape installations. As this chapter will demonstrate, *installing* landscapes correctly can take longer and cost more than doing it poorly. If educational institutions continue to follow the low-bid model, their new landscapes are not likely to thrive and may require frequent treatment with fertilizers and pesticides and costly plant replacement.

2. The practices followed by most landscape installation and management contractors are based on traditional production of agricultural crops. These practices are not appropriate for permanent installations of landscape trees and shrubs; more appropriate practices are evolving from the relatively new fields of urban horticulture and arboriculture.

3. Faculty expertise (i.e. faculty with academic and practical knowledge of sustainable landscape management) is underutilized, if used at all. Instead, universities and schools often rely on consultants or others with only a superficial understanding of urban horticulture. This approach exemplifies Patton's [6], and important information." For example, in an otherwise excellent article on sustainable campuses, Moomaw [7] states "A number of universities and colleges in the southwestern United States are growing water-conserving desert plants, rather than lawns and plantings more appropriate to rainy Seattle, to create a more sustainable aesthetic." An urban horticulturist would be quick to point out that turf and other plant materials with high irrigation needs are at odds with sustainability efforts anywhere; an urban horticulturist in Seattle would also point out that Seattle is not rainy in the summer when water demand is the highest. Likewise, Conroy [8] equates "indigenous" with "low-maintenance," when in fact many native plants are not well adapted to urban conditions [9 Chalker-Scott, 2009] and require more care than well-adapted, noninvasive, introduced species. Furthermore, Conroy [8] states that "where codes permit, graywater (wastewater from tars, showers, washing machines or other equipment not involving human waste or food processing) also can be used [for landscape irrigation]," completely ignoring the negative effect contaminated water can have on landscape soils and plantings. Lovell and Johnston [10] maintain that urban landscapes could be improved by "incorporating theoretical and applied principles from the fields of landscape ecology, agroecology, and ecological design," yet completely ignore the central role of applied plant and soil sciences. Finally, some college campuses consider their landscapes environmentally sustainable [11 Abercrombie, 2005], but embrace products and practices with no scientifically-documented value, representing instead a waste of energy and resources.

Landscape failure is endemic in urban areas, yet evidence remains largely anecdotal. However, tree longevity statistics indicate typical trees live 25 to 30 years in heavily used city parks and 12 to 18 years along suburban street rights-of-way, while the trees in the small planting holes cut into the sidewalks and parking lots of large cities are replaced every 3 to 4 years [12 Perry 1984]. Certified arborists and urban horticulturists agree that the leading cause of death of urban trees and shrubs is poor selection, installation, and/or management. We need a new paradigm for the sustainable management of permanent landscapes, modeled after a forest ecosystem rather than a crop production system. The best management practices (BMPs) described briefly in this chapter are valid for urban sites regardless of scale and can be applied equally to ornamental, native, and restoration plantings. [Further details on these practices can be found in *Sustainable Landscapes and Gardens: good science – practical application* [13 Chalker-Scott, ed., 2009] and in a series of on-line columns (http://www.theinformedgardener.com).]

Sustainable Installation and Management of Permanent Landscapes

I. Site Analysis (Adapted from [14] Chalker-Scott, 2009)

A successful, sustainable landscape depends on the assessment of the environmental conditions, many of which are not inherently obvious and require careful scrutiny.

Soils: The physical and chemical characteristics of the soil on site must be known prior to plant selection and site preparation. Most campus soils will have little in common with whatever native soil(s) used to be on site. Soil textural analysis, bulk density, organic matter content, pH, and nutrient composition will guide selection of appropriate plants for the site.

Water: Natural water availability can vary dramatically even in small landscapes. Water movement is affected by site slope, soil type, soil compaction, presence of hardscaped surfaces, and other above- and below-ground characteristics. Soil testing will help determine water availability, as will an easily-performed field percolation test. Irrigation sources should also be considered at this time in terms of availability and water quality. For instance, use of gray or recycled water can introduce salts and other minerals that can impose a secondary drought stress on susceptible plants and such landscapes need to feature drought-tolerant species.

Temperature: Temperature gradients should be assessed, especially on urban campuses. Urban areas experience the "heat island" phenomenon, which results in higher levels of water loss from the soil and plants. Surfaces such as asphalt that absorb sunlight and release heat further exacerbate this problem. Consider aspect differences: in the northern hemisphere north-facing landscapes are cooler than those facing south but will also be more likely to freeze in the winter.

Light: Light levels in urban environments are significantly different from those found in nature. Many of the light-related disorders seen in landscape plants can be avoided by proper analysis of light conditions prior to installation. Seasonal variability in the amount of light (the photoperiod) needs to be considered as well as the angle of the sun, which is steeper in the summer. For instance, north-facing landscapes in the winter receive little to no direct sunlight, and the photoperiod is quite short. By summer, day length has doubled and the sun's angle now allows light to reach areas previously shaded. Light availability is further influenced by the presence or absence of leaves on deciduous trees, so their impacts also need to be considered, especially as new or existing plantings mature and reduce light levels further.

Urban areas also experience significant light pollution, which serves to disrupt a plant's ability to determine seasonal changes. Plants key in on relative amounts of light and dark, interpreting long days as "summer" and short days as "winter." Urban lights, especially sodium halide and other high-intensity sources, artificially lengthen the photoperiod so that many plants perceive an endless summer. Such plants are not able to enter dormancy and become cold hardy. This is commonly seen in trees near street lights, where the branches closest to the light source retain their green color long into the fall until the leaves eventually succumb to cold temperatures without turning color first. Native trees and those adapted to similar climates are not significantly hurt by this phenomenon and need to be specified for such landscapes in place of less cold hardy species.

Wind: Summer winds will increase evapotranspiration from the leaves; winter winds will decrease the air temperature and promote freezing; and offshore winds from oceans or brackish waters will deposit salt on foliage. All three of these phenomena can injure sensitive plants through heat-, freeze- and salt-induced drought. Thus, prevailing wind directions on site must be considered in landscape design planning.

Biotic factors: Be aware of regionally significant diseases and pests, including rats and other urbanized pests, when selecting plant species.

II. *Plant Selection* (Adapted from [9] Chalker-Scott, 2009)

Plant materials selected for a campus landscape are more than just design elements: the appearance, functions, and environmental characteristics of a landscape will change as plant materials establish and mature. It is critical to the sustainability of any campus landscape to consider the ecological appropriateness of species selected for a site. Too often materials are selected that quickly outgrow their space or become invasive, thus requiring intensive management to control or replace. Thus, there are plant selection criteria that extend far beyond aesthetics.

Landscape function: Before appropriate plants can be selected, their desired function(s) must be determined:

- Screening – visual and/or noise control
- Environmental modification – light, temperature, humidity, wind
- Behavioral modification – deterring animals, pedestrians, criminal activity
- Wildlife habitat – birds, butterflies
- Erosion control – slopes, sandy soils
- Groundcover/living mulch – turf alternatives, natural weed control

Once function has been determined, lists of appropriate plant species will be more clearly defined.

Ecological appropriateness: As discussed earlier, environmental conditions of the site are important to assess prior to planting. Once known, these conditions will again help to formulate lists of plants most appropriate to the site and thus most sustainable over the lifetime of the landscape.

The cause du jour in sustainable landscapes is the use of native plants (e.g., [17 Kermath, 2007; 18] Womack, 2009). In theory, this seems to make perfect sense: native species are adapted to local climates, soils, and animal life. They will enter and break dormancy at the appropriate time, flower at the same time that native pollinators are available, and tolerate seasonal moisture patterns. Theoretically, native plants will not displace other native plants in the landscape, though some are more aggressive than others and will overrun slower-growing species. Additionally, native plants are adapted to native insect pests and diseases and should be more resistant to these stresses. Native plants already "fit" into the landscape, both in terms of their relationships with other native organisms and in their natural appeal to many people.

Unfortunately, many urban areas no longer resemble the native landscapes that preceded development. Plants adapted to shaded forest understories are unlikely to do well in urban landscapes, where environmental conditions are significantly different. The combination of urban soil problems, increased heat load, reduced water, and other stresses mean that many native species do not survive in urban landscapes. Trees under stress, including natives, are more susceptible to opportunistic insects and pathogens. When site conditions are such that many native plants are unsuitable, the choice is either to have a restricted plant palette of natives or expand the palette by including non-native species.

There are practical, functional, ecological, and aesthetic reasons for using introduced species. From a practical standpoint, there are often not many native plant species available locally. Introduced plants can provide functions that native species may be unable to do in the landscape of interest. For instance, there are a number of species that are phytoremediators and are able to remove pollutants from the soil and water. In the absence of native tree and shrub species that provide wildlife habitat, introduced species with similar characteristics can provide the ecological requirements necessary for native wildlife to survive. Finally, there are the aesthetic benefits of broadening the plant palette. Though it may seem less important from a scientific standpoint, in fact studies have shown that attractive landscapes can improve human health and well-being, to the extent that healing gardens are now common in many medical facilities.

Introduced species do have drawbacks: for example, they are less likely to be adapted to local pests and diseases. The most significant problem, however, is invasiveness. What appear to be desirable characteristics for a sustainable landscape – "fast-spreading", "self-sowing", and "tolerates poor soil" are also indicators of potential invasiveness. Not only do exotic invasive plants create monocultures in a landscape and thus reduce its biodiversity, they also can escape managed landscapes and establish in remnant natural areas, eliminating native flora and indirectly the wildlife that depend on them. Lists of regionally and nationally exotic ornamentals (noxious weeds) are widely available on the web (see web resources). *The deliberate usage of exotic invasive species on university campuses is widespread and negates any efforts towards sustainable landscaping.* It is easy to identify state-listed noxious weeds (though removal can be tedious) from campus and replace them with non-invasive species suited to site conditions and usage. To ignore the problem not only sends the wrong message to students, faculty, staff, and the community at large, but suggests that talk of campus sustainability is merely lip service unsupported by action.

Desirable characteristics: At this point, plant materials lists can be further refined by considering their local availability as well as life history, physiological, and morphological characteristics:

- Durability under environmentally hostile conditions
- Long lived
- Low potential for root damage to foundations or pavement
- Mature size appropriate for site
- Minimal water needs once established

- No interference with visibility for pedestrians or vehicles
- No major disease or insect problems
- No messy fruit or pods on materials near sidewalks or roads
- Not "attractive nuisances" (e.g. attractive yet poisonous fruit)
- Not invasive
- Sturdy; not prone to breakage or otherwise becoming hazardous

Selecting quality plants: Both trunk and crown characteristics must be assessed prior to accepting landscape plant materials from either a nursery or a landscape contractor. It is up to college administration to insist that plant quality be part of the contractual agreement between the university and the plant supplier. Characteristics of good and poor quality plants are discussed in detail elsewhere [15 Chalker-Scott & Hummel, 2009].

The principal problems seen in newly purchased trees and shrubs are structural defects in the root systems. Kinking and circling roots will eventually become girdling roots, which inhibit normal water and nutrient flow, thereby stressing the plant and leading to its decline and early death. Such trees are also more susceptible to disease and insect attack. Root systems compromised by girdling roots are more likely to fail and contribute to blow-down, threatening both human and property safety.

III. *Site Preparation* (Adapted from [14] Chalker-Scott, 2009)

Tree preservation: If new plantings are being installed where trees and shrubs already exist, then tree protection zones must be established. This is especially important if any heavy equipment will be used, since the physical damage and compaction these machines cause is a major killer of urban landscape plants. Two zones must be established: (1) a crown protection zone to buffer the trees and shrubs from direct damage (e.g. trunk injuries and broken branches) and (2) a root protection zone to prevent fatal root damage and soil destruction. The first zone should extend to the plant's dripline if possible and no work should be allowed within this zone. The second zone is much bigger – a tree's root zone can be two to three times the diameter of the crown. Root zones that will be subjected to heavy equipment should be proactively mulched with a thick, coarse mulch that will alleviate the compaction and retain moisture. These are two relatively simple precautions to take that will have significant impact on preserving tree health.

If a root protection zone is not established it is unlikely that effects to tree health will be seen the first few years. Eventually, however, crown stunting or dieback will begin as roots succumb to compaction stress and can no longer supply adequate water to the leaves. Disease and insect damage usually become more obvious as well. This mortality spiral occurs when otherwise healthy trees are stressed by an environmental factor (in this case root zone compaction) and become susceptible to opportunistic pests and disease. Landscape managers often erroneously ascribe tree decline to the opportunistic pests or pathogens, and apply massive amounts of pesticides, which do not address the underlying problem and contribute to pesticide overuse. Preventing the problem at the outset with appropriate soil protection is a smarter, more sustainable approach.

Modification of soil conditions: There are sustainable methods of modifying soil conditions if necessary. While none of these are permanent, they are repeatable and therefore sustainable.

    a. *Changing soil structure:* It is difficult and expensive to change soil structure. Other than adding topsoil to a denuded construction site, there are few, if any, good reasons to amend landscape soils. Under no circumstances should planting holes or other small areas be amended prior to installing woody plant materials. If soil amendment is necessary, the entire site must be modified to avoid creating restrictive interfaces through which water, oxygen and roots cannot easily move.

The routine amendment of non-agricultural soils with high amounts of organic matter prior to installing trees and shrubs is unsustainable and unscientific. It is based on the traditional agricultural practice of readying a field for annual crop production. In this scenario, vegetation is removed yearly and soil must be amended on an annual basis to return nutrients to the soil through the decomposition of organic matter. The system is adapted to an annual disturbance cycle. In contrast, urban landscapes with trees, shrubs and turf are not annual crops, nor are these types of landscapes adapted to an annual disturbance. Amending soils after landscapes have been installed is impossible to do without damaging root systems and disrupting the system.

Improper soil amendment also can lead to nutrient overload. Many years of extensive research confirm that the ideal soil for plant growth contains between 4-10% organic matter (OM) by volume. The only natural exceptions to this are wetland soils, which are part of highly productive, poorly drained ecosystems with plants adapted to such conditions. It is a poor horticultural practice to overapply organic matter, in terms of soil, plant, and watershed health. The organic matter content of a permanent landscape installation should never exceed 10% of the volume of soil (this does not count the mulch layer).

A final reason to avoid overamendment of soil with organic matter is the eventual decomposition and disappearance of OM from the soil profile. OM by its nature is biodegradable; within a few years all of the OM used as a soil amendment will be gone. Part of the organic material is replaced naturally by dead plant roots, soil organisms, etc. On the other hand, a soil amended with 33% OM will lose one third of its volume when this OM is degraded, with only a small portion returned through natural processes. The end result will be a landscape soil that has subsided and compacted, often below grade. Examples of landscape subsidence can be seen in every urban area because of the unsustainable practice of heavily amending soils prior to installing trees and shrubs. Thus, the overuse of OM amendment ostensibly to "improve drainage and soil structure" will instead create a landscape soil that is quite the opposite once the OM has decomposed. While the rate of decomposition will depend on the materials used as amendment, ranging from weeks to several years, a permanent landscape should have a lifetime of decades or centuries.

Subsidence of landscape soil is not easily remedied, as adding more soil will smother fine roots of trees and shrubs and induce disease conditions where trunks are buried in soil. The best solution is to not create the problem in the first place; improper soil amendment creates barriers to water, air and root movement; overloads soil and water systems with nutrients; and leads to compaction and subsidence. Organic matter in permanent landscapes should be applied as a mulch – the same way that organic matter enters a forest ecosystem. This should be the model we follow for managing permanent urban landscapes – not the annual crop production model.

b. *Changing soil water:* Improving soil water movement and retention is relatively easy without resorting to the unsustainable practice of amending soil prior to planting. OM added as a topdressing (mulch) will absorb water and slowly release it to the soil below, exactly as the duff layer in the forest. Furthermore, water evaporation from the soil is reduced along with compaction, so that soil water levels and temperatures are moderated. Inorganic mulches, such as gravel, can also help retain soil moisture by reducing evaporation. Use of hydrogels as an amendment is not recommended, as they quickly degrade and disappear along with any benefit they may confer.

Decreasing soil water content is more difficult but it can be accomplished through use of French drains or site grading. A hydrologist may need to be consulted to help with significant drainage issues.

c. *Changing soil oxygen:* Compaction is the primary cause of hypoxia (low oxygen) in urban soils, so disrupting the compacted layers will remedy this problem. Physical disruption is best performed when the soil is dry, as working wet soils will lead to increased compaction and destroy soil structure. Aeration of the soil with air spades, drills, etc. is preferable to tillage in existing landscapes. Tilling will destroy soil structure, damage soil organisms, and severely damage tree and shrub roots, which extend far past the dripline of their crown.

A less invasive way to combat compaction is to apply a thick, coarse, organic mulch over the impacted soil. The application of a good quality organic mulch will allow the soil ecosystem to recover; moisture is retained, temperatures are moderated, and compaction will loosen as roots and soil organisms begin to move through the layers. Biological disruption is not a quick process, but it is easy, inexpensive, natural, and sustainable. Within a few weeks to a few months the soil will be significantly improved and easier to manage.

An increasingly frequent practice is the incorporation of vertical plastic pipe during tree installation. **These** 3-4" aeration tubes are sometimes perforated and run from the bottom of the planting hole to the soil surface. No scientific evidence suggests that passive aeration pipes will improve soil oxygen levels in field situations or assist in root establishment. In addition, use of petroleum-based, non-biodegradable materials does not fit a sustainable management philosophy.

d. ***Changing soil nutrition:*** **Mo**st managed urban soils contain adequate levels of nearly all nutrients except nitrogen. (A soil test will identify what mineral nutrients are deficient or unavailable in the landscape.) Neither organic matter nor fertilizer should be worked **into** the soil prior to planting; this traditional crop production practice is not appropriate for an urban landscape. The more appropriate model of a forest ecosystem obtains its nutrients from the spongy, decomposing duff layer on the forest floor. Application of a good quality organic mulch mimics these natural processes, not only providing a slow release of nutrients, but enhancing beneficial microbes and soil organisms as well.

IV. *Installation* (Adapted from [19] Chalker-Scott, 2009; [21 22]2005a,B)

The proper preparation of both plant materials and the planting area is crucial to the long-term health of permanent landscapes. Proper installation takes longer, especially if the root system requires corrective pruning, but results in a healthier plant that establishes quickly in the landscape.

Seasonal considerations: Spring is not always the best time to plant trees and shrubs. The climate in the western half of North America differs dramatically from the east in that summer rainfall is minimal. West of the Rocky Mountains regions may experience 2, 6, or even 10 months of low rainfall. In Omaha, Nebraska (where Arbor Day originated), the average total precipitation during the three summer months is 10.6 inches; in Seattle, Washington, the average total is a mere 3.2 inches. This is insufficient rainfall for anything but *established*, native or Mediterranean-climate plants growing under near-optimal conditions: most if not all urban landscapes do not fall into this category.

In moderate climates that do not experience severe freezing the best time to install trees and shrubs is in the fall, when soil moisture levels are optimal. In colder climates fall planting is still preferred as long as root zones can be protected from hard freezes by the use of mulch. In either case fall planting allows root growth to progress through the winter (roots never go dormant), allowing the tree to become better established before summer drought occurs. Several studies have demonstrated that shrubs and trees planted during the fall suffer less environmental stress than those planted in the spring or summer [23 Hanson *et al.*, 2004 among others].

Root Preparation

a. *Removing* foreign materials: All containers, tags, plastic, wire, and burlap must be removed. Several scientific publications conclude that burlap and wire baskets interfere with root growth, causing girdling and other root problems (e.g., [24] Kuhns 1997). These underground barriers to root establishment are without doubt one of the leading causes of urban tree failure and early mortality.

b. *Removing growth media:* It is vital that landscape soils are uniform in their composition and texture. Container media are soilless mixes composed of organic matter and pumice. If the container medium is transplanted with the plant, a soil interface is created that inhibits water and air movement between the root ball and the surrounding soil. The interface will inhibit root development outside the planting hole and increases water stress and thus plant mortality. Potting material should be shaken or washed off the root system before plants are installed. Likewise, balled-and-burlapped trees need to be bare-rooted prior to installation: differences between the clay root ball and landscape soil will impede water movement and therefore inhibit root establishment.

c. *Correcting root problems:* As discussed earlier, poor quality plant materials often have serious root problems as a result of improper production techniques. If poor quality plant **material** has not been rejected earlier, it is still possible to correct root defects by careful pruning. Roots that are pruned at transplant time will respond by generating new, flexible roots that help them establish in the landscape. Information from a number of scientists suggests that as much as 80% of the root system can be removed without permanent injury to the plant, though irrigation in the first season will need to be substantial.

Digging the hole: Planting holes should mirror actual root systems, not erroneous perceptions of root systems; a planting hole should resemble a saucer rather than a cup.

Installing plants: Roots must be spread radially over a planting mound in the middle of the hole to ensure future stability of the root system.

Backfilling: Backfill with the same soil that came out of the hole. Water in well, filling any holes with backfill soil, allowing gravity to distribute soil around roots. Avoid tamping down the soil, as this reduces soil oxygen and increases root stress.

V. *Aftercare* (Adapted from [19-21] Chalker-Scott, 2009; 2005a,B)

Appropriate staking: Improper and neglected staking is·yet another significant cause of tree injury and death, primarily from staking the tree too high, too tightly, or for too long. Rather than helping a tree develop root and trunk growth that allows it to stand independently, improper tree staking replaces a supportive trunk and root system. This artificial support causes the tree to put its resources into growing taller but not growing in girth. When the stakes are removed, the lack of trunk and root development makes these trees prime candidates for breakage or blow-down. If the staking material is not removed, girdling and trunk damage or death can occur when secondary growth of the trunk creates an ever-tightening noose of wire.

Staking plants material may be necessary, especially if with tall or top-heavy specimens. Trees should be staked low and loose with 3-4 stakes to allow proper trunk and root development while providing temporary support and protection. Materials used to tie the tree to the stakes should be flexible (no wire) and allow the tree to sway back and forth, which induces secondary growth (taper development). This is especially true in urban areas because of poor, shallow soils that hinder root development and the likelihood of mechanical injury from people and vehicles.

Once trees are firmly established, all staking material must be removed. Removal may be as early as a few months, but must be no more than one year after planting to avoid the problems outlined above. If the tree cannot stand on its own after one year there is little chance it ever will.

Irrigation: Fall installations may require irrigation during the following summer to help them establish; spring installations will require much more. This is true even of drought tolerant species: no newly transplanted plant is able to withstand drought. Use of mulch (discussed below) will help soils retain moisture and thus reduce irrigation needs. Once plants are well established, a more conservative irrigation schedule can be implemented. The vertical aeration tubes mentioned earlier are sometimes installed as a means of delivering irrigation water; again, there is no scientific evidence supporting this practice.

Fertilizer: Nitrogen fertilizer is adequate for transplanting landscape plants; avoid use of "transplant fertilizers" that contain phosphate (discussed below). Difficult-to-transplant species may be aided by application of auxin-containing products in addition to nitrogen. Fertilizer should be applied to the soil surface and not incorporated.

Mulch: All sustainable landscapes need to be mulched to conserve soil water and nutrients and to prevent weed infestation. The importance of a good organic mulch cannot be overstated and can determine success or failure of an urban landscape [25 Cahill et al., 2005]. Mulch the entire planting region with at least 4" of organic mulch, keeping a buffer between the trunk and the mulch to prevent disease. In regions where organic mulch is unavailable, stone mulches and other inorganic materials will work as well. Do not use landscape fabrics or plastics, as they are not conducive to healthy soil conditions and are therefore not sustainable.

Pruning: No pruning should be performed after installation except to remove diseased, damaged, or dead limbs; if such pruning is necessary, do not use wound dressings but allow the plant's natural wound response to occur unimpaired. Any other crown pruning will cause the plant to put its resources into new top growth at the expense of root growth. In addition to interfering with the plant's ability to establish its roots, the removal of a significant portion of the crown means the plant has lost biomass and cannot photosynthesize at its previous level. Plants left intact after transplanting appear to be dormant, but they actually are putting resources into root growth. When roots have become established, shoot growth resumes.

Inappropriate amendments: These products are heavily marketed towards urban landscape managers who waste resources and often damage soils and watersheds through their use.

a. *Antitranspirants:* Antitranspirants reduce water lost through leaf transpiration and are often used improperly as transplant shock reducers. In actuality, reducing transpiration is harmful to normal plant function; the increase in internal leaf temperature has been documented to kill some plants. Furthermore, it is impossible to prevent water vapor movement through the stomates without reducing gas exchange and photosynthesis. Interfering with the plant's ability to manufacture food by blocking stomates only increases plant stress, which could be lethal to plants already shocked from transplanting or other environmental perturbations.

b. *Phosphate fertilizers (triple phosphate, super phosphate, bone meal):* Phosphorus is usually adequate in non-agricultural soils and will cause significant problems in the landscape and nearby watersheds if it is added unnecessarily. High soil phosphate levels will inhibit development of beneficial mycorrhizae on establishing root systems. Shrub and tree species that are mycorrhizae-dependent are less efficient in absorbing water and minerals from the soil and are more likely to suffer transplant shock than plants with active mycorrhizae.

c. *Transplant vitamins:* Applying vitamin B-1, or thiamine, to root systems of plants does not stimulate root growth or reduce transplant shock. In fact, healthy plants and microbes will synthesize their own thiamine supply, so additional vitamin B-1 merely serves as an expensive nitrogen fertilizer.

d. *Hydrogels:* While hydrogels can help reduce water stress in newly installed landscapes, they are not sustainable over the lifetime of the landscape. Hydrogels function by releasing water slowly to the surrounding soil, reducing the need for irrigation. After a few years, however, hydrogels decompose, especially when exposed to fertilizer salts, ultraviolet radiation, and microbial activity. Thus, they cannot be considered long-term solutions to droughty soil conditions.

Suggestions for University and School Administrators Who Are Serious about "Green Landscapes

1. *Utilize faculty expertise at every level of landscape planning, implementation, and management.* This includes faculty in the disciplines of landscape architecture, hydrology, soil science, restoration ecology, conservation biology and urban horticulture. If your institution does not have faculty associated with urban plant systems, consult with appropriate faculty at other institutions.

2. *Encourage on-campus service learning experiences* for students enrolled in applied plant science fields. Campus landscapes with special functions (e.g. restoration, collections, demonstration gardens, etc.) can be planned, implemented, and managed by capstone courses on a continual, sustainable basis. The benefits to students and institutions alike have been documented repeatedly [4 Cahill and Chalker-Scott, 2002; 5 Chalker-Scott and Cahill, 2002; 26 Covington et al., 2000; 27 Fox et al., 2000; 28 Lavendel, 1999; 29 Public Schools of North Carolina, 1998).

3. *Expand efforts beyond university boundaries.* Environmental stewardship and community service are both enhanced by connecting college students with students in K-12 schools to design and implement sustainable landscapes [4 Cahill and Chalker-Scott, 2002; 5 Chalker-Scott and Cahill, 2002; 30 Moore and Bohning, 2007; 31 Reardon, 1999).

4. *Consider volunteers outside the traditional college student pool*, especially if long-term volunteers are an essential part of a management effort. Volunteers can be recruited from local communities, and can often include highly skilled individuals such as Master Gardeners [32 Chalker-Scott and Collman, 2006] and native plant stewards.

5. Use a *checklist of sustainable landscape indicators* during the planning, installation, and management of campus landscapes. The following is a list of suggested indicators based on this paper and referenced resources:
   • Have soil tests have been performed?
   • Has natural water availability and drainage been determined?

- If needed, has a source of supplemental water been identified?
- Is there an obvious temperature gradient on site?
- Are artificial lights on site?
- Will wind be a significant factor on the site?
- Are there regional plant pest or disease problems?
- Have the specific functions of the landscape been determined?
- Are the selected plant species appropriate for the desired function?
- Do the selected plant species have these desirable characteristics?
    - Durability under environmentally hostile conditions
    - Long lived
    - Low potential for root damage to foundations or pavement
    - Mature size appropriate for site
    - Minimal water needs once established
    - No interference with visibility for pedestrians or vehicles
    - No major disease or insect problems
    - No messy fruit or pods on materials near sidewalks or roads
    - Not "attractive nuisances" (e.g. attractive yet poisonous fruit)
    - Not invasive
    - Sturdy; not prone to breakage or otherwise becoming hazardous
- Are plant materials acceptable in terms of root and crown quality?
- Are existing trees protected during construction activities?
- Are plants installed during the appropriate season?
- Have woody roots been prepared and defects removed prior to installation?
- Does the planting hole contain only roots and unamended soil?
- If tree stakes are necessary, have they been installed properly?
- Is irrigation in place for the first season?
- Has an appropriate fertilizer been applied to the soil surface?
- Has a good quality mulch been applied over the root zone?
- Is there a management plan and budget in place to address these needs?
    - Irrigation schedule
    - Fertilizer schedule
    - Stake removal
    - Mulch replacement
    - Pruning
    - Pest management (including weeds, insects, rodents, disease)

Conclusion

It is ultimately the responsibility of campus administration to implement, encourage, and support efforts to create healthy urban landscapes or the efforts themselves will become unsustainable [33 Chalker-Scott and Tinnemore, 2008]. These projects often begin with significant start-up monies, but their permanence can be threatened by the lack of sustained funding. It is thus imperative to the long-term support and success of these projects that they are administratively housed in a president's office, which in turn helps "research universities track, coordinate, and communicate its service to the state and local communities". [34 Weerts, 2005]

Sustainable campus landscapes address current environmental issues including water quality protection and conservation, invasive species management, and native plant conservation that are important locally and globally. Ideally, these landscapes represent an integration of disciplinary applied sciences, student service learning, and day-to-day grounds management. This chapter not only addresses both the importance of healthy landscapes in urban settings, but more importantly the applied soil and plant sciences required to create and maintain truly sustainable systems.

References

[1]   Kenwik, R. A., Shammin, M. R. & Sullivan, W. C. (2009). Preferences for riparian buffers. *Landscape & Urban Planning,* **91**(2), 88-96.

[2]   Thomas, M. (2005). Brighton & Hove's school grounds biodiversity action plan. *Environmental Education,* **78**, 10.

[3]   Calhoun, T. & Cortese, A. D. (2006). We rise to play a greater part. *Planning for Higher Education,* **34**(2), 62-69.

[4]   Cahill, A. & Chalker-Scott, L. (2002). Sustainable community landscapes. In W. L. Filho (Ed.), *Teaching Sustainability at Universities: Towards Curriculum Greening. Environmental Education, Communication and Sustainability,* (Vol. 11, 363-377). New York, NY: Peter Lang Verlag.

[5]   Chalker-Scott L. & Cahill, A. (2002). Sustainable community landscapes. In H. Lotz-Sisifka, & N. Hamer (Eds.), *Proceedings from the 2002 Environmental Management for Sustainable Universities Conference* (63-75). Grahamstown, South Africa: Rhodes University.

[6]   Patton, M. Q. (1985). Extension excellence in the information age. *Journal of Extension* [http://www.joe.org/joe/1985summer/a1.html], **23**(2).

[7]   Moomaw, W. R. (2003). Aligning values for effective sustainability planning. *Planning for Higher Education,* **31**(3), 159-64.

[8]   Conroy, J. J. (2006). How green can you go? *American School and University High-Performance School Supplement,* (March), 30-34.

[9]   Chalker-Scott, L. (2009). Plant choices: Natives or introductions? In L. Chalker-Scott (Ed.), *Sustainable Landscapes and Gardens: Good Science – Practical Application* (8:1-9). Yakima, WA: GFG Publishing.

[10] Lovell, S. T. & Johnston, D. M. (2009). Creating multifunctional landscapes: how can the field of ecology inform the design of the landscape? *Frontiers in Ecology & the Environment,* 7(4), 212-220.

[11] Abercrombie, S. (2006). Pesticide-free campuses. *Environmental Practice,* 7(1), 10-12.

[12] Perry, T. O. (1984). Planting site for a 3" caliper tree with room to grow. In L. J. Kuhns, & J. C. Patterson (Eds.), *METRIA 5: Selecting and Preparing Sites for Urban Trees: Proceedings of the Fifth Conference of the Metropolitan Tree Improvement Alliance* (8-12). University Park, PA: The Pennsylvania State University.

[13] Chalker-Scott, L. (Ed.). (2009). *Sustainable Landscapes and Gardens: Good Science –
      Practical Application.* Yakima, WA: GFG Publishing.

[14] Chalker-Scott, L. (2009). The lay of the land: Site assessment and preparation. In L.
      Chalker-Scott (Ed.), *Sustainable Landscapes and Gardens: Good Science – Practical
      Application* (7:1-7). Yakima, WA: GFG Publishing.

[15] Chalker-Scott, L. & R. Hummel. (2009). Selecting quality plants: Better long-term
      value and satisfaction. In L. Chalker-Scott (Ed.), *Sustainable Landscapes and Gardens:
      Good Science – Practical Application* (11:1-8). Yakima, WA: GFG Publishing.

[16] Reichard, S. (2009). Invasive ornamentals. In L. Chalker-Scott (Ed.), *Sustainable
      Landscapes and Gardens: Good Science – Practical Application* (9:1-7). Yakima, WA:
      GFG Publishing.

[17] Kermath, B. (2007). Why go native? Landscaping for biodiversity and sustainability
      education. *International Journal of Sustainability in Higher Education,* **8**(2), 210-223.

[18] Womack, J. (2009). Going green by thinking blue. *School Planning & Management,* **48**
      (4), 38-55.

[19] Chalker-Scott, L. (2009). Installation and aftercare: Permanent landscapes. In L.
      Chalker-Scott (Ed.), *Sustainable Landscapes and Gardens: Good Science – Practical
      Application* (12:1-11). Yakima, WA: GFG Publishing.

[20] Chalker-Scott, L. (2005). Growing healthier trees. *Organic Gardening,* (Oct/Nov), 14-
      15.

[21] Chalker-Scott, L. (2005). Transplant science: will the patient live? *American
      Nurseryman,* **201**(6), 20-23.

[22] Hanson, A. M, Harris, J. R. & Wright, R. (2004). Effects of transplant season and
      container size on landscape establishment of *Kalmia latifolia* L. *Journal of
      Environmental Horticulture,* **22**(3), 133-138.

[23] Kuhns, M. R. (1997). Penetration of treated and untreated burlap by roots of balled-and-
      burlapped Norway maples. *Journal of Arboriculture,* **23**(1), 1-7.

[24] Cahill, A., Chalker-Scott, L. & Ewing, K. (2005). Wood-chip mulch improves plant
      survival and establishment at no-maintenance restoration site (Washington). *Ecological
      Restoration,* **23**, 212-213.

[25] Covington, W. W., Fulė, P. Z., Alcoze, T. M. & Vance, R. K. (2000). Learning by
      doing: education in ecological restoration at Northern Arizona University. *Journal of
      Forestry,* **98**(10), 30-34.

[26] Fox, B. E., Kolb, T. E. & Kurmes, E. A. (1996). An integrated forestry curriculum: the
      Northern Arizona University Experience. *Journal of Forestry,* **94**(3), 16-22.

[27] Lavendel, B. (1999). Ecological restoration in academia. *Ecological Restoration,* **17**(3),
      120-125.

[28] Public Schools of North Carolina, State Board of Education, and Department of Public
      Instruction. (1998). The school site planner: Land for learning.
      http://www.schoolclearinghouse.org/pubs/schsite.pdf.

[29] Moore, P. & Bohning, M. (2007). Connecting college students with K-8 students to
      create sustainable schools. *North American Association of Environmental Education
      Conference* (4). Virginia Beach, VA.

[30] Reardon, K. M. (1999). A sustainable community/university partnership: University of
      Illinois' East St. Louis Action Research Project. *Liberal Education,* **85**(3), 20-5.

[31] Chalker-Scott, L. & Collman, S. J. (2006). Washington State's Master Gardener program: Thirty years of leadership in university-sponsored, volunteer-coordinated, sustainable community horticulture. *Journal of Cleaner Production,* **14**, 988-993.

[32] Chalker-Scott, L. & R. Tinnemore. (2009). Is community-based sustainability education sustainable? *Journal of Cleaner Production,* **17**, 1132-1137.

[33] Weerts, D. J. (2005). Validating institutional commitment to outreach at land-grant universities: listening to the voices of community partners. *Journal of Extension* [http://www.joe.org/joe/2005october/a3.shtml], **43**(5), Article 5FEA3.

In: Progress in Education, Volume 21
Editor: Robert V. Nata , pp. 145-159

ISBN: 978-1-61728-115-0
© 2011 Nova Science Publishers, Inc.

Chapter 7

Usual Difficulties in the Application of Reinforcement Learning to Real-Life Problems: Proposals of Solving

José D. Martín-Guerrero, Emilio Soria-Olivas,
Marcelino Martínez-Sober, Antonio J. Serrrano-López,
Rafael Magdalena-Benedito and Juan Gómez-Sanchis
Intelligent Data Analysis Laboratory, Department of Electronic Engineering,
University of Valencia, Spain

Abstract

This chapter presents the use of Reinforcement Learning (RL) in two real-life problems. The use of RL seems to be adequate for many real problems in which there is a long-term goal to achieve clearly defined by means of rewards, and the way of achieving that goal is by means of some interactive actuations to change the state of the environment that characterizes the problem. However, the practical use of RL also involves some associated problems. This chapter presents the experience of the authors to deal with those difficulties in order to successfully solve the tackled problems, as it is shown in the obtained results.

1. Introduction

The use of Reinforcement Learning (RL) techniques is one of the most promising fields of Artificial Intelligence (AI) in terms of its practical application to real-life problems. The classical RL approach based on action-state-reward is suitable to tackle many real problems. This work presents two applications in very different fields, namely, marketing and pharmacokinetics. The marketing application is focused on maximizing the profits of a marketing campaign by individualizing it for each customer using historic data. The pharmacokinetics application is based on obtaining the optimal administration of Erythropoietin (EPO) for anaemic patients undergoing chronic renal failure; the goal is to keep patients within a narrow range of Haemoglobin (10-12 g/dl) administering doses of EPO as low as possible in order to avoid side affects and reduce costs for the Health Care System. The previous two applications fit the schema of many other real problems that can be summarized in the following items:

1. All the knowledge of the problem is stored in the variables that define the problem.

2. Working with data-driven problems involves difficulties, such as the presence of noise (unreliable information or data).

3. There are many variables involved in the definition of the problem (high-dimension).

The previous three characteristics lead to some difficulties in the application of RL algorithms:

- How should states be defined? In other words, which strategy would be the most suitable one for the definition of the states?

- How to deal with the problem of sparsity in high-dimension problems?

- What is the best strategy for the definition of rewards?

This work shows the experience of the authors in dealing with those difficulties, and the proposed approaches to solve them. The proposed approaches come basically from Artificial Neural Networks (ANNs), e.g., Multilayer Perceptrons (MLP) for function approximation and Self-Organizing Maps (SOMs) to cluster similar states in order to have a natural and small representation of the different states present in the data.

2.   Optimization of EPO Dosages in Patients Undergoing Chronic Renal Failure

2.1.   Description of the Problem

Anemia is a nearly universal sequel in an End-Stage Renal Disease (ESRD) patient. Until the advent of EPO, ESRD patients faced severe anemia and cardiovascular complications, or the requirement for multiple transfusions. The addition of this expensive drug to the already burdensome cost of the Medicare ESRD program involves considerable expenses for the Health Care System (HCS). It is crucial to make a good use of this drug by means of personalized dosages and number of administrations. This will guarantee an adequate pharmacotherapy as well as a reasonable cost of the treatment.

Anemia treatment has two stages: correction and maintenance. In the correction stage, an Erithropoyetic Stimulating Factor (ESF) is used since it is recommended to increase the Hemoglobin (Hb) level within 4–8 weeks. In the maintenance stage, and depending on the patient's response, some changes may be done either in dosages or weekly number of administrations. It is important to point out that there is an important risk of side effects associated with ESFs if Hb levels are too high or they increase too fast. These side effects are basically related to trombo embolisms and vascular problems [Lynne Peterson, 2004]. Oftentimes, the relationship between the drug dose and the patient's response is complex. To facilitate drug administration, practitioners attempt to use protocols. Such protocols are developed from average responses to treatment in populations of patients. Nevertheless, achieving a desired therapeutic response on an individual basis is complicated by the differences within the population.

The Dialysis Outcomes Quality Initiative of the National Kidney Foundation recommended Hb maintained within the narrow range of 11 − 12 g/dl [National Kidney Foundation, 2000], although nowadays the most accepted recommendation by nephrologists and pharmacists is to maintain Hb within 11 and 13 g/dl [Steensma et al., 2006]. In this study, our target is to maintain Hb levels within 11.5 and 12.5 g/dl. This narrower range allows to increase the sensitivity of alert criteria.

Several attempts at the automation of the EPO delivery have already been reported based on parametric identification in a Bayesian framework [Bellazzi, 1992], on a fuzzy rule-based control strategy [Bellazzi et al., 1994], and on Artificial Neural Networks (ANNs) [Jacobs et al., 2001, Martín et al., 2003]. All these works are based on approximators or predictors that can obtain the Hb concentration or the optimal EPO dosage for the next control in order to attain a certain Hb concentration. This is an interesting approach but it shows a major flaw, namely, this kind of predictors optimize the output variable a predefined number of steps ahead, but it is extremely difficult to obtain long-term predictors because the models are restrictive in terms of both the number of considered delays and steps ahead.

What makes RL a suitable technique for this problem is its way of tackling the problem as achieving long-term stability in patients' Hb level. This processing is much closer to medical reasoning than the processing followed by any of the other approaches proposed previously (Bayesian theory, fuzzy logic, ANNs, etc.). This is because RL finds a suitable policy, i.e., given a patient in a certain state, RL provides the sequence of actions that will lead the patient to the best possible state. The goodness of the state is appropriately defined by means of the rewards assigned to the different possible values of Hb levels.

There are two basic RL approaches: on-policy and off-policy [Sutton and Barto, 1998]. An on-policy RL method modifies the starting policy towards the optimal one. In our particular application, patients would be probed by possibly non-optimal policies during an episodic learning process. Construction of such a policy requires sufficiently many occurrences of all possible state transitions, potentially causing over-dosing or under-dosing. As a result, on-policy episodic RL tools can discover a useful dosing policy, as a product of a learning process, which may be however unacceptably long and dangerous in real-time pharmacotherapy.

In an off-policy approach, the optimal policy can be computed while the agent is interacting with the environment by means of another arbitrary policy. In this work, we use the most widely known off-policy RL method (Q-learning). Therefore, our goal is to stabilize the Hb level within the target range of 11.5 − 12.5 g/dl. The Q-learning mechanism avoids probing the system by suboptimal dosing policies during long training episodes for evaluation of the state/action pairs. The proposed learning system determines the optimal drug dose using reinforcements, which are produced immediately after state transitions occurring within the patient dynamics during treatment [Martín et al., 2006, Martín et al., 2007]

2.2. Data Collection

Patients with secondary anemia due to Chronic Renal Failure (CRF) in periodic hemodyalisis were included in this study. All patients were treated in the University Hospital Dr. Peset (Valencia, Spain). Patients were monitored monthly. We used two sets of patients:

a cohort of 64 patients treated during 2005 and 77 patients analyzed during 2006. Several factors for each patient were usually collected in their follow-up: plasmatic concentration of Hb (g/dl), Hematocrit concentration (%), ferritin (mg/l), administration of Intra-Venous Iron (IV Fe) (mg/month), number of administrations of IV Fe, weekly dosage of EPO beta (International Units, IU), weekly dosage of darbepoetin alpha (μg), number of administrations of these ESFs, and other variables that the Pharmacy Unit staff considered irrelevant for our study, namely, age, weight, sex, Calcium (mg/l), Phosporus (mg/l), Phosphate (IU), PTH-I (pg/ml), dosage of Calcitriol and number of administrations of Calcitriol.

2.3.   Experimental Setup

In order to accommodate our data to RL algorithms, we considered each monthly test as an episode. After a preprocessing stage, seven variables were selected to define the state space: Hb level, ferritin, dosage of IV Fe, dosage of EPO beta, dosage of Darbepoietin alpha and number of administration of these ESFs.

Percentile analysis as well as expert advice were used to define the most adequate thresholds for the ranges used to discretize the variables. In particular, the variable Hb was divided into seven ranges[1], ferritin into five ranges, IV Fe dose into four ranges, EPO beta into five ranges, number of administrations of EPO beta into five ranges, and finally, both Darbepoietin alpha and number of administrations of Darbepoietin alpha into four ranges.

Nine actions were chosen according to nephrologists: increase/decrease EPO beta dosage; increase/decrease Darbepoietin alpha dosage; increase/decrease number of administrations of EPO beta; increase/decrease number of administrations of Darbepoietin alpha; maintain dosage and number of administrations with no changes. Since patients were treated using either one kind of EPO or the other, there was not any action involving changes in the kind of EPO. Rewards depended on the Hb level, since the final goal was to maintain patients within 11.5 g/dl and 12.5 g/dl. Rewards were defined according to experts' advice, as shown in Eq. (1).

$$
reward = \left\{
\begin{array}{ll}
10, & if\ Hb \in [11.5 - 12.5]g/dl \\
\\
0, & \begin{array}{l} if\ Hb \in [10.0 - 11.5]g/dl \\ or\ Hb \in [12.5 - 13.0]g/dl \end{array} \\
\\
-5, & \begin{array}{l} if\ Hb \in [9.0 - 10.0]g/dl \\ or\ Hb \in [13.0 - 14.0]g/dl \end{array} \\
\\
-10, & otherwise
\end{array}
\right\}
\tag{1}
$$

We used an ANN, such as the Multilayer Perceptron (MLP), as function approximator [Haykin, 1999]. The inputs to the MLP are given by the variables that define the state and also by the taken action. The desired output of the MLP is given by Eq. (2). Once the

---

[1]These seven ranges were the same as those used to select the different values of rewards. These values were selected by the nephrologists due to their medical relevance.

model is trained, it can approximate the reward associated to any combination of states and actions. The use of this function approximator has two basic approaches; the first one is based on swapping the tabular Q-learning algorithm with the function approximator in all cases; and the second one, is based on swapping only if the action-state combination has not yet been previously experienced. The latter makes more sense, since it only uses the approximator when it is impossible to obtain a policy by using tabular methods.

$$target = r_{t+1} + \gamma Q_t(s_{t+1}, a_{t+1}) \tag{2}$$

2.4. Results

Using data from 2005, we obtained a policy that turned out to be considerably better than that used in the hospital in terms of the percentage of patients that were within the targeted range of Hb. Evaluation was carried out off-line using historic data. The best results were obtained using the tabular Q-learning algorithm for already experienced situations and the function approximator for those cases that had not yet been previously experienced. In particular, being N_m the number of monitorings and I the best value of the Q function at the last episode, i.e., the value associated to that action which guarantees the maximum value of the Q-function (greedy approach), the hospital policy evaluated by the SARSA algorithm showed a value of $\sum_{i=1}^{N_m} I_h(i) = 2359.7$, whereas the RL policy had a value of $\sum_{i=1}^{N_m} I_q(i) = 2922.0$, which involved an increase of 19%.

Our proposed policy guaranteed that Hb levels of patients were closer to the desired range of Hb than using the hospital protocol. In particular, analyzing the long-term results after one year of treatment, there was an increase of 25% in the number of patients that were within the desired range of Hb or in those ranges that were immediately next to the desired one. This ensured stable conditions in patients undergoing CRF and maximized patients' quality-of-life. Moreover, the proposed policy might involve a considerable economic saving for the hospital. The percentage of patients undergoing CRF represents between 0.1% and 0.2% of the population. The investment in ESFs of the Pharmacy Unit (PU) of the hospital analyzed in this study is around €30,000 per year. This PU has estimated than an optimal policy would save between €100 and €200 per patient and year, which would involve a rough saving of €1,000,000 for all Valencian Region[2].

The application of the previously obtained policy to the cohort of patients treated during 2006, showed an improvement in the value of $\sum_{i=1}^{N_m} I(i)$ equal to 15%. Therefore, it involved that a higher percentage of patients were within the desired range of Hb (or at least, closer to the desired range), when using the RL policy than following the hospital policy. In particular, there was an increase of 22% in the number of patients that were within the desired range of Hb at the end of year 2006. It guarantees a better Quality-of-Life, and it also involves considerable economic savings for the HCS.

Therefore, the achieved results are promising, since they indicate that the RL policy is robust and generalizable to patients different from those used to obtain the policy. To end up all the validation process, some measures should still be carried out, e.g., a complete

---

[2]Region of Valencia is a Spanish region with approximately 5 millions of inhabitants and an autonomous government, which manages its own Health Care System.

calculation of the economic savings involved (taking into account all the factors, such, as potential admissions in hospitals, expenses in drugs related to the treatment and the state of the disease, ...). It would also be very interesting to analyze the monthly evolution of the ratio of patients that are within the desired range of Hb; this would help answer questions like: How long does it take for a certain patient to reach this desired target? Are they stable?, i.e., once they are within the desired target, what is the probability to be out of the range again in the future? Is the evolution slow and progressive? The answers of these questions could be used together with experts' advice to improve the definition of the rewards.

3.   Optimization of a Marketing Campaign

3.1.   Description of the Problem

The latest marketing trends are more concerned about maintaining current customers and optimizing their behavior than getting new ones. For this reason, relational marketing focuses on what a company must do to achieve this objective [Reichheld, 2001]. The relationships between a company and its customers follow a sequence of action-response system, where the customers can modify their behavior in accordance with the marketing actions developed by the company.

One way to increase the loyalty of customers is by offering them the opportunity to obtain some gifts as the result of their purchases from the company. The company can give *virtual credits* to anyone who buys certain articles, typically those that the company is interested in promoting. After a certain number of purchases, the customers can exchange their virtual credits for the gifts offered by the company.

The problem is to establish the appropriate number of virtual credits for each promoted item and for each individual customer. In accordance with the company policy, it is expected that the higher the credit assignment, the higher the amount of purchases. However, the company's profits are lower since the marketing campaign adds an extra cost to the company. The goal is to achieve a trade-off by establishing an optimal policy. We propose the use of RL to solve this task since previous applications have demonstrated its suitability in this area [Abe et al., 2004, Sun, 2003], in particular to solve the mailing problem.

The main difference between the mailing problem and the credit assignment problem is that the action space becomes multi-valued instead of binary. In the mailing problem only two actions can be considered: to send a catalog or not to send a catalog. In a credit assignment application, the optimal policy should recommend how many credits should be assigned to each transaction.

Marketing problems tend to have a very complex characterization of the transactions that are involved. This highly dimensional attribute requires the implementation of RL algorithms by means of state aggregators or function regressors, which under certain conditions may lead to convergence problems [Sutton and Barto, 1998]. In this work, we propose two different approaches. First, the state space is clustered by using a vectorial quantization carried out by algorithms based on the Self-Organizing Map (SOM); this approach enables us to work with RL tabular methods. Second, an MLP is used to predict the response of customers when different actions are carried out by the company. This prediction is then used to obtain an optimal policy.

3.2. Data Collection

Data were collected from a company[3] that was interested in designing a campaign to encourage their clients to buy more of their products. Data involved 1,264,862 transactions, 1,004 different articles, 3,573 customers and 5 (monthly) episodes. This marketing campaign was based on assigning virtual credits to customers. That assignment was carried out manually based on internal criteria.

The information used for this study corresponds to the first five months of the campaign. The main characteristics of the campaign are the following:

1. The company assigned virtual credits to customers according to the items bought by them. When customers had enough credits, they could exchange their credits for gifts.

2. Customers could obtain virtual credits by buying specific items which were indicated as "encouraged". The company selected these promoted items monthly (according to internal criteria).

3. Since the assignment of these virtual credits involved a cost to the company, immediate profits decreased as a direct consequence of the campaign.

The credit assignment took place at the end of every episode and was computed by taking into account how many "encouraged" articles were bought by customers during that month. The so-called Life-Time Value (LTV) at time t (reward) for a certain customer was obtained as follows:

$$LTV(t) = \sum_i P_i(t) \cdot A_i(t) - K_C V_C(t) \tag{3}$$

where A_i is the amount of type i articles purchased by the customer; P_i is the price of type i articles; V_C is the number of virtual credits assigned to the customer; and K_C is a coefficient that reports the costs incurred by the company due to credits. The aim of this work is to increase LTV for every customer by using RL as the strategy to achieve an optimal policy.

Since it was not possible to carry out the improvement of the policy on-line, a batch method was used. Episodes were repeatedly shown to the RL algorithm until the convergence of the policy was achieved.

3.3. Experimental Setup

3.3.1. Action and State Spaces

The first task to tackle in an RL algorithm is the design of state and action spaces. This requires an exhaustive analysis of both the clients and their actions. The vast amount of information stored by the company showed that there were many features that defined the customer behavior. Specifically, the following features were included in the study:

---

[3]The name of the company cannot be made public due to a confidentiality agreeement.

1. The identification of the shop that sold the products.

2. The geographical area where the client made the purchase.

3. The date of the purchase transaction.

4. The number of items purchased by the client.

5. Family[4].

6. The item identification number.

7. Whether the items were regular items or "encouraged" items.

8. Price of the item purchased.

An initial classical data mining study was carried out to analyze the data. This study showed that neither geographical nor temporal information were relevant; therefore, this information was removed from further analyses.

Marketing studies consider that an optimal set of features to profile the future behavior of a customer is given by the so-called RFM variables [Pfeifer and Carraway, 2000]:

- **Recency (R)**: the most recent date when the customer made a transaction (usually a purchase, but it can also be a refund request, for instance).

- **Frequency (F)**: the number of times the customer made a purchase.

- **Monetary (M)**: the monetary quantity of products purchased by the customer.

It has been confirmed experimentally that the most valuable customers have high frequency and monetary values, and low recency values [Pfeifer and Carraway, 2000]. Although this set of features is the most suitable one to define the state space, we avoided using the same information in the definition of the state space and in the computation of the long-term reward. Therefore, the monetary feature was split into two different ones:

- **Amount**: the number of items purchased in an episode by each customer.

- **Average price**: the average price of all the purchases in an episode.

In addition, another feature was considered in the state space. Since customers obtained virtual credits by purchasing some items marked as "encouraged", it made sense to add a feature that showed how many "encouraged" items were bought by customers.

The action to be taken was the assignment of a certain number of virtual credits to customers depending on their purchases. Since there was a wide range of credits, their quantization was required to have a manageable number of possible actions. This quantization procedure was carried out taking into account the different gift values for a certain number of credits. The company established 10 categories of gifts according to their price, and hence, the action space was also divided into 10 categories.

---

[4]Articles were grouped into families. A family was a label which gathered similar products.

3.3.2. The SOM Approach

A SOM was trained with all the input patterns from the data collection, and then, the most representative neuron for a particular input vector was computed. That neuron is usually called Best Matching Unit (BMU), and in our case, represents the state of the customer. This approach located similar customers in the same state; i.e., an aggregation of states was obtained. Given an input vector $s_t = s_t(R, F, A, A - P, E)^5$, its BMU was computed. This value was used as an entry for the Q-table. Therefore, the input patterns actually contained information about the marketing-oriented features.

An additional advantage of this proposal is that the interpretation of results was quite straightforward due to the intuitive maps provided by the SOM. Moreover, there was no need to use function regressors, thereby avoiding the danger of non-convergent policies.

3.3.3. The MLP Approach

The input space was made up of the set of transaction features, and the output space consisted of the long-term rewards. Moreover, in the prediction problem, it was necessary to include not only the state features, but also the features of the actions taken by the company. It was then feasible to predict the Q-values when taking different actions in the same state. The best MLP model had one hidden layer made up by eight neurons. This architecture was obtained by a cross-validation procedures, after testing different architectures. The objectives of the training were computed using MC methods because they ensured convergence of the regression algorithm.

3.4. Results

Since the algorithms used in this work were off-policy, the data had to be arranged in episodes and the evaluation was carried out off-line. Each episode was made up of the transactions of each customer in each one of the five temporal (monthly) steps that appeared in the data set.

3.4.1. SOM Results

Figure 1 (a) shows that the policy followed by the company was very deterministic. Three zones are well defined. The darkest area depicts high number of credits given to customers; the gray area depicts intermediate amounts, and the white area indicates that no credits were given to customers. This guideline of the company policy is a disadvantage for the RL algorithms since they need all actions to be taken in all states. In spite of this lack of exploration, the RL algorithm was able to find a good enough solution for this problem. In fact, when computing the $Q(s, a)$ function by means of the SOM approach, several modifications of the actual policy were suggested as shown in Figure 1 (b). There are two main parts in this comparison map: the upper-right and the lower-right areas (in which no modifications were suggested), and the central area where the optimal policy suggested an increase in the number of credits given to customers. The former represents well-defined

---

[5]$R \equiv$ recency, $F \equiv$ frequency, $A \equiv$ the amount of items purchased, $A - P$ is the average price, and E indicates whether or not the products are "encouraged".

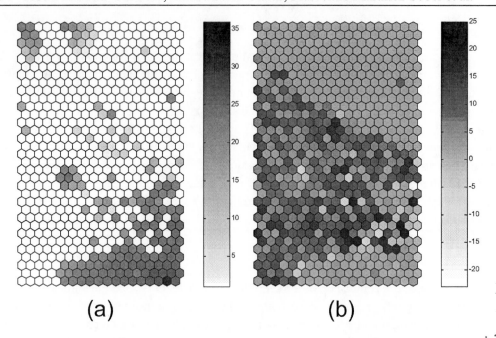

(a)   (b)

Figure 1. Policy followed by the company (a) in terms of the number of assigned credits and improvements suggested by the SOM-RL algorithm (b) in terms of the difference of assigned credits with respect to the company policy. In the company policy map, (a), the darkest area depicts a high number of credits given to customers; the medium gray area shows intermediate numbers, and the white area indicates that no credits were given to customers. In the comparison map, (b), the darkest areas mean that an increase in the credit assignment is recommended by the optimal policy; medium gray areas mean no modification in the company policy is suggested and the light gray areas (very small) indicate that a decrease in the credit assignment should be made.

customers ("loyal" customers in the case of the lower-right area and "negligible" customers for the company in the case of the upper-right area). The central area represents "average" customers.

3.4.2.   MLP Results

The data was split into three data sets: a training data set formed by 33.3% of the patterns to train the network; a validation data set (33.3% of the patterns) to carry out a cross-validation; and finally, a test data set that consisted of the remaining 33.3% of the patterns, which had not yet been seen by the network. Unbiased models with good generalization capabilities were obtained in this way. It should be pointed out that cross-validation procedures were applied to estimated values, not to policies.

Very similar values of the Mean-Square Error (MSE) were obtained in these three data sets. In particular, errors showed low values, which corresponded to an accurate regression. Once the MLP was trained, it was used to estimate the optimal policy. The results achieved with this algorithm were difficult to visualize because the input space had 11 dimensions.

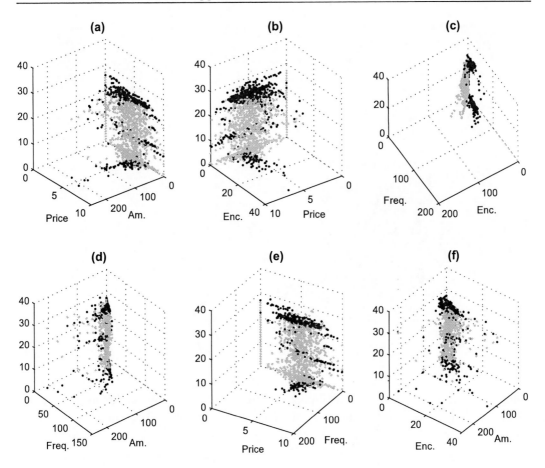

Figure 2. Several plots showing the comparison of the optimal policy and the company policy with the features of the state space. The gray dots represent the company policy, while the black dots represent the optimal policy. The xy-plane is defined by sets of two features, while z-axis represents the number of given credits.

Figure 2 shows several plots comparing the optimal policy and the company policy with the features that characterize states. Note that in Figure 2 (c) (which shows both policies versus the characteristics "Frequency" and "Encouraged"), the company policy assigned virtual credits to those customers who were prone to buying "encouraged" articles. The optimal policy suggested that credits should be assigned to customers who purchased products more frequently even when these products were not "encouraged".

The overall behavior of the optimal policy was more "aggressive" than the company policy. For instance, in the company policy, actions were spread over the entire action space, whereas the two main groups in the optimal policy were located at the top and at the bottom of the action space. Similar states seemed to lead to opposite actions. The explanation of this behavior might be related to the features used to define the state space. The fact that opposing actions were recommended in similar states suggests that these features might be an incomplete state representation.

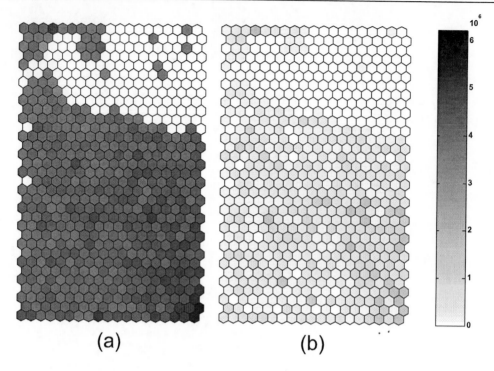

(a)   (b)

Figure 3. Q-function in a SOM topology for the optimal policy (a) and for the company policy (b). The darker the color, the higher the value of the action-value function $Q^\pi(s, a)$. The RL policy provides much larger profits than the company policy. The gray-shade bar shows the value of $Q^\pi(s, a)$ for the different gray shades.

Figure 3 shows how the optimal policy helps the company to increase its profits considerably. In those areas in which improvements were suggested, the Q-values for the optimal policy were four or even five times larger than the Q-values of the company policy.

The results yielded by the MLP approach are shown in Figure 4. The black dots are more uniformly distributed than the gray dots, which might be due to the fact that the optimal policy tried to make customers loyal to the company by ensuring a certain minimum number of sales. The behavior of the company policy was either excellent or very poor. The Q-values obtained by the RL policy were not as high as some of the results obtained by the company policy in some cases. Nonetheless, the RL policy was less likely to obtain poor results than the company policy.

Figure 5 shows the relative profit increase following the RL policy instead of the company policy. VIP customers refer to a selected group of customers that has a special relationship with the company. An RL policy provided much higher profits than the company policy when it was evaluated using historic data. Although it is a promising result, a validation with new data is required to claim that RL can indeed get higher profits.

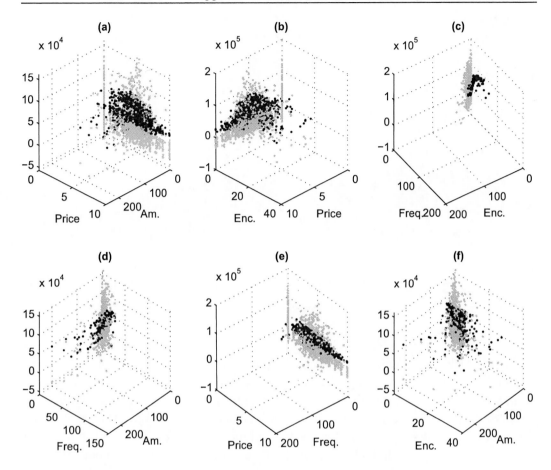

Figure 4. Q-function for the MLP approach. Gray dots stand for the profits expected if the company policy is followed, whereas black dots correspond to the RL policy values. The xy-plane is defined by sets of two features, whereas z-axis represents the value of the Q-function.

4.   Conclusion

We have presented a work focused on the application of RL to two real problems. We have shown how to deal with usual difficulties when applying RL to real problems, thus showing that RL is a suitable approach to many real problems once those difficulties are overcome. In the problem of optimization of anemia management, we have found policies to maximize the ratio of patients that are within a targeted range of Hb. It is remarkable the novelty of an RL application to Pharmacy, which is a field of knowledge very different to the typical ones that are related to RL. The proposed approach is completely general and can be applied to any problem of drug dosage optimization.

Moreover, two different RL approaches (state aggregation by SOM and action-value function approximation by MLP) in targeted marketing have been developed and benchmarked. The application of both algorithms has proven to be appropriate for problems

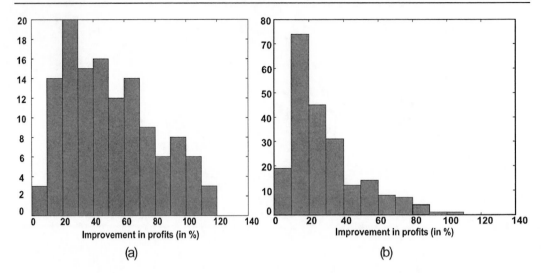

Figure 5. Histograms showing relative profit increase when using the RL policy instead of the company policy. Non-VIP customers are shown in (a) and VIP customers in (b).

of this kind because promising results have been achieved. The SOM approach is more straightforward to understand than the MLP approach due to the properties of the SOM algorithm, which allows an intuitive representation of the results. The results suggest that the use of SOM could be recommended to improve a marketing campaign. The MLP regressor is more powerful because the generalization process is more robust than in the SOM algorithm, but is is more difficult to extract information from the achieved modeling.

References

[Abe et al., 2004] Abe, N., Verma, N., Schroko, R., and Apte, C. (2004). Cross channel optimized marketing by reinforcement learning. In *Proceedings of the KDD*, pages 767–772.

[Bellazzi, 1992] Bellazzi, R. (1992). Drug delivery optimization through bayesian networks: an application to erythropoietin therapy in uremic anemia. *Computers and Biomedical Research*, **26**:274–293.

[Bellazzi et al., 1994] Bellazzi, R., Siviero, C., and Bellazzi, R. (1994). Mathematical modeling of erythropoietin therapy in uremic anemia. Does it improve cost-effectiveness? *Haematologica*, **79**:154–164.

[Haykin, 1999] Haykin, S. (1999). *Neural Networks: A Comprehensive Foundation*. Prentice Hall, Upper Saddle River,NJ, USA, 2nd edition.

[Jacobs et al., 2001] Jacobs, A. A., Lada, P., Zurada, J. M., Brier, M. E., and Aronoff, G. (2001). Predictors of hematocrit in hemodialysis patients as determined by artificial neural networks. *Journal of American Nephrology*, **12**:387A.

[Lynne Peterson, 2004] Lynne Peterson, L. (May 2004). FDA Oncologic Drugs Advisory Committee (ODAC) meeting on the safety of erythropoietin in oncology. *Trends in Medicine*, pages 1–4.

[Martín et al., 2003] Martín, J. D., Soria, E., Camps, G., Serrano, A., Pérez, J., and Jiménez, N. (2003). Use of neural networks for dosage individualisation of erythropoietin in patients with secondary anemia to chronic renal failure. *Computers in Biology and Medicine*, **33**(4):361–373.

[Martín et al., 2006] Martín, J. D., Soria, E., Chorro, V., Climente, M., and Jiménez, N. V. (2006). Reinforcement learning for anemia management in hemodialysis patients treated with erythropoietic stimulating factors. In *European Conference on Artificial Intelligence 2006, Proceedings of the Workshop "Planning, Learning and Monitoring with uncertainty and dynamic worlds"*, pages 19–24, Riva del Garda, Italy.

[Martín et al., 2007] Martín, J. D., Soria, E., Martínez, M., Climente, M., De Diego, T., and Jiménez, N. V. (2007). Validation of a reinforcement learning policy for dosage optimization of erythropoietin. In *Twentieth Australian Joint Conference on Artificial Intelligence - AI07. Lecture Notes in Computer Science AI 2007: Advances in Artificial Intelligence, LNAI 4830*, pages 732–738, Surfers Paradise, QLD, Australia.

[National Kidney Foundation, 2000] National Kidney Foundation, K. D. O. Q. I. (2000). Guidelines for anemia of chronic kidney disease. NKF K/DOQI Guidelines. www.kidney.org.

[Pfeifer and Carraway, 2000] Pfeifer, P. E. and Carraway, R. L. (2000). Modelling customer relationships as markov chains. *Journal of Interactive Marketing*, **14**(2):43–55.

[Reichheld, 2001] Reichheld, F. F. (2001). *The loyalty effect: the hidden force behind growth, profits, and lasting value*. Harvard Business School Press, Boston, MA, USA.

[Steensma et al., 2006] Steensma, D., Molina, R., Sloan, J., Nikcevich, D., Schaefer, P., Rowland, K. J., Dentchev, T., Novotny, P., Tschetter, L., Alberts, S., Hogan, T., Law, A., and C.L., L. (2006). Phase III study of two different dosing schedules of erythropoietin in anemic patients with cancer. *Journal of Clinical Oncology*, **24**(7):1079–1089.

[Sun, 2003] Sun, P. (2003). *Constructing Learning Models from Data: The Dynamic Catalog Mailing Problem*. Phd thesis, Tsinghua University.

[Sutton and Barto, 1998] Sutton, R. and Barto, A. (1998). *Reinforcement Learning: An Introduction*. MIT Press, Cambridge, MA, USA.

In: Progress in Education, Volume 21
Editor: Robert V. Nata , pp. 161-190

ISBN 978-1-61728-115-0
© 2011 Nova Science Publishers, Inc.

Chapter 8

A COMPARATIVE STUDY OF DISCRETIZATION APPROACHES FOR STATE SPACE GENERALIZATION IN THE KEEPAWAY SOCCER TASK

Javier García,[*] *Iván López-Bueno,*[†] *Fernando Fernández*[‡]
and Daniel Borrajo[§]
Computer Science Department, Universidad Carlos III de Madrid
Avenida de la Universidad 30, 28911 Leganés, Madrid, Spain

Abstract

There are two main branches of reinforcement learning: methods that search directly in the space of value functions that asses the utility of the behaviors (*Temporal Difference Methods*); and methods that search directly in the space of behaviors (*Policy Search Methods*). When applying Temporal Difference (TD) methods in domains with very large or continuous state spaces, the experience obtained by the learning agent in the interaction with the environment must be generalized. The generalization can be carried out in two different ways. On the one hand by discretizing the environment to use a tabular representation of the value functions (e.g. Vector Quantization Q-Learning algorithm). On the other hand, by using an approximation of the value functions based on a supervised learning method (e.g. CMAC Q-Learning algorithm). Other algorithms use both approaches to benefit from both mechanisms, allowing a higher performance. This is the case of the Two Step Reinforcement Learning algorithm. In the case of Policy Search Methods, the Evolutionary Reinforcement Learning algorithm has shown promising in RL tasks. All these algorithms present different ways to tackle the problem of large or continuous state spaces. In this chapter, we organize and discuss different generalization techniques to solve this problem. Finally, we demonstrate the usefulness of the different algorithms described to improve the learning process in the Keepaway domain.

Keywords: Reinforcement Learning, Temporal difference learning, Evolutionary computation, State space generalization, Discretization, Keepaway soccer

[*]E-mail address: fjgpolo@inf.uc3m.es
[†]E-mail address: ivan.lopezbueno@gmail.com
[‡]E-mail address: ffernand@inf.uc3m.es
[§]E-mail address: dborrajo@ia.uc3m.es

1. Introduction

Many model-free Reinforcement Learning (RL) techniques rely on learning value functions. Ideally, we could assume that the estimated values of the value function could be represented as a look-up table with one entry for each state or state-action pair. However, complex (most real world) domains represent a challenge to the use of such tables, because they usually have continuous (or very large) state/action spaces. This fact poses two problems: the size of the state-action tables (presenting unrealistic memory requirements); and the correct use of the experience (an agent is not able to visit all states or state-action pairs, or the time needed to fill the look-up table easily becomes too large). This problem is known as the curse of dimensionality and requires some form of generalization. Generalization techniques have been extensively studied before the popularity of RL [1], so many of the existing generalization methods are commonly combined with RL. Some approaches have used decision trees [2], neural networks [3], or variable resolution dynamic programming [4].

Another alternative consists on discretizing the continuous variables. Then, the new discrete version of the problem is solved with RL techniques. However, if we choose a bad discretization of the state space, we might introduce hidden states into the problem, making it impossible to learn the optimal policy. If we discretize too fine grain, we loose the ability to generalize and increase the amount of training data that we need. This is especially important when the task state is multi-dimensional, where the number of discrete states can be exponential in the state dimension.

Thus, it seems reasonable to replace the discrete look-up tables of many RL algorithms with function approximators or by discretizing the environment to use a reduced tabular representation of the value functions, capable of handling continuous variables in several dimensions and generalizing across similar states.

All these traditional techniques require a policy representation through state enumeration. Another group of techniques perform a direct policy search. These methods are often more applicable to problems with large or infinite state spaces, because they do not need a policy representation through state enumeration. Policy search methods represent a policy through a set of parameters, θ. This set of parameters can be expressed in different ways (e.g. weights in a neural network), which generally increase linearly in both the number of dimensions and the size of these dimensions. For this reason, policy search methods are always more amenable to problems whose state space is large or infinite.

The goal of this chapter is to introduce the reader to the generalization problem in complex RL domains and to organize and discuss different generalization techniques to solve this problem. We will review and compare Vector Quantization (VQ) [5], CMAC [6], other generalizations techniques such as decision trees [7] and regression trees [8], and a policy search method [9]. All these techniques, coupled with RL methods, will be applied in the Keepaway Soccer Task [10].

The remainder of the chapter is organized as follows. Section 2 begins with a brief summary of the generalization problem, introducing some of the main approaches used. Section 3 describes how vector quantization is used to solve the generalization problem in the Vector Quantization Q-Learning (VQQL) algorithm. The CMAC Q-Learning algorithm is shown in Section 4. Section 5, where the Two Step Reinforcement Learning algorithm

(2SRL) is reviewed, shows two approaches based, one on supervised learning function approximation (ISQL), and the other on state space discretizations. Section 6 overviews the Evolutionary RL method and Section 7 describes the keepaway task and presents empirical results on the benchmark version of this task for the different algorithms described. Section 8 concludes.

2. Related Work

In [11], the authors characterize two main branches of RL: methods that search directly in the space of value functions that measure the utility of the behaviors (*Temporal Difference Methods*); and methods that search directly in the space of behaviors (*Policy Search Methods*). The authors focuses entirely on the first set of methods. Temporal difference (TD) methods are one popular way to solve RL problems, that learn a value function that estimates the expected reward for taking an action in a particular state. Policy search methods can also address RL problems by searching in the space of behaviors for one that receives the maximal reward [12].

When applying TD methods in domains with very large or continuous state spaces, the experience generated by the learning agent during its interaction with the environment must be generalized. The generalization methods are often based on the approximation of the value functions used to calculate the action policy and tackled in two different forms [13]. On the one hand, by discretizing the state space to use a tabular representation of the value functions. On the other hand, by using an approximation of the value functions based on a supervised learning method.

The first one consists on discretizing the state space to obtain a compacted and discrete one, so tabular representations of the value functions can be used. Uniform discretization has reached good results [14], but only in domains with few features describing the states, where a high resolution does not increase the number of states very much. A very large state space produces unpractical computational requirements, and unpractical amounts of experience in model based methods [15].

Continuous U Trees has also been used for discretizing the state space [16]. Thus, the Continuous U Tree transfers traditional regression trees techniques to RL techniques. In [17], the authors try to improve the applicability and efficacy of RL algorithms by adaptive state space partitioning. They proposed the TD learning with adaptive vector quantization algorithm (TD-AVQ) wich is an online method and does not assume any priori knowledge with respect to the learning task and environment. The paper [18] introduces new techniques for abstracting the state space of a Markov Decision Process (MDP). These techniques extend one of the minimization models, known as $\epsilon - reduction$, to build a partition space. The state space built has a smaller number of states than the original MDP. As a result, the learning policies on the state space built should be faster than on the original state space. The discretization approach is used in Section 3, where the VQQL algorithm is described.

The second approach for learning the Q function is based on the supervised learning of tuples $< s, a, q_{s,a} >$, where s is a state, a is an action, and $q_{s,a}$ is the $\hat{Q}$ value approximated for the state s and the action a. Any supervised learning method can be used, each of them with a set of parameters θ to be computed [19; 20; 21]. Many different methods of function approximation have been used successfully, including CMACs, radial basis functions, and neural networks [1]. This approach is studied in Section 4 where a CMAC is used as function approximation, and in Section 5, where we define the Iterative Smooth Q-Learning (ISQL) algorithm, based on the Smooth Value Iteration algorithm [22], which will be tested using different function approximators.

Policy search methods, are a reasonable alternative to TD methods. The general idea behind these methods is to search for the optimal policy in the space of all possible policies (behaviors) by directly examining different policy parameterizations, bypassing the assignment of the value. In [23], the authors discuss direct search methods for unconstrained optimization. They give a modern perspective on this classical family of algorithms. In [24], they focus on the application of evolutionary algorithms to the RL problem, emphasizing alternative policy representations, credit assignment methods, and problem-specific genetic operators. Some strengths and weaknesses of the evolutionary approach to RL are discussed, along with a survey of representative applications. In [25], the authors present a method for structuring a robot motor learning task. By designing a suitably parameterized policy, they show that a simple search algorithm, along with biologically motivated constraints, offers a competitive means for motor skill acquisition. Surveys of policy search methods can be found in [26; 27]. This approach is used in Section 6, where the evolutionary RL algorithm is described.

Although there have been several generalization approaches that can be used to effectively solve the state space generalization problem, there is a lack of comparative studies in common difficult tasks as the one we propose in this chapter. In addition, rarely these studies help isolate factors critical to the performance of each method and the yield insights [12; 28].

3. Vector Quantization and RL

Vector Quantization (VQ) is a clustering method that permits to find a more compact representation of the state space. VQ appeared as an appropiate way of reducing the number of bits needed to represent and transmit information [29]. This technique is extensively employed for signal analog-to-digital conversion and compression, which have common characteristics to MDP problems. VQ is based on the principle of block coding. In the past, the design of a vector quantizer was considered to be a challenging problem due to the need for multi-dimensional integration. In [30], the authors proposed a VQ design algorithm based on a training sequence. A VQ that is designed using this algorithm is cited in the literature as LBG-VQ (which refers to the initials of the authors: Linde, Buzo and Gray). In the case of large state spaces in RL, the problem is analogous: *how can we compactly represent a huge number of states with very few information?*. As an example, RL and VQ are used in [31] for image compression. In that work, they present the FRLVQ algorithm (Fuzzy Reinforcement Learning Vector Quantization) which is based on the combination of fuzzy K-means clustering and topology knowledge. In each iteration of the RL algorithm, the size and direction of the movement of a codevector is decided by the overall pair-wise competition between the attraction of each training vector and the repellent force of the corresponding winning codevector. In [5], VQ is applied again to the RL problem. The authors present the *VQQL* model, that integrates Q-Learning as the RL technique, and VQ as state generalization technique. They use the Generalized Lloyd Algorithm, a numerical clustering method, for the design of vector quantizers. Figure 1 shows how to represent the action policy following this approach.

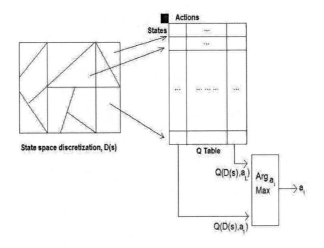

Figure 1. Generalization by discretizing the environment, and using a tabular representation of the value functions.

Next, we review how to apply VQ to RL. First, we review the main concepts of VQ and, then, the VQQL algorithm is described in detail.

3.1. Vector Quantization

A vector quantizer Q of dimension K and size N is a mapping from a vector (state or action) in the K-dimensional Euclidean space, R^k, into a finite set C containing N states. Thus,

$$Q : R^k \to C$$

where $C = y_1, y_2, ..., y_N$, $y_i \in R^k$. Given C, and a state $x \in R^k$, $VQ(x)$ assigns x to the closest state from C,

$$VQ(x) = \arg\min_{y \in C}\{dist(x,y)\}$$

where $dist(x,y)$ is a distance function in the R^k space (typically the euclidean distance). To design the vector quantizer we use the Generalized Lloyd Algorithm (GLA), also called *k-means*. GLA is a clustering technique that consists of a number of iterations, each one recomputing the set of more appropriate partitions of the input states and their centroids. The centroids, together with the distance metric, define the Voronoi regions. The VQQL algorithm uses each of those regions as a unique state, obtaining a state space discretization, that permits learning with reduced experience. An example of 2-dimensional

VQ is shown in Figure 2. There are 16 partitions and a point associated with each partition. In this figure, every pair of values falling in a particular partition are approximated by a grey point associated with that partition.

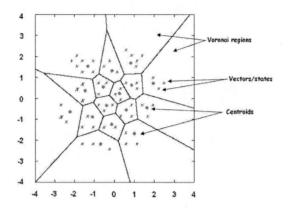

Figure 2. Example of Vector Quantizer.

3.2. VQQL

The integration of VQ and Q-learning yields the VQQL (Vector Quantization Q-Learning) algorithm, that is shown in Table 1. The vector quantizer is designed from the input data C obtained during an interaction between the agent and the environment. The data set C is composed of tuples in the form $< s_1, a, s_2, r >$ where s_1 and s_2 belong to the state space S, a belongs to the action space A and r is the immediate reward. In many problems, S is composed of a large number of features. In these cases, we suggest to apply feature selection to reduce the number of features in the state space. Feature selection is a technique for selecting a subset of relevant features for building a new subset. So feature selection is used to select the relevant features of S to obtain a subset S'. This feature selection process is defined as $\Gamma : S \rightarrow S'$. The set of states $s' \in S'$, C'_s, are used as input for the Generalized Lloyd Algorithm to obtain the vector quantizer. The vector quantizer $VQ^{s'}$ is a mapping from a vector $s' \in S'$ into a vector $s' \in D_{s'}$, where $D_{s'}$ is the state space discretization $Ds' = s'_1, s'_2, ..., s'_n$ for $s'_i \in S'$.

In the last part of the algorithm, the Q-table is learned from the obtained discretizations using the set C' of experience tuples by equation 1.

$$Q(s_t, a_t) \rightarrow Q(s_t, a_t) + \alpha[r_{t+1} + \gamma max_a Q(s_{t+1}, a) - Q(s_t, a_t)] \qquad (1)$$

To obtain the set C' from C, each tuple in C is mapped to the new representation. Therefore, every state in C is firstly projected to the space S' and then discretized, i.e. $VQ^{S'}(\Gamma(S))$.

Table 1. VQQL Algorithm.

VQQL
1. Gather experience tuples
1.1. Generate the set C of experience tuples of the type $< s_1, a, s_2, r >$ from an interaction of the agent in the environment, where $s_1, s_2 \in S$, $a \in A$ and $r \in \Re$ is the immediate reward.
2. Reduce (optionally) the dimension of the state space
2.1. Let C_s be the set of states in C
2.2. Apply a feature selection approach using C_s to reduce the number of features in the state space. The resulting feature selection process is defined as a projection $\Gamma : S \to S'$
2.3. Set $C'_s = \Gamma(C_s)$
3. Discretize the state space
3.1. Use GLA to obtain a state space discretization, $D_{s'} = s'_1, s'_2, ..., s'_n$, $s'_i \in S'$, from C'_s.
3.2. Let $VQ^{S'} : S' \to D_{s'}$ be the function that, given any state in S', returns the discretized value in D_s.
4. Learn the Q-Table
4.1. Map the set C of experience tuples to a set C'. For each tuple $< s_1, a, s_2, r >$ in C, introduce in C' the tuple $< VQ^{S'}(\Gamma(s_1)), a, VQ^{S'}(\Gamma(s_2)), r >$
4.2. Apply the Q-Learning update function defined in equation 1 to learn a Q table Q: $D_{s'} \times a \to \Re$, using the set of experience tuples C'
6. Return Q, Γ and $VQ^{S'}$

4. CMAC and RL

In RL, though, generalization is commonly achieved through function approximation (as an instance of supervised learning): by learning weights from a set of features over the agent past and present perceptions. In this case, CMAC is often used as the approach for function approximation. CMAC (*Cerebellar Model Arithmetic Computer*) was originally designed for robotic systems and today is still widely used [6]. CMAC architecture was motived by the biological motor control functions of human cerebellum. According to [32], a CMAC is most closely comparable to a neural network that is trained using back-propagation, but almost always outperforms the neural network. So, CMAC can be adapted to function as a data analysis tools beyond its original purpose as robot controller. In [33], the authors adapted the CMAC algorithm for use in representing a general multi-variable function and applied the algorithm to mapping a geological surface. The CMAC discretization of the variable space is quite similar to that used in the Averaged Shifted Histogram (ASH) proposed by [34]. The results presented in [10] indicate that using a CMAC to approximate the value function led to results that were better than hand-coded approaches.

Thus, CMAC has been widely used for applications in function approximation [6; 35; 36; 37]; in robotics for path planning for manipulators [38; 39]; industrial processes [40]; and character recognition [41]. CMAC is widely used in robotic control and it has been used in various adaptive control tasks [42; 43; 44], and it has received extensive attention and extensive mathematical analysis [45]

CMAC is well known as a good function approximator and it local generalization ability has been beneficial in RL. In this section, CMAC together with Q-Learning is reviewed. First, we describe CMAC as function approximation, and later the CMAC-QL algorithm is described in detail.

4.1.   CMAC

Consider a problem in which the state set is continuous and 2-dimensional. In this case, a state is a vector with two components. One kind of feature are those corresponding to circles in state space. If a state is in a circle, then the corresponding feature has the value 1, otherwise the feature has the value 0 [1]. Figure 3 shows an example where the binary feature vector corresponding to the state $S' = (S_1', S_2')$ is $\phi(S') = 0, 1, 0, 0, 1, 0$.

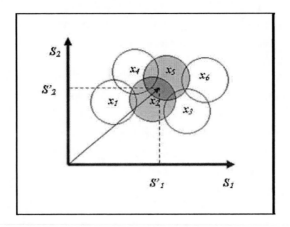

Figure 3. *Tile coding.*

For each state, a vector of binary features is built. This vector represents a coarsely code for the true location of the state in the space. Representing a state with features that overlap in this way is known as coarse coding.

CMAC, also known as tile coding, is a form of coarse coding [10; 1]. In CMAC the features are grouped into partitions of the input state space. Each of such partition is called a *tiling* and each element of a partition is called a *tile*. Each *tile* is a binary feature. The tilings are overlaids, each offset from the others. In each tiling, the state is in one tile. In Figure 4, we present an example of tile-coding which represents a 2-dimensional input state space S where two tilings were overlaid, each one with an offset from the other of 1/2 of the tile width. The set of all these active tiles, one per tiling and two per state, is what makes up the binary feature vector. As an example, the binary features vector for the state (0.38, 0.38) is $\phi_s = 0_0, 0_1, ..., 1_5, 0_6, ..., 1_{26}, 0_{27}, ..., 0_{31}$.

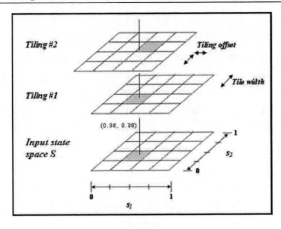

Figure 4. *Tile coding.*

4.2. CMAC-QL

When we combine CMAC with Q-Learning, it results in the CMAC-QL algorithm. In CMAC-QL, the approximate value function, Q_a, is represented not as a table, but in a parameterized form with a parameter vector $\vec{\theta_t}$. This means that the approximate value function Q_a totally depends on $\vec{\theta_t}$. In CMAC, each tile has an associated weight. The set of all these weights is what makes up the vector $\vec{\theta}$. The approximate value function, $Q_a(s)$ is then computed using equation 2.

$$Q_a(s) = \vec{\theta}^T \vec{\phi} = \sum_{i=0}^{n} \theta(i)\phi(i) \tag{2}$$

The CMAC process to compute the Q function is shown in Figure 5.

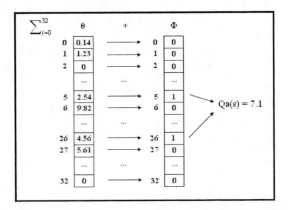

Figure 5. CMAC process to compute the Q value for an action *a*.

The Figure 5 shows a vector $\vec{\theta_t}$ of size 32 an a vector of features ϕ_s of the same size. The

Q function is computed by the scalar product of these vectors. The CMAC-QL algorithm, described in Table 2, uses CMAC to generalize the state space. In this case, a data set C is obtained during an interaction between the agent and the environment. This data set C is composed of tuples in the same form as in VQQL, $< s_1, a, s_2, r >$. Again, s can be also composed of a large number of features and feature selection can be used to select a subset S' of the relevant features of S. Later, the CMAC is built from C'_s. For each state variable x'_i in $s' \in S'$ the tile width and tiles per tiling are selected taking into account their ranges. In this chapter, a separate value function for each of the discrete actions is used. Finally, the Q function is approximated using equation 2.

Table 2. CMAC-QL Algorithm.

CMAC-QL
1. Gather experience tuples
1.1. Generate the set C of experience tuples of the type $< s_1, a, s_2, r >$ from an interaction of the agent in the environment, where $s_1, s_2 \in S$, $a \in A$ and $r \in \Re$ is the immediate reward.
2. Reduce the dimension of the state space
2.1. Let C_s be the set of states in C
2.2. Apply a feature selection approach using C_s to reduce the number of features in the state space. The resulting feature selection process is defined as a projection $\Gamma : S \to S'$
2.3. Set $C'_s = \Gamma(C_s)$
3. Design CMAC
3.1. Design a CMAC function approximator from C'_s
4. Approximate the Q function
4.1. Map the set C of experience tuples to a set C'. For each tuple $< s_1, a, s_2, r > \in C$, introduce in C' the tuple $< \Phi(\Gamma(s1)), a, \Phi(\Gamma(s_2)), r >$ where Φ is the binary vector of features
4.2. Update the weights vector θ for the action a using $\Phi(\Gamma(s_1))$, $\Phi(\Gamma(s_2))$ and r.
4.3. Apply the approximate value function defined in equation 2 to approximate the Q function for the action a using θ and $\Phi(\Gamma(C_s))$.
6. Return Q, Γ and θ

5. Decision/Regression Trees and RL

The value function can be approximated using any general function approximator such as neural network, or decision/regression trees. Two Steps Reinforcement Learning (2SRL), uses decision and regression trees as discretization methods of the state space [7]. It computes the action-value function in model free RL. The method assumes a reduced set of actions and finite trials, where positive and discrete rewards can be obtained only when a goal area is achieved. It is based on finding discretizations of the state space that are adapted to the value function being learned, trying to keep the convergence properties of the discretization methods using non-uniform discretizations [46]. The method is based on two learning phases. The first one is a model free version of the Smooth Value Iteration algorithm [22], that is called Iterative Smooth Q-Learning (ISQL). This algorithm, that executes an iterative supervised learning of the Q function, can be used to obtain a state space discretization too. This new discretization is used in a second learning phase, that is called Multiple Discretization Q-Learning (MDQL), to obtain an improved policy.

However, the method presented a main drawback: it requires a discrete reward function. Using such discrete reward function permits ISQL to learn a function approximation of the Q function applying classification algorithms such as J48, an algorithm to learn decision trees [47]. However, many domains, like the Keepaway [10], have continuous reward functions. In this case, 2SRL needs to discretize the reward space by hand, and to test different discretizations to obtain an accurate one. To apply the same ideas of 2SRL in domains with continuous rewards requires that the function approximation used in the ISQL phase be a regression approach. As before, the approximation method should generate a discretization of the state space, so such discretization can be used in the second learning phase. Fortunately, there are different approaches in the literature for regression that generate state space discretizations of the input space. Classical ones are M5 [47] or PART [48], which generate regression trees and regression rules respectively.

In this section, first decision and regression trees are introduced as discretizacion techniques. Finally, the Two Step Reinforcement Learning algorithm is described.

5.1. Decision/Regression Trees

An approach for representing the value function in RL is to use a neural network. This approach scales better than others, but is not guaranteed to converge and often performs poorly even on relatively simple problems. Our alternative is to use a decision/regression tree to represent the value function. Also, decision and regression trees divide the state space with varying levels of resolution, as shown in Figure 6.

In a decision tree, each decision node contains a test on the value of some input variable. The terminal nodes of the tree, the leafs, contain the predicted class values. Examples of algorithms to build decision trees are ID3, or J48 [47].

Regression trees may be considered as a variant of decision trees, designed to approximate real-valued functions instead of being used for classification tasks. A regression tree is built through a process known as binary recursive partitioning. This is an iterative process of splitting the data into partitions and then splitting it up further on each of the branches. The process continues recursively on each branch until an end condition is true, and the current node becomes a terminal node. Examples of algorithms to build regression trees are PART [48] and M5 [47].

5.2. Two Steps RL

Two Steps RL (2SRL) computes the action-value function in model free RL. This technique combines function approximation and discretization in two learning phases:

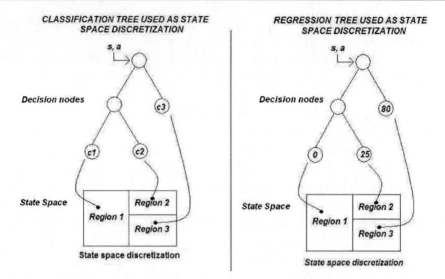

Figure 6. Decision and regression trees allow the state space to be divided.

- ISQL phase: iteratively refines a $Q(s,a)$ function approximation. For each iteration, it obtains a state space discretization.

- MDQL phase: runs the Q-Learning algorithm using the state space discretization obtained from the approximation of the $Q(s,a)$ function.

Iterative Smooth Q-Learning algorithm (ISQL) derives from Discrete Value Iteration [49], where a function approximator is used instead of the tabular representation of the value function. Thus, the algorithm can be used in the continuous state-space case. The algorithm is described in Figure 7. The update equation of the Q function used is the stochastic Q-Learning update equation. The figure shows the adapted version of the original ISQL algorithm that allows continuous rewards.

The algorithm assumes a discrete set of L actions, and hence, it will generate L function approximators, $Q_{a_i}(s)$. It requires a collection of experience tuples, T. Different methods can be applied to perform this exploration phase, from random exploration to human driven exploration [50]. In each iteration, from the initial set of tuples, T, and using the approximators $\hat{Q}_{a_i}^{iter-1}(s)$, $i = 1, \ldots, L$, generated in the previous iteration, the Q-learning update rule can be used to obtain L training sets, $T_{a_i}^{iter}$, $i = 1, \ldots, L$, with entries of the kind $< s_j, c_j >$ where c_j is the resulting value of applying the Q update function to the training tuple j, whose state is s_j.

In the first iteration, $\hat{Q}_{a_i}^0(s)$ are initialized to 0, for $i = 1, \ldots, L$, and all $s \in S$. Thus, when the respective c_j are computed, they depend only on the possible values of the immediate reward, r. A requirement of the 2SRL approach is that the classification/regression techniques used in the ISQL phase to generate a $Q(s,a)$ function approximation must learn by dividing the space in regions, so that these regions can be used as a state space discretization. In the second phase, the obtained discretizations can be used to tune the action value function generated in the previous phase, following a multiple (one per action) discretization based approach.

Iterative Smooth Q-Learning with Regression

- Inputs:

    1. A state space X

    2. A discrete set of L actions, $A = \{a_1, \ldots, a_L\}$

    3. A collection T of N experience tuples of the kind $< s, a_i, s', r >$, where $s \in X$ is a state where action a_i is executed, $s' \in X$ is the next state visited and r is the immediate reward received

- Generate L initial approximators of the action-value function $\hat{Q}^0_{a_i} : X \rightarrow \mathcal{R}$, and initialize them to return 0

- $iter = 1$

- Repeat

    - For all $a_i \in A$, initialize the learning sets $T^{iter}_{a_i} = \emptyset$

    - For $j = 1$ to N, using the jth tuple $< s_j, a_j, s'_j, r_j >$ do

        * $c_j = \alpha c_j + (1 - \alpha) \max_{a_r \in A} \gamma \hat{Q}^{iter-1}_{a_r}(s'_j)$
        * $T^{iter}_{a_j} = T^{iter}_{a_j} \cup \{< s_j, c_j >\}$

    - For each $a_i \in A$, train $\hat{Q}^{iter}_{a_i}$ to approximate the learning set $T^{iter}_{a_i}$

    - $iter = iter + 1$

    Until r_{max} is propagated to the whole domain

- Return $\hat{Q}^{iter-1}_{a_i}, \forall a_i \in A$

Figure 7. *Iterative Smooth Q-Learning* algorithm for domains with continuous rewards.

Figure 8 shows how to translate the refined function approximation obtained in the first phase to state space discretization in the second phase of 2SRL. An approximation like M5-Rules has been used, and L rule sets have been obtained (one for each action).

The left part of the approximator rules *RuleSet i* will be used as the discretization $D_i(s)$, and the right part of the rules of *RuleSet i* will be located in column i of the generated Q table, providing an initialization of the Q table in the second learning phase.[1] Each RuleSet may have a different number of rules, so the number of rows of the table is given by the maximum number of rules of the L approximators, and zero values can be used to complete the columns with less rules.

If we use J48 as the approximation technique, we obtain a classification tree where the regions of the state space discretization are each leaf of the tree. In Figure 9 we can see how to use a classification tree as space state discretization in the MDQL phase.

If we use M5 as an approximation technique, we obtain a regression tree where its leafs have a numerical value. We can use these numbers to initialize the Q table in the MDQL phase. Each leaf also represents a region of the state space discretization. In Figure 10 we can see how to use the numbers in the leafs of the tree to initialize the Q table.

---

[1] We can also initialize to 0 and do not use the right part of the rules.

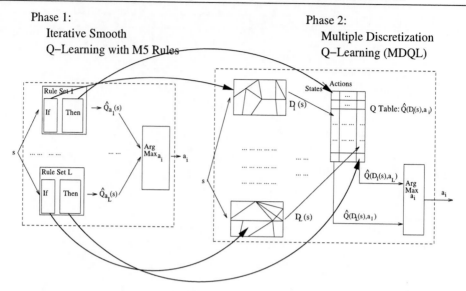

Figure 8. The two steps of the 2SRL algorithm with Regression.

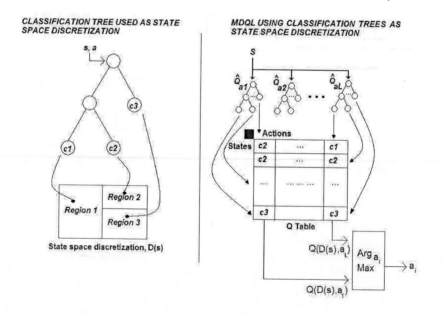

Figure 9. MDQL phase of 2SRL algorithm with classification trees.

Once the translation from the first scheme (ISQL) to the second one (MDQL) is done, a new learning phase can be executed using the Q-learning update function shown in equation 1.

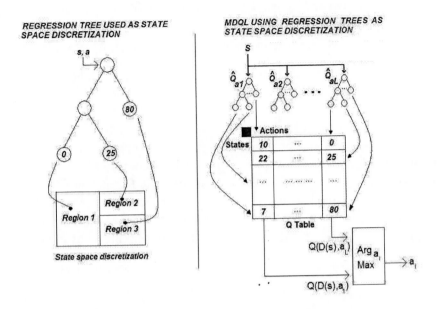

Figure 10. MDQL phase of 2SRL algorithm with regression trees.

The MDQL learning phase can be executed with new experiences or with the same ones used in the first phase. In the experimentation performed next, the first approach is applied using new experiences. This second phase can be executed exactly as it was defined in the original 2SRL algorithm, so additional explanation of this phase, and how to connect both phases, can be found in [7].

6. Evolutionary Computation and RL

Another category of RL methods are policy search methods. The main difference between policy search methods and other RL methods lies on how the search for a best policy is performed. Policy search methods search directly in the space of policies. The advantages of direct search methods compared to standard RL techniques are that they allow direct search in the policy space, whereas most RL techniques are restricted to optimize the policy indirectly by adapting state-action value functions or state-value functions, and they are usually easier to apply in complex problems and more robust.

In [51], the authors use a policy search method as a technique for finding sub-optimal controllers when such structured controllers exist. To validate the power of this approach, they show the presented learning control algorithm by flying an autonomous helicopter. In a similar way, [52] considers several neuroevolutionary approaches to discover robust controllers for a generalized version of the Helicopter hovering problem. In the same research line, [9] present a method to obtain a near optimal neuro-controller for the autonomous helicopter flight by means of an "ad hoc" evolutionary RL method. Evolutionary algorithms are powerful direct policy search methods. They has shown promising in RL tasks. In this section, first evolutionary algorithms are described from a direct policy search method perspective. Finally, the Evolutionary RL algorithm is explained in detail.

6.1. Evolutionary Algorithms as Direct Policy Search Method in RL

In Evolutionary Algorithms RL, the solutions take the form of policies used by decision making agents that operate in dynamic environments. Agents are placed in the world where they make decisions in response to environmental conditions. The Evolutionary Algorithm selects policies for reproduction based on their performance in the task, and applies genetic operators to generate new policies from the promising parent policies.

Evolutionary algorithms learn a decision policy of the form $f(s) \rightarrow a$ that maps a state description s to an action a. So, the fundamental difference between Evolutionary Algorithms and TD methods concerns the decision policy representation. TD methods define a value function of the form $f(s, a) \rightarrow v$ (Figure 11). Evolutionary Algorithm use a direct mapping that associates state descriptions directly with the recommended action.

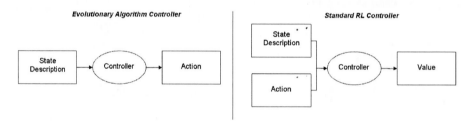

Figure 11. Mappings of Evolutionary Algorithms and TD methods.

6.2. Evolutionary RL

In this chapter, we apply an evolution strategy to the adaptation of the weights of artificial neural networks for RL tasks [9]. In this case, each artificial neural network is used for representing the policy of an agent. When using neural networks for representing the policy directly, the neural network weights parameterize the policies space that the network can learn. This parameterization is usually very complex, since there are strong correlations. The ability of an optimization algorithm to find dependencies between network parameters seems to be an important factor of the good performance.

In Evolutionary RL [9], each agent manages a population of N individual solutions (or candidate solutions). Each individual solution is a artificial neural network, all with the same topology but different weights. Each neural network receives as input the state perceived from the environment and the last action and returns as output the action to be executed. The algorithm evolves towards better solutions using four steps: selection of the best individual solutions, correlation, soft mutation and strong mutation. This evolution strategy adapts the weights of the neural networks in every generation. Figure 12 shows the different steps to evolve a population.

The weights of the initial population are radomly generated and adapted in every evolution. In every generation, each individual solution executes a number of τ episodes ob-

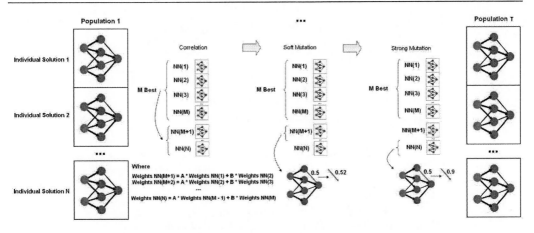

Figure 12. Evolutionary RL with Neural Networks.

taining the cumulative reward (the fitness in the evolutionary algorithm). When all the individual solutions have their own fitness, the population is evolved using the evolutionary operators (i.e. selection of the best individual solutions, correlation, soft mutation and hard mutation). In the correlation step, the individual solutions are ordered by their fitness or cumulative reward. The M best individual solutions propagate their weights to the rest of the population in the way shown in Figure 12. The correlation step is an effective form of guaranteeing offspring viability since weights can be set in order to generate individuals very close to one of its parents. In addition, this strategy guarantees the interrelation of the system since this causes a chain of correlations that propagates over the whole population. In the mutation steps, the algorithm randomly changes the weights of the last $N - M$ individual solutions. In soft mutation this change is a slight change, while in strong mutation it is a big change. The algorithm is shown in Table 3.

7.　Evaluation

RoboCup simulated soccer presents many challenges to RL methods: a large state space, hidden and uncertain states, multiple and independent agents learning simultaneously, and long and variable delays in the effects of actions. It has been used as the basis for international competitions and research challenges [53]. It is a distributed, multi-agent domain with teammates and adversaries. There are hidden states, meaning that each agent has only a partial view of the world at any moment. The agents have noisy sensors and actuators, meaning that they do not perceive the world exactly as it is, nor can they affect the world exactly as intended. In addition, the perception and action cycles are asynchronous, prohibiting the traditional AI paradigm of using perceptual input to trigger actions. Communication opportunities are limited, and the agents must make their decisions in real-time. These domain characteristics make simulated robot soccer a realistic and challenging domain. In this chapter, we present the results in the Keepaway domain [10], a subtask of the full and complex RoboCup soccer domain. This subtask of soccer, involves 5-9 players rather than the full 22. In the next section we describe the Keepaway domain. The next sections show the results obtained in this domain for the RL algorithms described previously:

Table 3. Evolutionay RL Algorithm.

Evolutionay RL Algorithm
1. Generate a initial population of N individual solutions
1.1. All the neural networks have the same topology
1.2. The weights are randomly initialized
2. For each individual solution
2.1. The agent interacts with the environment for τ episodes
2.2. Obtain the cumulative reward of this interaction using the individual solution.
3. Evolve the population, applying
3.1. Selection of the M best individual solutions
3.2. Correlation of the M best individual solutions
3.3. Soft mutation of the $N - M$ individual solutions
3.4. Strong mutation of the $N - M$ individual solutions
4. Return to 2 if the number of evolutions $< T$
5. Return Population T

VQQL, CMAC-QL, 2SRL and Evolutionary RL.

7.1. Keepaway Domain

In this subtask, the keepers try to maintain the possession of the ball within a region, while the takers try to gain it. An episode ends when the takers gain the possession of the ball or the ball leaves the playing region. When an episode ends, the players are reset for another episode. In our experiments each keeper learns independently. From a point of view of a keeper, an episode consists of a sequence of states, actions and rewards in the form:

$$s_0, a_0, r_1, s_1, ..., s_i, a_i, r_{i+1} \tag{3}$$

where a_i is selected based on some perception of s_i. We reward the keepers for each time step they keep possession, so we set the reward r_i to the number of time steps that elapsed while following action $a_{i-1} : r_i = t_i - t_{i-1}$. The keepers goal is to select an action such that the remainder of the episode will be as long as possible, and thus maximizes the total reward.

The state space is composed of several features that can be considered continuous. These features use information derived from distances and angles between the keepers, takers and the center of the playing area. The number of features used for each state depends on the number of players. In 3vs2 Keepaway (3 Keepers against 2 Takers) there are 13 features (Table 4).

The action space is composed of two different macro-actions, *HoldBall()* and *PassBall(k_i)* where k_i is the teammate i. The actions are available only when the keeper is in possession of the ball. In all the experiments reported, the 3vs2 keepaway is used and the size of the playing region is 25×25. In addition, the parameter setting for VQQL, CMAC-QL and 2SRL, obtained after an exhaustive experimentation, are the following: $\gamma = 1$ and

Table 4. The 13 state variables in 3vs2.

Feature	Description
dist(K_1, C)	Distance between $Keeper1$ and the center of the playing region.
dist(K_2, C)	Distance between $Keeper2$ and the center of the playing region.
dist(K_3, C)	Distance between $Keeper3$ and the center of the playing region.
dist(T_1, C)	Distance between $Taker1$ and the center of the playing region.
dist(T_2, C)	Distance between $Taker2$ and the center of the playing region.
dist(K_1, K_2)	Distance between $Keeper1$ and $Keeper2$.
dist(K_1, K_3)	Distance between $Keeper1$ and $Keeper3$.
dist(K_1, T_1)	Distance between $Keeper1$ and $Taker1$.
dist(K_1, T_2)	Distance between $Keeper1$ and $Taker2$.
Min(dist(K_2, T_1), dist(K_2, T_2))	Minimum distance between $Keeper2$ and $Taker1$ and between $Keeper2$ and $Taker2$
Min(dist(K_3, T_1), dist(K_3, T_2))	Minimum distance between $Keeper3$ and $Taker1$ and between $Keeper3$ and $Taker2$
Min(ang(K_2, K_1, T_1), ang(K_2, K_1, T_2))	Minimum between the ang(K_2, K_1, T_1) and ang(K_2, K_1, T_2)
Min(ang(K_3, K_1, T_1), ang(K_3, K_1, T_2))	Minimum between the ang(K_3, K_1, T_1) and ang(K_3, K_1, T_2).

$\alpha = 0.125$. In all cases, an $\epsilon - greedy$ strategy is applied, increasing the value of epsilon from 0 (random behaviour) to 1 (fully greedy behaviour) by 0.0001 in each episode.

7.2. Results of VQQL

In this setting, we use VQ to discretize the state space. First, for each keeper, we design the vector quantizer composed of N centroids from the input data obtained during a random interaction between the keeper and the environment. Then, the Q function is learned, using Q-Learning, generating the Q table composed of N rows and a column for each action. The size of the discretized state space is 64. In 3vs2, we obtain the results shown in Figure 13. The *y-axis* represent the average time that the keepers are able to keep the ball from the takers and the *x-axis* is training time. In the graphs, there are ten learning curves. The average values raises from 7 seconds up to around 18 seconds.

7.3. Results of CMAC-QL

The intervals of the variables in the 3vs2 case in a 25×25 region are defined in Table 5. In our experiments we use single-dimensional tilings. For each variable, 32 tilings were overlaid, each offset from the others by a 1/32 of the tile width. For each state variable, we specified the width of the tiles based of the width of the generalization that we desired. For example, distances were given widths of about 3.0 meters, whereas angles were given widths of about 10.0 degrees. This is the same parameter setting used in [10].

Then, the size of the primary vector $\vec{\theta}$ in 3vs2 is 4224 ($x_{1_{tiles}} + x_{2_{tiles}} + ... + x_{13_{tiles}}$). In our work, we use a separate value function for each of the discrete actions. So there would

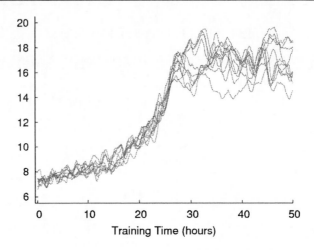

Figure 13. VQQL Results.

Table 5. Number of tiles per tiling.

Feature	Interval	*Tile* width	Tiles per tiling
dist(K_1, C)	[0, 17.67]	3	6
dist(K_1, K_2)	[0, 35.35]	3	11
dist(K_1, K_3)	[0, 35.35]	3	11
dist(K_1, T_1)	[0, 35.35]	3	11
dist(K_1, T_2)	[0, 35.35]	3	11
dist(K_2, C)	[0, 17.67]	3	6
dist(K_3, C)	[0, 17.67]	3	6
dist(T_1, C)	[0, 17.67]	3	6
dist(T_2, C)	[0, 17.67]	3	6
Min(dist(K_2, T_1), dist(K_2, T_2))	[0, 35.35]	3	11
Min(dist(K_3, T_1), dist(K_3, T_2))	[0, 35.35]	3	11
Min(ang(K_2, K_1, T_1), ang(K_2, K_1, T_2))	[0, 180]	10	18
Min(ang(K_3, K_1, T_1), ang(K_3, K_1, T_2))	[0, 180]	10	18

be roughly 4224 tiles for the *HoldBall()* action, 4224 tiles for the *PassBall*(k_1) action and 4224 tiles for the *PassBall*(k_2) action (about 12672 in total). We obtain the results shown in Figure 14. In the graph, there are ten learning curves. The average values raises from 7 seconds up to around 25 seconds.

7.4. Results of Two Steps RL

We use both M5 (regression) and J48 (C4.5, classification) algorithms to approximate the Q function for each iteration of the ISQL phase. In the case of
J48 [47], we have applied the original 2SRL algorithm discretizing the reward function.

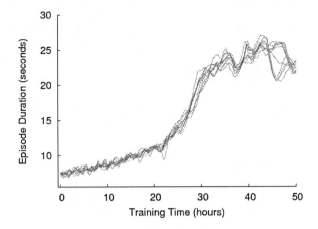

Figure 14. CMAC-QL Results.

We test different discretizations to obtain an accurate one. In this section we only show the best results obtained when we discretize the reward function by hand, using 88 classes. For M5 [47], we use the continuous rewards adapted version.

The first tuple set was obtained with a random policy working in the keepaway domain.

We tested two different approaches for the approximation. The first approach uses only one approximation $\hat{Q}_{(}s, a_i)$ where the action is an input parameter. The second approach uses multiple approximations $\hat{Q}_{a_i}(s)$, one per action, to approximate the Q function. The Q table is initialized using the values obtained in the leaves of the M5/J48 tree. In 3vs2, we obtain the results shown in Figure 15.

For each graph in Figure 15, we can see 10 evolution curves using the same configuration and the same approximation approach. The title at the top of each graph shows the approximation approach used. The *y-axis* is the average episode length and the *x-axis* is the training time. The J48 curves were generated using the best discretization of the reward space obtained by hand with 88 classes. We can observe how the policy improves during the training time.

7.5. Results of Evolutionary RL

In this case, a population of 100 individuals for each keeper is evolved using the evolutionary algorithm. In each generation, each individual plays five episodes in the keepaway domain. The cumulative reward achieved by playing all individuals in the population determines the probability that an individual will be selected when the next generation is created. Each individual is an artificial neural network with 14 nodes in the input layer. Inputs to each network describe the agent's current state and the last action selected (13 inputs for the state features and 1 for the last action selected). There are eight nodes in the hidden layer and three nodes in the output layer. There is one output for each available action and the agent takes whichever action has the highest activation.

Each candidate network is evaluated by allowing it to control the keepers' behavior and observing how much reward it receives. The policy's fitness is the sum of the rewards accrued while under the network's control. It is necessary to evaluate each member of the

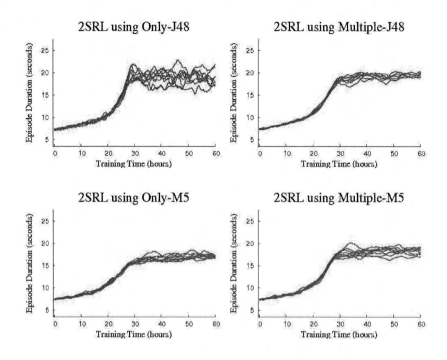

Figure 15. 2SRL algorithm results in Keepaway 3vs2.

population for many episodes to get accurate fitness estimates. In these experiments, each policy in keepaway is evaluated for an average of five episodes. Figure 16 shows 10 learning curves. The average values raise from seven seconds up to around 14 seconds.

7.6. Summary of the Results

The results of the four algorithms described in previous sections (VQQL, CMAC-QL, 2SRL and Evolutionary RL) are summarized in Figure 17. The graph in Figure 17 shows the mean and the standard deviation for the different algorithms. We can see the best result is achieved by CMAC-QL. In this case, the mean value grows from 7 seconds to 25 seconds approximately. Using the keepaway domain, our experiments show that Q-learning with CMAC can significantly improve the performance of other techniques. We believe this performance is approximately equal to the best result published to date, and it matches the best results published by other researchers [10]. In any case, the effectiveness of the CMAC function approximator combined with Q-Learning is widely demonstrated on several control problems [54].

In the second place, we can see the results obtained by 2SRL when J48 trees is used as approximation technique. In this case, the mean value raises from 7 seconds up to around 20 seconds. The discretization is obtained after an exhaustive experimentation evaluating different discretizations. In contrast, M5 does not need to discretize by hand the reward space and it obtains similar results than J48. When we use M5 as approximation technique, the mean grows from 7 seconds to 18 seconds approximately. We are using one state space

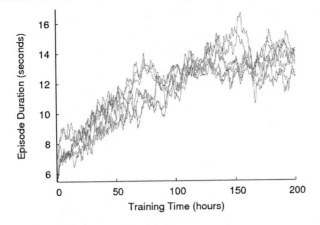

Figure 16. Evolutionary RL Results.

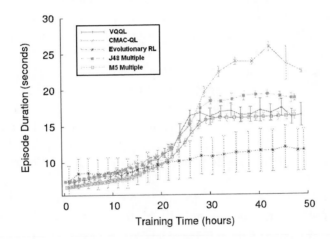

Figure 17. Mean and standard deviation obtained for the different algorithms in the keep-away domain.

discretization per action. This is a difference with previous work based on state space discretizations that typically use the same discretization for each action. Here we show that in model free methods where the action-value function, $Q(s, a)$ must be approximated, it is possible that each action requires a different number of resources or state space discretizations.

In the third place, we find the results of the VQQL algorithm. VQQL's mean grows from 7 seconds to 19 seconds approximately. The results show that VQ is a successful method to solve the states generalization problem of RL algorithms. The experiments show how VQ and the generalized Lloyd algorithm allows us to dramatically reduce the number of states needed to represent a continuous environment (only 64).

Finally, we can see the results obtained by Evolutionary RL. In this case, the mean raises from 7 seconds up to around 12 after 50 hours of training. In section 7.5., the performance grows from 7 seconds to 14 seconds approximately after 200 hours of training. The results in the Keepaway task show that Evolutionary algorithms can obtain good policies at the

RL task. In this chapter, a comparison between TD methods and Evolutionary algorithm is given. A detailed comparison can be found in [12; 28]. These studies conclude that the choice between using Evolutionary algorithms and a TD method should be made based on some of the given task's characteristics. In deterministic domains, the fitness of an individual can be quickly evaluated and Evolutionary algorithms RL are likely to excel. If the task is fully observable but nondeterministic, TD methods may have an advantage. If the task is partially observable and nondeterministic, each method may have different advantages: TD methods in speed and Evolutionary algorithms in asymptotic performance.

8. Conclusions

There are many approaches to tackled the state space generalization problem in RL tasks. Although, there is a lack of comparative studies that directly compare such approaches. As a result, there are currently no general guidelines describing the methods' relative strengths and weaknesses. This chapter presents the results of a detailed empirical comparison between the different state space generalization approaches reviewed in the Keepaway domain, a standard RL benchmark domain based on Robot Soccer.

The chapter began by suggesting two distinct approaches to solve RL problems with large or continuous state spaces; one can search in the value function space or in the policy space. Different TD methods and Evolutionary Algorithms RL, examples of these two approaches, are reviewed in this chapter. Unfortunately, conventional TD methods cannot be applied to problems with large or continuous state spaces; some form of generalization is required. This generalization is carried out in two different ways: by discretizing the state space to use a tabular representation of the value functions, or by using an approximation of the value function. As an example of the first approach, the chapter reviewed the VQQL algorithm which use vector quantization to discretize the state space. For the second approach, the CMAC-QL algorithm, which uses a CMAC function approximator, is explained in detail. There are even algorithms that use both approaches. The 2SRL algorithm is the algorithm representative of this category reviewed in this chapter.

In this chapter, we have also shown that the use of vector quantization for the generalization problem of RL techniques provides a solution to how to partition a continuous environment into regions of states that can be considered the same for the purposes of learning and generating actions. The experiments demonstrate vector quantization drastically reduces the state space and, in addition, it also solves the problem of knowing what granularity or placement of partitions is more appropriate. In relation to the CMAC-QL algorithm, this chapter reviewed the application of Q-Learning with linear tile-coding function approximation to a complex, multiagent task. CMAC is a function approximation method that strikes an empirically successful balance along representational power, computational cost and ease to use. The sucess of CMAC in practice depends in large part on parameter choices. The results obtained in this chapter by the CMAC-QL algorithm show that RL can work robustly in conjunction with function approximators. In addition, the results demonstrate that CMAC can learn better policies in this domain than VQ.

Then, we have described the 2SRL algorithm, that is composed of two main learning phases based on two approaches: supervised function approximation, using the Iterative Smooth Q-learning algorithm, and state space discretization methods, using the Multiple

Discretization Q-Learning. The algorithm has two main advantages. First, the two phases have shown better results over methods based on only one of the approaches. So, this method can be applied to approaches which only execute the first phase. In experiments, M5 and J48 are used to approximate the Q function in the first phase and we use the same approximators as discretization of the continuous keepaway state space, obtaining very successful results. The Q-RRL algorithm [55] is a Relational Reinforcement Learning algorithm very similar in structure to the Iterative Smooth Q-Learning algorithm presented here, but using relational data instead of feature based data. Furthermore, Q-RRL uses a logical Q-tree to approximate a Q-table, so a state space discretization is obtained in the same way that was presented in this chapter for J48 tree or M5. So, a second learning phase could be added over that state space representation obtained after executing Q-RRL to tune the Q-Learning approximation obtained. The second advantage is that the number of parameters and/or knowledge that must be introduced in order the algorithm to work correctly is very low, and hence, easily applicable to new domains.

Evolutionary RL algorithms is a general purpose optimization technique and can be applied to a wide variety of problems. We have used an Evolutionary RL algorithm to perform policy search RL and represent population of neural network action selectors. The results show that Evolutionary RL can learn good policies in the keepaway domain, though it requires a high number of evaluations to do so. In this chapter we can see RL problems can also be tackled without learning value functions, by directly search in the space of policies. Evolutionary methods, which simulate the process of Darwinian selection to discover good policies, are one way of conducting this search.

Evolutionary methods have fared better empirically on certain benchmark problems, especially those where the agent's state is partially observable [56; 57; 58]. In contrast, value functions methods have stronger theoretical guarantees [59; 60]. Evolutionary methods have been criticized because they do not exploit the specific structure of the RL problem. There have been few studies that directly compare these methods [57; 61], and in these studies rarely isolate factors critical to performance of each method [12; 28].

Unfortunately, since the TD and evolutionary research communities are disjoint and usually focus on different applications, there are no accepted benchmark problems or evaluation metrics.

The experiments presented in this chapter provide a preliminary basis about which methods to use to tackle RL task with large or continuous state space. Additional studies using more domains and different algorithms are necessary to draw definitive guidelines about when to use a technique or another one.

References

[1]　Richard S. Sutton and Andrew G. Barto. *Reinforcement Learning: An Introduction (Adaptive Computation and Machine Learning)*. Mit Pr, May 1998.

[2]　David Chapman and Leslie Pack Kaelbling. Input generalization in delayed reinforcement learning: An algorithm and performance comparisons. pages 726–731. Morgan Kaufmann, 1991.

[3]   Long Ji Lin. Scaling up reinforcement learning for robot control. In *ICML*, pages 182–189, 1993.

[4]   Andrew Moore. Variable resolution dynamic programming: Efficiently learning action maps in multivariate real-valued state-spaces. In L. Birnbaum and G. Collins, editors, *Machine Learning: Proceedings of the Eighth International Conference*, 340 Pine Street, 6th Fl., San Francisco, CA 94104, June 1991. Morgan Kaufmann.

[5]   Fernando Fernández and Daniel Borrajo. Vqql. applying vector quantization to reinforcement learning. In *RoboCup-99: Robot Soccer World Cup III*, pages 292–303, London, UK, 2000. Springer-Verlag.

[6]   J. S. Albus. A new approach to manipulator control: the cerebellar model articulation controller (cmac). *Journal of Dynamic Systems, Measurement and Control*, **97**:220–227, 1975.

[7]   Fernando Fernández and Daniel Borrajo. Two steps reinforcement learning. *Int. J. Intell. Syst.*, **23**(2):213–245, 2008.

[8]   Iván López-Bueno, Javier García, and Fernando Fernández. Two steps reinforcement learning in continuous reinforcement learning tasks. In *IWANN '09: Proceedings of the 10th International Work-Conference on Artificial Neural Networks*, pages 577–584, Berlin, Heidelberg, 2009. Springer-Verlag.

[9]   José Antonio Martin H. and Javier de Lope Asiaín. Learning autonomous helicopter flight with evolutionary reinforcement learning. In Roberto Moreno-Díaz, Franz Pichler, and Alexis Quesada-Arencibia, editors, *EUROCAST*, volume 5717 of *Lecture Notes in Computer Science*, pages 75–82. Springer, 2009.

[10] Peter Stone, Richard S. Sutton, and Gregory Kuhlmann. Reinforcement learning for RoboCup-soccer keepaway. *Adaptive Behavior*, 13(3):165–188, 2005.

[11] Leslie Pack Kaelbling, Michael L. Littman, and Andrew W. Moore. Reinforcement learning: A survey. *Journal of Artificial Intelligence Research*, 4:237–285, 1996.

[12] Matthew E. Taylor, Shimon Whiteson, and Peter Stone. Temporal difference and policy search methods for reinforcement learning: An empirical comparison. In *Proceedings of the Twenty-Second Conference on Artificial Intelligence*, pages 1675–1678, July 2007. Nectar Track.

[13] Juan Carlos Santamara, Juan Carlos Santamar'ia, Richard S. Sutton, and Ashwin Ram. Experiments with reinforcement learning in problems with continuous state and action spaces. *Adaptive Behavior*, 6:163–218, 1998.

[14] Rémi Munos. A study of reinforcement learning in the continuous case by the means of viscosity solutions. *Machine Learning*, 40(3):265–299, 2000.

[15] Fernando Fernandez State Space Representations and Daniel Borrajo. On determinism handling while learning reduced. In *In Proceedings of the European Conference on Artificial Intelligence (ECAI 2002*, 2002.

[16] William Taubman Bryant Uther. *Tree Based Hierarchical Reinforcement Learning.* PhD thesis, Pittsburgh, PA, USA, 2002. Chair-Veloso, Manuela.

[17] I. S. K. Lee and H. Y. K. Lau. Adaptive state space partitioning for reinforcement learning. *Engineering Applications of Artificial Intelligence*, **17**:577–588, 2004.

[18] Mehran Asadi and Manfred Huber. State space reduction for hierarchical reinforcement learning. In Valerie Barr and Zdravko Markov, editors, *FLAIRS Conference.* AAAI Press, 2004.

[19] Dimitri P. Bertsekas and John N. Tsitsiklis. *Neuro-Dynamic Programming (Optimization and Neural Computation Series, 3).* Athena Scientific, May 1996.

[20] John N. Tsitsiklis and Benjamin Van Roy. Feature-based methods for large scale dynamic programming. In *Machine Learning*, pages 59–94, 1994.

[21] Leemon Baird and Andrew Moore. Gradient descent for general reinforcement learning. In *In Advances in Neural Information Processing Systems 11*, pages 968–974. MIT Press, 1998.

[22] Andrew Moore Justin Boyan. Generalization in reinforcement learning: Safely approximating the value function. In G. Tesauro & D.S. Touretzky & T.K. Lee, editor, *Neural Information Processing Systems 7*, pages 369–376, Cambridge, MA, 1995. The MIT Press.

[23] Robert Michael Lewis, Virginia Torczon, Michael, and Michael W. Trosset. Direct search methods: Then and now. *Journal of Computational and Applied Mathematics*, **124**:191–207, 2000.

[24] David Moriarty Moriarty, Alan C. Schultz, and John J. Grefenstette. Evolutionary algorithms for reinforcement learning. *Journal of Artificial Intelligence Research*, **11**:241–276, 1999.

[25] M. T. Rosenstein and A. G. Barto. Robot weightlifting by direct policy search. In *IJCAI'01: Proceedings of the 17th International Joint Conference on Artificial Intelligence*, volume **2**, pages 839–844, San Francisco, CA, USA, 2001. Morgan Kaufmann Publishers Inc.

[26] Douglas Aberdeen. A (revised) survey of approximate methods for solving partially observable markov decision processes. Technical report, National ICT Australia, 2003.

[27] Leonid M. Peshkin. *Reinforcement Learning by Policy Search.* PhD thesis, Providence, RI, USA, 2002. Adviser-Kaelbling, Leslie.

[28] Shimon Whiteson, Matthew E. Taylor, and Peter Stone. Critical factors in the empirical performance of temporal difference and evolutionary methods for reinforcement learning. *Journal of Autonomous Agents and Multi-Agent Systems*, 2009.

[29] Allen Gersho and Robert M. Gray. *Vector Quantization and Signal Compression*. Kluwer Academic Publishers, Norwell, MA, USA, 1991.

[30] Y. Linde, A. Buzo, and R. Gray. An algorithm for vector quantizer design. *Communications, IEEE Transactions on*, **28**(1):84–95, 1980.

[31] J. Zhang W. Xu, A.K. Nandi. A new fuzzy reinforcement learning vector quantization algorithm for image compression. In *Proceedings of the IEEE International Conference on Acoustics, Speech and Signal Processing*, Hong Kong, June 2003.

[32] George Burgin. Using cerebellar arithmetic computers. In *AI Expert 7*, pages 32–41, 1992.

[33] Alexander Hagens and John H. Doveton. Application of a simple cerebellar model to geologic surface mapping. *Comput. Geosci.*, **17**(4):561–567, 1991.

[34] David W. Scott. *Multivariate Density Estimation: Theory, Practice and Visualization (Wiley Series in Probability and Statistics)*. Wiley-Interscience, September 1992.

[35] J. S. Albus. Data storage in the cerebellar model articulation controller (cmac). *ASME Journal of Dynamical Systems, Measurement and Control*, pages 228–233, 1975.

[36] J. S. Albus. *Brains, Behaviour and Robotics*. Byte Books, Subsidiary of McGraw-Hill, 1981.

[37] E. Ersü and J. Militzer. Software implementation of a neuron-like associative memory system for control applications. In *2nd IASTED Conference on Mini- and Micro-Computer Applications – MIMI '82*, Davos, Switzerland, March 1982.

[38] C. K. Tham and R. W. Prager. *Reinforcement Learning for Multi-linked Manipulator Control*. Cambridge University Engineering Department, Trumpington Street, Cambridge CB2 1PZ, UK, 1992.

[39] C. K. Tham and R. W. Prager. *Reinforcement Learning Methods for Multi-linked Manipulator Obstacle Avoidance and Control*. Cambridge University Engineering Department, Trumpington Street, Cambridge CB2 1PZ, UK, 1993.

[40] H. Tolle, P. C. Parks, E. Ersuand, Hormel, and J. Militzer. Learning control with interpolating memories - general ideas, design-lay-out, theoretical approaches and practical applications. **56**(2):291–317, 1992.

[41] W. T. Miller, K. F. Arehart, and S. M. Scalera. On-line hand-printed character recognition using cmac neural networks. In *In Lendaris, G. G., Grossberg, S., & Kosko, B. (Eds.), World Congress on Neural Networks, WCNN'93*, pages 10–13, 1993.

[42] W. Thomas Miller. Real-time application of neural networks for sensor-based control of robots with vision. *IEEE Transactions on Systems, Man, and Cybernetics*, **19**(4):825–831, 1989.

[43] W. Thomas Miller, III, and Andrew L. Kun. *Dynamic Balance of a Biped Walking Robot*. MA: Academic Press, Boston, 1997.

[44] Michael Lang. *A Real-time Implementation of a Neural-network Controller for Industrial Robotics*. PhD thesis, Toronto, Ont., Canada, Canada, 1998. Adviser-D'Eleuterio, G. M.

[45] W. Thomas Miller, Filson H.Glanz, and L. Gordon Kraft. Cmac: An associative neural network alternative to backpropagation. In *Proc. IEEE*, volume 78, pages 1561–1567, 1990.

[46] Rémi Munos and Andrew W. Moore. Variable resolution discretization in optimal control. *Machine Learning*, **49**(2-3):291–323, 2002.

[47] Ian H. Witten and Eibe Frank. *Data Mining: Practical Machine Learning Tools and Techniques, Second Edition (Morgan Kaufmann Series in Data Management Systems)*. Morgan Kaufmann Series in Data Management Systems. Morgan Kaufmann, 2 edition, June 2005.

[48] Eibe Frank and Ian H. Witten. Generating accurate rule sets without global optimization. pages 144–151. Morgan Kaufmann, 1998.

[49] Richard Bellman. *Dynamic Programming*. Dover Publications, March 2003.

[50] William Donald Smart. *Making Reinforcement Learning Work on Real Robots*. PhD thesis, Providence, RI, USA, 2002. Adviser-Kaelbling, Leslie Pack.

[51] J. Andrew (Drew) Bagnell and Jeff Schneider. Autonomous helicopter control using reinforcement learning policy search methods. In *Proceedings of the International Conference on Robotics and Automation 2001*. IEEE, May 2001.

[52] Rogier Koppejan and Shimon Whiteson. Neuroevolutionary reinforcement learning for generalized helicopter control. In *GECCO 2009: Proceedings of the Genetic and Evolutionary Computation Conference*, pages 145–152, July 2009.

[53] H. Kitano, M. Tambe, P. Stone, M. Veloso, S. Coradeschi, E. Osawa, H. Matsubara, I. Noda, and M. Asada. The robocup synthetic agent challenge,97. In *International Joint Conference on Artificial Intelligence (IJCAI97)*, 1997.

[54] Richard S. Sutton. Generalization in reinforcement learning: Successful examples using sparse coarse coding. In *Advances in Neural Information Processing Systems 8*, pages 1038–1044. MIT Press, 1996.

[55] Saso Dzeroski, Luc De Raedt, and Kurt Driessens. Relational reinforcement learning. *Machine Learning*, **43**(1/2):7–52, 2001.

[56] Faustino J. Gomez and Jürgen Schmidhuber. Co-evolving recurrent neurons learn deep memory pomdps. In *GECCO '05: Proceedings of the 2005 Conference on Genetic and Evolutionary Computation*, pages 491–498, New York, NY, USA, 2005. ACM.

[57] Faustino Gomez, Juergen Schmidhuber, and Risto Miikkulainen. Efficient non-linear control through neuroevolution. In *Proceedings of the European Conference on Machine Learning (ECML)*, 2006.

[58] Kenneth O. Stanley and Risto Miikkulainen. Evolving neural networks through augmenting topologies. *Evolutionary Computation*, **10**:2002, 2001.

[59] Michael Kearns. Near-optimal reinforcement learning in polynomial time. In *Machine Learning*, pages 260–268. Morgan Kaufmann, 1998.

[60] T. L. Dean M. L. Littman and L. P. Kaelbling. On the complexity of solving markov decision processes. In *In Proceedings of the 11th International Conference on Uncertainty in Artificial Intelligence*, 1995.

[61] David E. Moriarty and Risto Miikkulainen. Efficient reinforcement learning through symbiotic evolution. In *Machine Learning*, pages 11–32, 1994.

In: Progress in Education, Volume 21
Editor: Robert V. Nata , pp. 191-216

ISBN: 978-1-61728-115-0
© 2011 Nova Science Publishers, Inc.

Chapter 9

MULTIPLE AGENT SYSTEMS
IN THE TIME-FREQUENCY DOMAIN

*John Hefferan**
Defence Science and Technology Organisation

Abstract

The detection and filtering of communication signals possessing time-frequency (tf) diversity is considered in this chapter. When viewed as an optimization problem in tf space, multiple intelligent agents are used to learn characteristic features of the transmitted signals. The agents are shown to detect and reconstruct specific signals possessing tf diversity in a co-ordinated manner.

The intelligent agents sensing this particular communications environment control a group of narrowband radio receivers. Multiple agent reinforcement learning is used to effectively co-ordinate agent behaviour as they respond to information retrieved from the tf environment. This approach has a further advantage of potentially increasing the rate of information processing following training, due to the parallel nature of the multiple agent implementation.

A review of some of the complex issues inherent in multiple agent reinforcement learning is presented. The concept of agent mediation in a multi-agent reinforcement learning environment is introduced.

Intelligent agents define the management and specialist tasks. Each is sensitive to different features of the signal of interest (SOI) likely to be present in the tf fragments detected. These include energy threshold agents, demodulator agents, spectral content agents and signal envelope agents which are introduced and discussed. A two-stage learning algorithm incorporating firstly, multi-agent clustering in the tf space. This is followed by a second phase consisting of an optimization of team membership by agents leading on to the reconstruction of one or more SOI.

Two multi-agent systems are introduced as examples that attempt to detect and filter signals possessing known features of interest contained within the wider received spectral band. Various learning policies are investigated and the performance of the systems are considered.

Finally, advantages and some of the co-ordination issues involved in the fusion of spatially diverse agent information are also discussed.

Keywords: multiple agent, time-frequency, wideband

*E-mail address: john.hefferan@dsto.defence.gov.au

1. Introduction

Modulated carrier electromagnetic transmission conventionally requires the receiver to possess detailed knowledge of how the original message signal was broadcast in order to correctly recover it. The transmission carrier frequency and modulation method are fundamental properties of the original transmission that the receiver requires. However, recently, time and frequency spreading techniques have become more widely used by transmitters in order to reduce susceptibility to narrowband channel noise and improve the usage of frequency bandwidth by transmitters. In situations where the specific transmission information for signals is unknown a conventional approach has been for the output of a single or multichannel wideband receiver to be analysed [1]. This conventional approach could be thought of as a single agent approach to analyse received tf data. This approach has been useful when the carrier frequency, or one of its signal components, was a constant feature of the power spectrum and could be detected by integrating the spectral region around the carrier frequency of the transmission. However, when time-dependencies are used by the transmitter during the signal transmission, individual receivers without full knowledge of the transmitted signal in time must keep track of potentially many concurrent signal transmissions in order to determine the correct state sequence through time-frequency space.

In this chapter a multi-agent approach is introduced to the problem of detecting (and characterizing) electromagnetic signals present in a wide bandwidth frequency and time environment. The advantage of processing many regions of the time-frequency environment concurrently, together with the opportunity to trial several learning policies has prompted this approach. Using many, digitally controlled, narrowband receivers is now a feasible alternative to the conventional use of a single wideband tuner.

A review of reinforcement learning and multi-agent approaches is presented in sections 2 and 3 of this chapter. The nature of the time-frequency space as an agent environment is then discussed in section 4 prior to the introduction of the learning algorithm in sections 5 and 6. Then, in sections 7 and 8 the algorithms are used to detect and then filter, signals present in synthetic examples of communications environments. Finally, some further applications and areas of work are discussed.

2. Reinforcement Learning

As depicted in Figure 1, we can describe a process whereby a single agent, at a discrete time t and based on information it has gathered from its environment, decides on which action to take given that it is currently in a particular state $s(t)$. At this level the agent gathers information from its environment at time t and examines the consequences of its possible range of actions. The action it chooses may move the agent into a new state at time $t+1$.

Each state will possess some intrinsic value $V(s(t))$ and the agent can explore the space available by making actions and testing the value of subsequent states. A characteristic feature of reinforcement learning [2] is that when the learning agent reaches a state of high value it is rewarded. The agent remembers this and, in future trials, the state sequence leading to the high value state is more likely as the actions taken leading to these states have been reinforced. The ultimate goal is to maximize the total reward. Figure 1 identifies

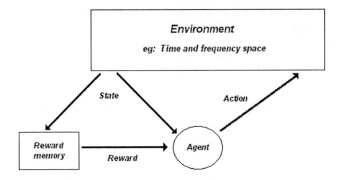

Figure 1. Overview of the Reinforcement Learning model with Reward Memory.

this reward memory as augmented information available to the agent at each state. We will briefly discuss some of the main concepts behind reinforcement learning as explained well in other literature. Chapter 16 of Alpaydin [3] provides an excellent introduction to the area.

Of course, from a given vantage point in time, the further into the future the agent looks, the less certain it can be that an optimal decision policy has been found (there are just too many possibilities). This uncertainty can be taken into account to some extent by discounting the reward term the further away from the goal state we venture whilst in the learning mode.

Bellman's [4] fundamental relationship, restated here in equation 1 succinctly summarizes this process:

$$Q^*(s_t, a_t) = E[r_{t+1}] + \gamma \sum (P(s_{t+1}|s_t, a_t) \max_{a_{t+1}} Q^*(s_{t+1}, a_{t+1}) \tag{1}$$

Here, $Q^*(s_t, a_t)$ is the value of the state action pair (s_t, a_t) when following the optimal policy and $E[r_{t+1}]$ is the expected reward at $t + 1$. The second main term on the right hand side of equation 1 is the discounted sum of the probability of being in state $t + 1$ given s_t and a_t multiplied by the maximum value state-action pair at $t + 1$ across all actions at $t + 1$ using the optimal policy. This term effectively looks ahead into the range of possible actions and assesses their currently known value weighted by the probability of being in that state. γ is the discount factor that, as explained above, reduces the effect of the more uncertain value estimates in future states.

In many situations we do not have enough knowledge of the environment to fully specify a model, as defined by $p(r_{t+1}|s_t, a_t)$ and $P(s_{t+1}|s_t, a_t)$, the reward function and state transition probabilities respectively. Hence, we may therefore need to use a model-free learning algorithm. For the simple case of there only being a single reward and next state possible then (1) becomes:

$$Q(s_t, a_t) = r_{t+1} + \gamma \max_{a_{t+1}} Q(s_{t+1}, a_{t+1}) \tag{2}$$

Equation 2 first chooses the action that maximizes the value of the next state and action pair, then adds the discounted resulting value to the known next-state reward amount $r(t+1)$

to give the value of the present state and action pair $Q(s_t, a_t)$.

When the rewards and results of actions are not deterministic then (2) becomes:

$$Q(s_t, a_t) = E[r_{t+1}] + \gamma \sum_{s_{t+1}} P(s_{t+1}|s_t, a_t) \max_{a_{t+1}} Q(s_{t+1}, a_{t+1}) \tag{3}$$

Watkins and Dayan [5] have developed a learning rule from 3 that possesses a variable learning rate η. $\hat{Q}(s_t, a_t)$ is the current estimate of the Q value for the state and action pair at time t. Known as Q-learning, the algorithm is:

$$\hat{Q}(s_t, a_t) \leftarrow \hat{Q}(s_t, a_t) + \eta \left[r_{t+1} + \gamma (\max_{a_{t+1}} \hat{Q}(s_{t+1}, a_{t+1})) - \hat{Q}(s_t, a_t) \right] \tag{4}$$

Here, $\hat{Q}(s_t, a_t)$ approaches its mean value as η is gradually decreased in time. Q-learning reduces the difference between the current Q value and the retained estimate from one time step later. This algorithm is a form of Temporal Difference learning [6]. It is an off-policy algorithm as no action policy is referred to in order to guide the next move, it is decided only upon perceived value.

Sarsa [2] is an on-policy version of Q-learning where the action chosen is set by the current policy and we are, in effect, estimating the value of that policy. Finally, Temporal Difference learning can be used to learn state values $V(s)$ rather than the value of state and action pairs $Q(s, a)$ [6]. The learning rule then becomes:

$$V(s_t) \leftarrow V(s_t) + \eta [r_{t+1} + \gamma(V(s_{t+1})) - V(s_t)] \tag{5}$$

Here, updates decrease the temporal difference between the current estimate and the refined, later prediction. As η is gradually decreased the estimate converges to the optimal value function $V^*(s)$ [3] p.385.

3. Multiple Agent Reinforcement Learning

In the case of single entity reinforcement learning, the agent acts independently with a guiding policy to direct its actions. During the optimization process over successive epochs the agent learns characteristic features of the environment that it is gaining information from. Specific actions are progressively reinforced as a result of cumulative reward at different states being acquired by the agent - the rewards effectively resulting from the agents own independent actions. During the learning process the agent becomes successively more confident (reinforced) about the actions to take when in particular states in order to maximize the long-term reward.

When there is only one agent acting in an environment the agent may implement a reinforcement learning algorithm with relative confidence, knowing that the algorithm has some guarantees about convergence in time [3]. However, when two or more learning agents are acting in the same environment it is possible that some interference between agents could occur. We would like to know whether the presence and actions of a population of agents effect the learning process being carried out in any particular individual agent.[1]

---

[1]See, for example [7] for an overview of some of the important issues.

From a reinforcement learning perspective, the effect of an agent population on the learning process of any particular agent in the same environment impinges on two aspects of that learning. Firstly, the extent to which the independent actions of agents effect the learning process is dependent upon the *visibility* of other agents (ie: whether agents are aware of the existence and state of other agents during learning). Secondly, the individual agent's learning process may be influenced if other agents in the population are able to affect the relative value of future states as perceived by the individual agent.

This interference between agents in an uncontrolled multi-agent learning scenario is potentially destabilizing. Hence, the approach taken in this chapter is to reduce the agent visibility to smaller subspaces relevant to the problem being solved and then to allow careful negotiation among the remaining visible agents. The goal is for agents within each others field of visibility to reach mutually beneficial state transitions. In this chapter this approach is termed agent mediation.

3.1.   Agent Mediation

The concept of agent mediation in this context refers to the tailoring of the scope of active steps that can be taken by agents to resolve the individual assessment of state values cooperatively during the learning process.

In effect we are mediating the actions of a potentially large population of agents, each implementing reinforcement learning with the goal of attempting to solve a problem collectively. Some of the specific steps that we take in this chapter are to specify a depth of influence, information to be shared and to agree on action policies.

3.1.1.   Depth of Influence of an Agent's Action on Other Agents

The *range of effect* or *depth of influence* that an agent possesses in its environment is an important factor affecting the impact that a particular agent has on the agent population as a whole. For example, we may define a depth of influence for agent (A) as I_A. Agents present within the I_A range are the only agents able to directly influence the learning process of agent (A). An important effect of the I_A value is to limit the number of agents able to be affected by agent (A) irrespective of how many agents are aware of it. Hence, the reduction in computational complexity aids in the modeling of agent interactions and the effects of neighboring agents may be accounted for in the estimation of state value. Furthermore, agents present in the same environment with orthogonal specialist abilities may have a non-intersecting depth of influence on each other.[2] With respect to their assessment of state value, agents with these orthogonal specialist abilities effectively form mutually independent agent populations.

3.1.2.   Information Shared between Agents

Information sharing between agents in the environment may influence the decisions made by agents when assessing the value of subsequent states. Agent-specific information

---

[2]See section 5 of this work for a description of the specialist agent in this context

about other agents within a visible field may be transmitted to the other agents within their depth of influence.

Information from these other visible agents may include static parameters such as their own depth of influence, its perceived self-value and its perceived value of the current state of the system. More dynamic parameters associated with the learning process in the agents including the agent's past trajectory through the environment and its history of perceived state values may also be shared.

Static and dynamic information from each visible agent may be shared to a greater or lesser extent. The availability of the current state value and reward matrices relevant to agents for an agreed future time horizon enable agents to take account of other agents range of probable actions.

3.1.3.   Current Policies

Agents conform to policies at various levels during the learning process. These include:

1. **Current Individual Policy.**
   At an individual level, each agent consults its own guidance policy when making decisions based on the values it has detected in its surrounding states.

2. **Population Guidance Policies.**
   For example, an explore vs exploit policy mixture may be implemented by the agent population as a whole, irrespective of the specific policies of individual agents. The sensitivity of an agent's decision on action at any particular state is closely linked to the explore vs exploit ratio in use at that state. Actions taken by other agents independently may significantly change the value of resultant states to an agent. Being bound by a greedy, relatively insensitive, exploitative policy may decrease the chance of convergence or, at least, increase the number of learning iterations required to reach it. Implementing a decision policy that reduces the sensitivity of an agent to uncontrollable changes made by other agents in the shared environment would be of value.

3. **Global Co-ordination Policies.**
   Implemented globally across all agents, these policies allow oversight of the progress of the learning process and the degree of convergence to a desired state. This absolute metric of performance allows the detection of agents whose learning has failed when their performance is compared with that of other agents in the broader population.

3.2.   Multiple Agent Instances

In specific environments the selection of an appropriate agent mediation policy attempts to reduce the effect of the presence of multiple learning agents. Prior research has studied the influence of the amount of knowledge mutually shared between agents present in the environment. We consider here three possible scenarios that may arise when a population of agents using reinforcement learning attempts to solve a problem collectively in an environment.

3.2.1. Agents Do not Share Information

If agents ignore each other they are effectively carrying our reinforcement learning without sharing information [8][9]. Hence, in this case, agents implement reinforcement learning independently. Sen, Sekaran and Hale have used this method with agents working in the same environment to solve the block-pushing problem [8]. In their work they found that two agents were able to successfully complete the task without sharing information - effectively working together to achieve a common goal independently and without being aware of each other's capabilities. In this case independent actions resulted in a global reward measure (the block position) which was available to each agent. Hence, it is possible, given appropriate information on progress towards a common goal for multiple agents to independently learn the actions that result in them making a constructive contribution to a combined solution to the task.

It is also worth mentioning here that awareness of other agents can, in fact, harm performance as described in [10]. In one case they examined, insufficient exploration of the state space by the multiple concurrent learners resulted in premature convergence. The effect of adding multiple learners is therefore not necessarily beneficial and requires careful matching of the multiple agent learning rule to the environment and goals presented to the agent population.

3.2.2. Agents Broadcast Information before Making Decisions

It is a goal of information sharing among agents to perform at least as well as independent learners. This has been found to be achievable [11] although it was found that there are risks involved when an agent population attempts to collaborate on a given task.

As described above (and in Tan[12]), awareness of other agents can actually harm performance. Extra, insufficient information was shown to interfere with learning and so this finding leads us to conclude that some form of tailoring of information to be shared may be necessary in order to actually facilitate learning with multiple agents.

Agents can openly share information with each other via a communications link. There is a communication cost when information from other agents is broadcast over a link of this type. This communication cost has previously been measured in bits [12] however increased bandwidth (ie: bits per unit time) is an alternative measure of communication cost. The bandwidth capacity of a given communications link in a multiagent system may also be called the channel or information capacity [13] required for a given number of agents. As an example of this, consider N agents present in an environment with full awareness of each other and a requirement to broadcast a set packet of information at each state that it enters. In this case, each agent needs to transmit 100 bits of data to advertise their current state. A full exchange of state information will therefore require $100.N(N-1)$ bits to be transmitted across the communications link during each state. This $O(N^2)$ requirement together with the bandwidth of the communications link is illustrated in Figure 2.

Figure 2 shows that increasing the number of agents within a given depth of influence does not guarantee a more efficient system when implemented. The quantity of data transmitted during negotiations in this example is of $O(N^2)$ and for a given link bandwidth this effectively places an upper bound on the maximum number of agents capable of negotiating

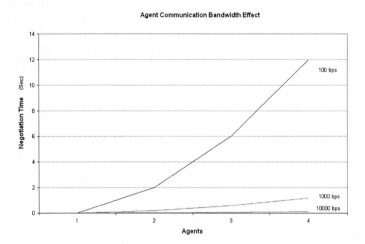

Figure 2. The effect of link bandwidth on agent communication.

within a set time constraint. This is of crucial importance if the task confronting the agent population is to gain knowledge from communications signals in real (or near real) time.

3.2.3. Knowledge of the Agent Population Is Mediated

In this instance we consider the case of a limiting mediation being applied to the data shared between agents. For example, only a fixed subset of agents are visible to any given agent. Each agent may only have a specific field of interest outside of which other agents are mutually ignored. The visible field is tailored to the specific subset of states in the environment that have importance to an agent in negotiations relevant to the overall goals in each of the learning phases.

4.   The Time-Frequency Domain as an Environment

Traditionally, electromagnetic energy received by means of a resonating device (antenna) is selectively tuned to the specific frequencies that the message carrying transmissions were broadcast on. As long as the modulating process is fully known, and subject to timing constraints, the transmitted message-stream may be recovered. In a digital modulation scheme some form of decoding may also be required. In general though, this reception process is usually carried out by a single receiver processing streams of time-varying input signals sequentially.

Modern wideband receiving systems are able to receive a frequency band of information whose upper and lower frequency bounds are limited by the response characteristics of the receiver system. For example, one version of the Esmeralda system [14] is able to receive and record received signals with a 20 MHz bandwidth. Using equipment capable of processing this frequency range for example, we may then store the received data for subsequent off-line processing. We are also able to plot the variation in spectral energy within this frequency bound vs. time as is depicted in Figure 3.

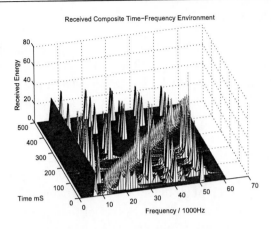

Figure 3. Received Energy Varying in the Time-Frequency Environment.

This three-dimensional representation of the received energy may be thought of as an environment where time and frequency are the independent variables. The two-dimensional tf space may be subdivided into a matrix of cells each of which possesses a uniform dimension in both the time and frequency axis. Furthermore, the two-dimensional spatial co-ordinates may be transformed from the tf space back to give us a one-dimensional index offset into the file containing the original received data stream whenever required.

5. The Specialist Agent

The ability of individual agents to detect relevant waveform attributes present in the tf environment that are present at its receiver input is central to the performance of the multiple agent population. Each of these detectable attributes are representative of the feature set associated with specific waveforms. It is the combined experience and perspective of many of these specialist agents that contribute to the overall detection decision.

Specialist agents may have a range of abilities and different populations of specialist agents are suitable for different tf environments. Some examples of the distinct features relevant to signal detection that specialist agents may detect include: energy threshold, modulation, spectral content and envelope.

5.1. Energy Threshold Agents

Perhaps the simplest form of specialist agent is the energy threshold agent. A blind threshold agent simply places higher value in destination states with a measured electromagnetic energy higher (or lower) than a predefined threshold level. If these agents are aware of the energy level of the current noise-floor in the tf environment they may also place value in states with a level greater than a defined marginal level above this noise-floor.

5.2. Demodulation Agents

The concept of the demodulator agent is introduced here as a specialist agent able to exploit the recorded time-series representation of the original received input signal from which the tf representation was derived. The agents state in the tf space is defined and, using the linkage of data back to the time-series at the correct time offset, is able to carry out a demodulation operation.

This specialist agent, depicted in figure 4 is, in this present context, a software frequency agile element capable of demodulating short bursts of modulated carrier wave transmissions at a given centre frequency (the carrier frequency f_c). Different populations of demodulator agents are required for the different modulation schemes likely to be present in the received tf environment. A key concept in this work is that of the time-frequency space as an environment for demodulator agents. The interaction of the agent with its environment is determined by the rule-set (ie: individual policy) that each of the agents possess.

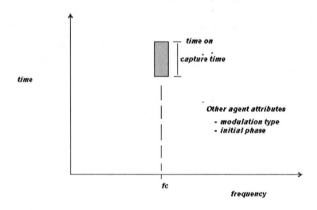

Figure 4. A Demodulator Agent.

5.3. Spectral Content Agents

Augmented demodulation agents able to perform a frequency analysis of a narrowband burst of the input signal can use the presence or absence of specific spectral components as an indicator of value. For example, in a preceeding paper [15] the presence of a 200Hz offset tone in received signal samples is used as an indicator of value in a multi-agent approach to the detection of a frequency agile signal. The spectral content agent recognizes and assigns value to specific spectral signatures present in the signal it processes.

5.4. Envelope Agents

The complex envelope $g(t)$ of a received signal fragment is defined by [16],

$$g(t) = a(t)cos\left[2\pi f_c t + \phi(t)\right]. \tag{6}$$

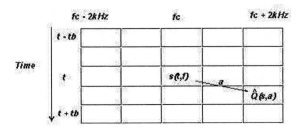

Figure 5. An example of the local region visible to an agent during phase 1 of learning.

The natural envelope of the signal $a(t)$ is usually obtained by rectification and lowpass filtering of the received signal time series. A specialist agent may use its estimate of the natural envelope of its data fragment as a template characterizing pre-demodulated features of the received signal.

6. Multiple Agent Learning (Phase 1)

The multiple agent learning algorithm introduced in this chapter consists of two phases. At the commencement of the first phase of the learning process for a given fixed tf environment, specialist agents are assigned to random locations within the tf space. Each agent is mobile and the environment that each agent finds itself in consists of a group of tf cells surrounding its present location. Figure 5 depicts a typical range of cells visible to each agent (ie: its depth of influence) during each learning cycle. During every learning cycle each agent decides whether to move in the tf space or not.

A simple form of mediated learning is used in this initial phase. Independent learning by each agent is augmented by the synchronised sharing of global state information at the completion of each learning cycle. Agents do not record the actions or effects of other agents in the environment thereby reducing the computational requirement. In this first learning phase agents are able to be treated as being independent and the results of their actions do not effect other agents directly. It is only in the subsequent cluster analysis phase that agent outcomes from the first learning phase are correlated.[3]

6.1. Local Value

Each grid space (t, f) (where t defines a short time duration) in the local environment is, in effect, a short duration narrowband segment of the wideband environment. Hence, agents are able to process this short segment in their range and then estimate a value. A local reward quantity, dependent on the feature that the agent is looking for in each state may then be calculated. Signal characteristics of the original transmission that could be used for the value term at this point include; demodulated spectral content and message characteristics,

---

[3] See [17] for an introduction to multi-agent intelligent clustering.

baud parameters and also unique transmitter characteristics in the time-frequency space (for example the transmitter's RF signature, or envelope).

A reinforcement learning rule may be used where different policies determine which action the agent will take depending upon its own current state and the state values that surround it. Restating equation 4 more simply [18], we can say that agent i, currently in state $s_k(t, f)$ at iteration k will determine its next state $s_{(k+1)}(t, f)$ and write,

$$\hat{Q}(s, a) \leftarrow r(s) + \gamma \max_{a'} \hat{Q}(s', a'). \tag{7}$$

Where $\hat{Q}$ is the current estimate of the Q function value for the state-action pair (s, a) and s' is the state resulting from applying action a in state s. The *discount* factor devaluing the effect of future states is again represented by γ.

6.2. Phase 1 Global Value

The co-ordinated performance of the population of agents in reaching a common goal (eg: detecting a specific energy transmission) is determined by calculating the *global value* of the population at each iteration k of the algorithm, Vg_k. The global value is an example of a global co-ordination policy and is a measure of how well the agent population as a whole has performed during the entire environment time window. It may be used to update, or mediate, the local estimates of the Q function at each agent. The higher the proportion of high value states found by the population then the higher is the global value obtained at a particular learning iteration.

6.3. Completing Phase 1

Learning in phase 1 continues until either an equilibrium point is reached[4] or an impasse is reached. An equilibrium occurs when no agents have moved following one of the synchronised learning cycles and an impasse occurs when some agents oscillate between states during successive learning cycles. A local learning policy is required in order to proceed past this point. The main functions of the mediation policy adopted here are to determine which action to take if an impasse has been reached and also, what negotiations will be allowed to occur between agents.

6.3.1. Local Guidance Policies (π_x)

Some specific examples of policies that may be used to guide agents include;

1. The greedy policy, is denoted by π_1 here. Each agent updates its Q table for each state in range and will choose the path with the highest calculated value as its destination during that iteration.

2. Local guidance policy π_2 contains an element of exploration for each agent. During each learning cycle, the agent calculates the Q value for surrounding states as with π_1. If the highest value state is the current state and has a local value $Q_k(t, f) < \delta$, then

---

[4]See Nash[19]

the agent will choose to move to the highest state in range other than its current state. This policy attempts to prevent agents becoming trapped at low value points in the environment by forcing a move to a different state when a low value is unavoidable using policy π_1. This provides the agent with a possible escape route.

3. Local guidance policy π_3 is an extension of π_2. It is a similar policy to π_2 with the exception that, if the agent is already in a state of low relative value, it is reset to a random position in the environment if there are no higher value local states visible. This policy is useful when there are relatively few agents in the environment as they are more likely to eventually locate a high value region.

7. Multiple Agent Learning Phase 2

The clustering of the multiple agents that occurs in phase 1 of the learning algorithm results in aggregations of individual specialist agents around regions of high perceived value in the time-frequency environment. Each of these aggregations is unique in that their constituent specialist agents have converged to a specific combination of features in the tf environment. For example, each specialist agent in a particular aggregation shares a common property. This property could include one or more of a common frequency, time-span or energy component.

Following the phase 1 learning we may coalesce agent aggregations into single representative agents that exhibit the chief characteristics of their parent aggregation. In this work we call these coalesced agents *derivative agents*. The main purpose of phase 2 of the learning process is to learn associations between derivative agents in the tf environment and form teams. In phase 2 of the learning algorithm each agent communicates with a mediated subset of agents in the population - those within its visible environmental field.

7.1. Derivative Agents

Unlike their specialist agent precursors, derivative agents are immobile in the tf space. They occupy one (or more) discrete points in the space and are defined by a table of *meta-data* derived from the original specialist agent aggregation parent. There is a hierarchical structure to the agent population evolution from individual specialist agents $\rightarrow$ agent aggregations $\rightarrow$ derivative agents. Meta-data that could be associated with a typical tf derivative agent includes centre frequency, start time, duration, envelope vector and mean energy level.

A further distinguishing characteristic of derivative agents is their depth of influence. Here, depth of influence refers to the group of tf grid spaces that each derivative agent is aware of. Figure 6 shows the depth of influence of a single derivative agent A in its detection of significant energy transmissions. The grid spaces that agent A needs to be aware of (for the purposes of the examples in this chapter) are those that enable time or frequency connectivity with other agents. These adjacent linkages are what will be reinforced by phase 2 of the learning rule.

The limited number of tf grid spaces visible to each derivative agent also reduces the computational complexity associated with the resultant mediated learning process. In the above figure there are a maximum number of 18 other agents possibly interacting with each

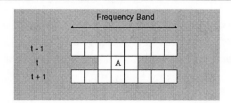

Figure 6. The maximum depth of influence (or visible range) of a derivative agent during phase 2 of learning.

derivative agent. The relative sparsity of derivative agents in many cases will also further reduce the actual number of interacting agents.

7.2. Derivative Agent Learning

The goal of phase 2 learning is to form associations between derivative agents that link them together into *teams* that correspond with signal transmissions present in the received communications environment. This second period of reinforcement learning explores the space of team membership amongst derivative agents.

At the commencement of this phase of learning, derivative agents are each assigned to their own individual starting team. A series of learning epochs then takes place where, in each epoch, agents negotiate with other agents present within their depth of influence. The aim of the negotiation is for each agent to improve its state value if possible by joining one of the teams associated with agents visible to it. Agents each maintain their own table of state/action values: $Q(s, a)$ tables where state corresponds to current team membership and action corresponds with joining the team of the visible agent in question. In the example above there are 18 entries in the $Q(s, a)$ table for each agent at each state. The update rule for the table entries for agent A, for example, is

$$\hat{Q}_A(s, a) = r(s') + \gamma \max_{a'} \hat{Q}_A(s', a'), \tag{8}$$

and ultimately,

$$r(s) = V_A(\text{Constant Carrier}(s)) + V_A(FH(s)) + V_A(\text{chirp}(s)). \tag{9}$$

Here, $V_A(\text{Constant Carrier}(s))$ is the value, from the view of a constant frequency carrier, that is associated with agent A's team membership state of s. Similarly, $V_A(FH(s))$ and $V_A(\text{chirp}(s))$ are team state s membership values from the viewpoint of Frequency Hopping (FH) and chirp signals for agent A. More specifically for the case of constant carrier value,

$$V_A(\text{Constant Carrier}(s)) = \frac{\sum_{team(s)} (\text{agents in tf contiguity})}{\sum_{team(s)} (\text{agents})} \tag{10}$$

Equation 10 gives a simple measure of value based on the fraction of agents in the team in question that are aligned in frequency and are continuous in time compared with the total number of agents in the team. When other value components are included as in equation 9 the resulting overall value of a team will be higher when a large proportion of its members possess characteristics of known communication signals in time and frequency.

Epoch learning continues until one of two conditions is met. Either an equilibrium is achieved when, following negotiations for all derivative agents at a particular state, none of them change teams or an impasse is achieved as described in phase 1. In this state of impasse agents may repeatedly swap teams after successive negotiations or revisit prior states a set number of times. It is worth pointing out here that revisiting prior states is allowable, up to the *thresholded* number of times, as past experience and the differing states of the visible agents may alter the negotiated outcome for a particular agent.

At the conclusion of each learning epoch the overall value of each resulting team is assessed. If the overall value of a team has increased then the reward matrix cross-terms for each of its constituent team members is also increased. That is,

$$R(i,j) \leftarrow R(i,j) + \text{ reward increment.} \tag{11}$$

Following the assessment of overall team values and the allocation of reward terms, the value of the entire collection of derivative agent teams is assessed. This measure can be thought of as a measure of completion which would be maximised.

7.3. Metrics to Assess Completion

Assessing the proximity of the derivative agent team allocations to actual signals of interest in the tf space requires an overall measure of agent allocation to teams and a measure of the teams *distance* from the tf trace of the typical signals that may be in the environment. A suitable metric that can be used to assess completion for the present purpose is whether teams are fully connected from a start-time to end-time of the tf frame. These boundaries can be either signal end-points or boundaries in time or frequency to the environment. A major goal is associated with identifying signals (possibly background signals) that fully traverse the received environment.

If the system has not reached one of the completion conditions then a new training epoch is initiated. The team allocations of the derivative agents are reset to the individual team state (i.e. one agent per team) and the reward matrix is retained. Hence, during subsequent learning epochs, the cumulative reward of agent team associations learned previously will have an influence on the decision-making process of individual agents when assessing future potential team partners.

7.4. Derivative Agent Policies

When the derivative agents are assessing whether to join a particular team belonging to one of the agents in its depth of influence, a population guidance policy such as exploit vs explore may be adopted. An exploit vs explore ratio may be defined to help prevent inadequate exploration of the state-space occurring. A ratio of 1:0 (i.e. fully exploitative) indicates that the agents will always choose the partner resulting in the highest subsequent state value. Whereas, a ratio of 1:1 means that there is an equal chance of an agent choosing to join a visible agent at random irrespective of the subsequent state value it has calculated. The exploit vs explore ratio may be changed during the learning epoch and would typically start with some exploration and progressively alter to become more fully exploitative.

The pseudocode in Text Box 1 describes the algorithm flow through phases 1 and 2.

```
    Text Box 1
                        Pseudocode of the Learning Algorithm
% Phase 1
%
% Read-in the Time-Frequency (tf) Environment
%
% Randomly distribute the specialist agents across the environment
%
% Repeat until (EQUILIBRIUM) OR impasse
%   For each agent:
%     Execute its specialist ability at its current location in tf space
%     Calculate the local value of this state and action
%     Implement the local agent policy within its visible field
%   end for
%
%   Calculate the Global Value of the specialist agent aggregated cluster groups following this iteration
%
%   Implement the Global value mediation policy for specialist agents
%
% end repeat until (EQUILIBRIUM) OR impasse
%
%
% Phase 2
%
% Allocate one derivative agent to each valid phase 1 aggregated cluster
%
% Initialise the state variables
%
% Initialise all the agent maps, lists and the reward matrix
% Set the list size for each agent's Q(s,a) list = N(visible agents)
% Assign each agent to a distinct team, N(Teams) = N(agents) initially
%
% Repeat until (COMPLETION METRIC) OR impasse
%
%   Repeat until (Nash Equilibrium) OR impasse
%     for each agent
%       for each visible agent
%       calculate the new (local) team values if we join their team
%       choose (and record) the preferred action based on the current exploit:explore policy
%     end for
%   end for
%
%     for each agent
%       resolve the preferred action with future intentions of visible agents
%     end for
%   end repeat
%
%   Assessment of Overall Value of each team
%   For each team, find it's most likely signal type, reward the agents
%   who are contributing to this type and remove the non-contributors
%   from the team. Re-assign them to an unused team number at random.
%
%   Assessment of Completion Metric
%   METRIC: One or more teams are fully connected from start to end of the tf frame
%
% end repeat if (COMPLETION METRIC) OR impasse
```

8.   Case Study 1 - A Wideband Signal Detector

8.1.   Introduction

In this section of the chapter we will apply the above method to the task of detecting the presence of a AM modulated carrier wave transmission whose carrier frequency hops over a fixed subset of frequencies at regular time intervals. Each resultant burst of carrier energy contains a time-sequenced fragment of the transmitted message signal and the sequence of frequencies in the hop sequence is determined by a pseudorandom code sequence at the transmitter. Under normal operation the code sequence is also known at the receiver and it is then able to reconstruct the transmitted signal by synchronously altering the receiver tuning. In cases where the hop sequence is unknown the receiver has a much more difficult task.

These Frequency Hopping (FH) signals have the advantage of a greater immunity to narrowband interfering signals than that of a single carrier frequency transmission. However, the difficulty in detecting and tracking a FH signal requires a more complex receiver. Conventionally, FH signal reception has been carried out by the analysis of the output of a single wideband receiver [1] using what could be interpreted as a single agent approach.

A multi-agent approach is introduced to the problem of detecting (and characterising) FH signals. The advantage of processing many regions of the time-frequency (tf) environment concurrently, together with the opportunity to trial several learning policies have prompted this approach. Using many, digitally controlled, narrowband receivers is also now a feasible alternative to using a single wideband tuner.

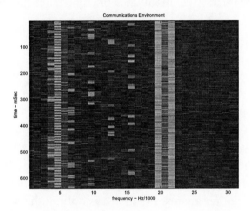

Figure 7. A time-frequency view of the spectral environment.

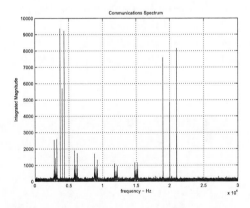

Figure 8. A communications spectrum with various transmissions present.

Figure 7 shows a representation of a wideband communications environment comprised of several fixed and variable frequency communications carriers in a background of Additive White Gaussian Noise (AWGN). A frequency hopping signal will appear as very short bursts appearing at a predetermined sequence of frequencies and will, in general, only be visible in a power spectral plot such as Figure 8 when the spectral plot is integrated over time and the FH signal revisits a set of fixed frequencies. Figure 7 is representative of the input tf raster environment of the agent population.

8.2.   Specialist Spectral Content Agent

The concept of a spectral content agent was introduced in section 5 above. The specialist agent used in this example is a software frequency agile element capable of demodulating short bursts of modulated carrier wave transmissions at a given centre frequency and performing basic spectral analysis on the demodulated waveform. The analog modulation (AM) used in this case may be defined as,

$$s(t) = m(t).cos(2\pi f_c t). \tag{12}$$

Here, the low frequency signal $m(t)$ modulates the higher frequency carrier.

8.3.   Multiple Agent Clustering

Independent learning by the multi-agent system is the simplest learning method to employ. Agents do not record the actions or effects of other agents in the environment thereby reducing the computational requirement. In cases where the multi-agent interactions effect the environment of other agents, this simplification cannot in general, be justified - the actions of other agents will have an effect on whether a particular agent can calculate the correct probability of entering a new state given its own action. In the first learning phase of this work however, agents are able to be treated as being independent and the results of their actions do not affect other agents directly. It is only in the subsequent cluster analysis phase that agent outcomes from the first learning phase are correlated.

Each spectral content agent is initially placed randomly at a point on the time-frequency plane of interest. In this example the boundaries of the environment are a frequency boundary of 1000 Hz $\leq f \leq$ 15000 Hz and a time boundary of $0 \leq t \leq$ 640 msec. A FH signal consisting of a 10msec burst time AM modulated carrier is present in the environment together with a variable background level of AWGN. A tf plot of a FH carrier modulated with a 200 Hz sine wave in a background AWGN level of 10dB SNR is shown in Figure 9

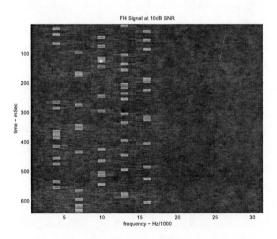

Figure 9. A frequency agile signal with a background noise level of 10dB.

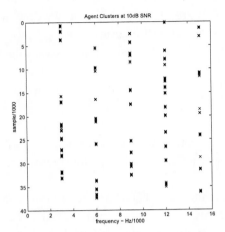

Figure 10. Multi-agent clusters following phase 1 of learning.

The environment of each agent consists of a group of tf cells surrounding its present location in tf space. Figure 5 above, depicts the range of cells visible to each agent during iterations of the first learning phase.

8.3.1. Specialist Agent Reward

An expression generating a reward value for specialist agents sensitive to a specific spectral component has been used in this example. The reward gained by agent (i) in each state $r_i(t, f)$ is defined as,

$$r_i(t, f) = S(200)/ \sum_{f=f_{lo}}^{f=f_{hi}} S(f). \tag{13}$$

The $S(f)$ is an estimate of the spectral energy at frequency f. Hence, from this expression, the particular state reward to an agent will be higher if the spectral component at 200 Hz is relatively high.

8.3.2. Cluster Analysis

The co-ordinated performance of the population of agents in detecting a FH wideband signal is determined by calculating the *overall* value of the population at iteration k, Vg_k. In this work the Vg_k value is determined by scanning down the time axis of the given environment and testing the output of the agent population at time segments equal to half the expected burst time of the FH signal. Hence, the value of the current state of all agents can be quantified by calculating the overall value. Vg_k is defined as,

$$Vg_k = \sum_t V_i(200). \tag{14}$$

Where $V_i(200)$ is the local value of agent (i) if present at contiguous time intervals through the entire environmental timeframe. The overall value is a measure of how well the agent population has been able to detect, in this case, a FH transmission with some known spectral content during the entire environment time window and may be used to update the local estimates of the state,action function at each agent. The longer the contiguous sequence of high value states found within the population then the higher is the overall value obtained.

As a result of the initial phase of learning, the agent population converges to states of high local value whilst concurrently maximizing the overall value of the population as a whole. As a result of this, the agent population effectively forms clusters around each likely burst of modulated energy detected in the tf environment. Figure 10 shows the clustering of the agent population following the initial learning layer when applied to the environment of Figure 9.

The multi-agent clusters that have been formed are now analysed and meta-data characterizing the associated derivative agent for each cluster is obtained. Measures that may be considered here in the search for FH signals are: the cluster start time, cluster duration, cluster centre frequency and number of agent members. We may also further analyse the cluster data as depicted in Figure 10 in an attempt to filter out clusters which are least likely to be part of a FH transmission.

At the conclusion of phase 1 of the learning process we have a set of derivative agents each centred on a specific point in the tf environment that its precursor specialist agents have found to be of high value. In the next section we will look at an example of how phase 2 of the learning process may be used to recognize, and take action on, structures in the aggregations of derivative agents.

9.   Case Study 2 - A Wideband Adaptive Filter

9.1.   Introduction

This section describes an application of the second phase of the learning algorithm. In this case, for simplicity, we use a tf environment represented by an 8x8 grid of spaces. This grid is assumed to represent the learning system after the completion of the phase 1 multi-agent clustering and with the clusters of *energy threshold* specialist agents coalesced into derivative agents with a maximum duration interval of one time unit. Figure 11 shows the state of the environment with the newly formed derivative agents. The 20 derivative agents are positioned over locations of maximal local value and can be seen to represent regions where relevant signal fragments are located.

9.2.   Team Building in TF Space

Individual derivative agents are aware of only a relatively small subset of the entire tf space when assessing possible actions. This depth of influence, or visible field as depicted in Figure 6, has been chosen so that derivative agents only need to track interactions with other agents adjacent in time. This progressive construction of teams linked by both specialist value and continuity in time, is a fundamental goal in this phase of the learning process.

During each iteration of the learning epochs each agent negotiates with other agents within its visible field. As the agents are stationary, the actions being considered are those of joining the other visible agent teams. The value function that each agent team consults is specifically designed to place higher value on groupings of agents that possess known characteristics of the signals of interest (SOI) in the tf space. For example, constancy of the central frequency of the agents is of value for fixed carrier SOI. Fixed multiples of burst length together with contiguous end-start times is of value for FH transmissions. Correlation of principal components is of value with a *chirping* SOI, that is, those signals that are of the form, $f(t) = M.f(t) + B$.

A level of exploitation vs exploration as part of a specific action policy guides the agents during their negotiations through the epoch. Discounted future states may play a role in each agents assessment of the value of a specific state,action pair. The cumulative reward matrix is, in this case, a sparsely populated square matrix of dimension 20.

9.3. The Reward Matrix

Epochs are completed whenever an equilibrium or impasse is reached and, at that time, the value of each team is assessed and those teams that have reached a state of high perceived value are rewarded. Each agent pairing in a successful team has its associated element in the reward matrix increased. This key action reinforces successful team formation during subsequent epochs as the reward matrix is retained and the cumulative reward influences the value of future agent negotiations. At the end of a learning epoch a policy may be implemented that re-assigns team members who have not significantly contributed to the overall team value to other (unallocated or randomly allocated) teams.

9.4. Completion Metric

Metrics to assess completion of the learning process may also gauge the extent to which the teams conform to actual distinct signals of interest. The actual metric used will vary depending on the complexity of the signal, the specialist agent tuning to characteristic features of the signal fragments and the interference present in the environment. Closely matching these metrics to the likely signals present will provide a better estimate of distance from the

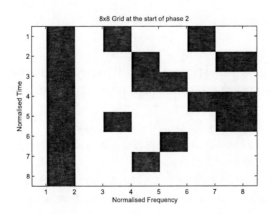

Figure 11. The derivative agent locations at the commencement of phase 2 of learning.

end-state of the learning process - the overall goal. A general condition that we may use in the 8x8 example from above is that one or more teams are fully connected from the start to the end of the tf frame. Here, fully connected means that the team possesses more than a predetermined threshold number of members. This completion metric therefore reinforces the formation of fewer, longer duration teams more likely to indicate signal transmissions rather than many independent bursts. Multiple independent energy bursts that are uncorrelated in time are often a characteristic of electromagnetic noise energy or background clutter in the received tf environment.

When the above method is used with the 8x8 grid example from Figure 11 above, eight of the derivative agents form a team on the constant frequency carrier signal located at a normalized frequency = 2 as shown in Figure 12.

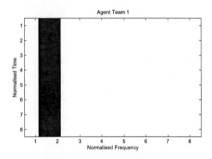

Figure 12. Derivative agent team identifying a constant frequency carrier transmission.

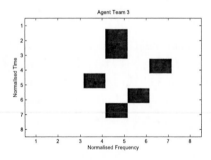

Figure 13. Derivative agent team identifying components of a frequency agile transmission.

The identification of the constant carrier signal by the derivative agents is an association of a recognized signal with specific derivative agent connections. This will allow the subsequent masking (or filtering) of this particular signal from further analysis of this tf environment.

The other energy bursts identified in the 8x8 tf space by the presence of a derivative agent are more difficult to classify as they present an overlapping FH and linear slope chirp signal. In this particular instance of the algorithm, no value was placed on the chirp signal structure and so the algorithms best attempt at reconstructing the FH sequence is shown in Figure 13. Other, isolated, or ambiguous energy bursts were, as would be expected, classed as being of low value. It is also worth noting that the derivative agents simulated in this 8x8 array had not been differentiated by tailored precursor specialist agents. The team's value to an agent was, in this case, based on the relative position and geometric similarity of the derivative agent to the existing team's principal features as they developed over time.

9.5. Noise Performance

The presence of additive channel noise at the receiver input will cause an increased background energy level in the tf environment as in Figure 9. The selective tuning of the specialist agent to specific signal features provides some immunity to this noise. Features that could be used include spectral components, timing information and externally provided features such as directionality of the energy burst for example. Figure 10 shows the agent clusters resulting from a group of specialist agent sensitive to energy bursts containing a spectral component. Specialist agents may also share meta-data related to a particular received fragment and use this information to augment their assessment of local value.

10. Further Applications

10.1. The Coordination of Spatially Diverse Agent Populations

Agent populations monitoring the received tf environment from differing geographical locations are potentially able to exploit the benefits of spatial diversity. There are well-documented advantages in positioning multiple receivers in different locations when tasked with receiving a common signal transmission. This is the Single Input Multiple Output (SIMO) wireless channel [20] which gives rise to receiver array gain.

Agents residing at differing locations, but monitoring the same region of time and frequency may detect a given signal of interest. The signals of interest will have been perturbed by additive noise that was generated over a different, unique propagation path from the transmitter to each receiver site. The fact that the noise is produced by independent processes, means that, when averaged over time at a common node, the additive noise will be reduced but the signal level will be reinforced. The result is an increase in the signal to noise ratio (SNR) in the combined output. This is illustrated in Figure 14 where one node is acting as a fusion node combining tf views from each of the remotely-located receiver sites. In the case where the interference is non-additive however, averaging may lead to a degraded noise environment from the perspective of the agents at the better-located sites. Different negotiation and sharing policies can be utilized with multiple agent populations in order to explore the broadened space that agents now have access to. Two cases are considered.

First, separate base-learners using different representations of the same event [3]. Each population uses its own locally received tf environment. The best performing agent group may transmit its progress to the other agent groups.

Second, the tf environments may be fused and averaged together as in Figure 14. The improved estimate of the tf environment is then distributed to each population, which, in most cases, will improve their base reference of actual energy distributions due to only the SOI in a given tf space. Subsequent multi-agent reinforcement learning will then occur over a large number of agents with effectively an enhanced tf estimate.

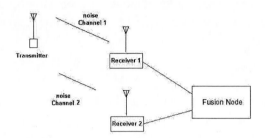

Figure 14. Spatially diverse agent populations.

10.2. Application to Speech Signals in TF Space

The characteristic spectral properties of speech signals present an opportunity for learning by specialist agents in an attempt to reconstruct segmented transmissions of analog speech signals in the tf domain. Pre-demodulation features of an unbiased transmitted signal may also provide a source of value to appropriate specialist agents. The signal envelope, for example, may possess a characteristic shape which is a function of differing voiced properties of the modulating speech signal. Specialist agents, sensitive to specific shape elements (or pattern fragments) in these signals are practical candidates for phase 1 clustering and phase 2 derivative agents using this method.

11. Conclusion

This chapter has introduced a multi-agent approach to the detection and recognition of communication signals present in a relatively wide bandwidth time-frequency environment. The two phase learning algorithm described employs a number of specialist agents in the first phase to explore a region of the local time-frequency space and respond to energy with features of interest to the agent. The second phase of learning uses derivative agents from the earlier phase and searches for groups, or teams, of agents who share common properties with signals of interest in the environment.

Using appropriate agent types, example applications of this approach to both detect and filter signals of interest has been demonstrated and discussed. Further tailoring of the specialist agents, together with refinement of the agent value functions will broaden the applicability of the method to other signals. Improved feature identification and analysis is possible and would potentially allow the identification of specific transmitter characteristics or signature. Other features in the modulation space (for example speech spectra or envelope distribution) may also be used as specialist agent capabilities.

Other externally provided indicators, for example, a directional antenna, giving a line of bearing to the source of incident signal energy would also provide further important feature to aid the cluster filter. The advantages gained from the fusion of external meta-data such as this, together with multiple agent receiver populations has also been discussed.

Although this chapter has been devoted to the analysis of two-dimensional time-frequency communications data, it is envisaged that the method described here could also be usable by parallel processing architectures tasked with the detection of entities within other multi-dimensional environments.

References

[1] H.-C. Horing, "Probability of intercept for frequency hop signals using search receivers," *News from Rohde & Schwarz*, no. 160, pp. 26–29, 1998, available online at http:\\www.rohde-schwarz.com, last accessed Mar. 4, 2010.

[2] R. Sutton and A. Barto, *Reinforcement Learning: An Introduction.* Cambridge MA.: The MIT Press, 1998.

[3] E. Alpaydin, *Introduction to Machine Learning.* Cambridge, MA: The MIT Press, 2004.

[4] R. Bellman, *Dynamic Programming.* Princeton, NJ: Princeton University Press, 1957.

[5] C. Watkins and P. Dayan, "Q-learning," *Machine Learning*, vol. 8, no. 3, pp. 279–292, 1992.

[6] R. Sutton, "Learning to predict by the methods of temporal difference," *Machine Learning*, vol. 3, pp. 9–44, 1988.

[7] N. Vlassis, *A Concise Introduction to Multiagent Systems and Distributed Artificial Intelligence. Synthesis Lectures in Artificial Intelligence and Machine Learning.* Morgan & Claypool Publishers., 2007, ch. 8.3.

[8] S. Sen, M. Sekaran, and J. Hale, "Learning to coordinate without sharing information," *Proc. Twelfth National Conf. on Artificial Intelligence*, pp. 426–431, 1994.

[9] E. Alonso, M. DÍnverno, D. Kudenko, M. Luck, and J. Noble, "Learning in multiagent systems," *The Knowledge Engineering Review*, vol. 16, no. 3, pp. 277–284, 2001.

[10] M. Mundhe and S. Sen, "Evaluating concurrent reinforcement learners," *Proc. Seventeenth International Joint Conf. on Artificial Intelligence*, 2000.

[11] C. Claus and C. Boutilier, "The dynamics of reinforcement learning in cooperative multiagent systems," *Proc. of the Fifteenth National Conf. on Artifical Intelligence*, 1998.

[12] M. Tan, "Multi-agent reinforcement learning: Independent vs. cooperative agents," *Proc. Tenth International Conference on Machine Learning*, 1993.

[13] C. Shannon, "A mathematical theory of communication," *The Bell System Technical Journal*, vol. 27, Oct. 1948.

[14] "Esmeralda - integrated station for spectrum monitoring," available online at www.thalesgroup.com, last accessed Mar. 17, 2010.

[15] J. Hefferan, "A multi-agent wideband signal detector," *Proc. of the KES International Symposium on Intelligent Decision Technologies KES IDT2009*, Apr. 2009.

[16] S. Haykin, *Communication Systems.* John Wiley & Sons Inc, 1983.

[17] J.-E. Park and K.-W. Oh, "Multi-agent systems for intelligent clustering," *Proc. World Academy Sc., Eng. and Tech.*, vol. 11, pp. 97–102, Feb. 2006.

[18] T. Mitchell, *Machine Learning.* McGraw Hill, 1997, ch. 13.

[19] J. Nash, "Equilibrium points in n-person games," *Proc. N.A.S.*, vol. 36, pp. 48–49, 1950.

[20] M. Jankiraman, *Space-Time Codes and MIMO Systems.* Norwood MA: Artech House Inc, 2004.

INDEX

M

N